Enduring Critical Poses

SUNY series, Native Traces

Scott Richard Lyons, editor

Enduring Critical Poses

The Legacy and Life of Anishinaabe
Literature and Letters

Edited by

Gordon Henry Jr., Margaret Noodin,
and David Stirrup

Published by State University of New York Press, Albany

© 2021 State University of New York

All rights reserved

Printed in the United States of America

No part of this book may be used or reproduced in any manner whatsoever without written permission. No part of this book may be stored in a retrieval system or transmitted in any form or by any means including electronic, electrostatic, magnetic tape, mechanical, photocopying, recording, or otherwise without the prior permission in writing of the publisher.

For information, contact State University of New York Press, Albany, NY
www.sunypress.edu

Library of Congress Cataloging-in-Publication Data

Names: Henry, Gordon, 1955– editor. | Noodin, Margaret, editor. | Stirrup, David, editor.
Title: Enduring critical poses : the legacy and life of Anishinaabe literature and letters / edited by Gordon Henry, Jr., Margaret Noodin, and David Stirrup.
Other titles: Native traces.
Description: Albany : State University of New York Press, [2021] | Series: SUNY series, native traces | Includes bibliographical references and index.
Identifiers: LCCN 2020039939 (print) | LCCN 2020039940 (ebook) | ISBN 9781438482538 (hardcover : alk. paper) | ISBN 9781438482521 (pbk. : alk. paper) | ISBN 9781438482545 (ebook)
Subjects: LCSH: Ojibwa Indians—Intellectual life. | American literature—Indian authors—History and criticism.
Classification: LCC E99.C6 E49 2021 (print) | LCC E99.C6 (ebook) | DDC 977.004/97333—dc23
LC record available at https://lccn.loc.gov/2020039939
LC ebook record available at https://lccn.loc.gov/2020039940

10 9 8 7 6 5 4 3 2 1

We dedicate this work to the memory of
all the Anishinaabe storytellers,
especially those known to us during our lifetimes,
who learned and shared the *aadizookaanag* and
dibaajimowinan of Anishinaabewakiing.

Contents

Acknowledgments ix

Introduction 1
    Gordon Henry Jr., Margaret Noodin, and David Stirrup

I. Majikawiz

1. Louise Erdrich's *Books and Islands in Ojibwe Country*:
   Writing, Being, Healing, Place 19
      Chris LaLonde

2. The Old World Display and the New World Displaced 33
      Nichole Biber

3. An Indian's Journey and Tribal Memory: David Treuer's
   Rez Life 51
      Padraig Kirwan

II. Bakaawiz

4. The Anishinaabe Eco-Poetics of Language, Life, and Place
   in the Poetry of Schoolcraft, Noodin, Blaeser, and Henry 79
      Susan Berry Brill de Ramírez

5. Ambiguity and Empathy in the Poetry of Gordon Henry Jr. 107
      Stuart Rieke

6. Justice *in absentia*: The Re-stor(y)ing of Native Legal Presence through Narratives of Survivance in Gerald Vizenor's "Genocide Tribunals"   119
     Sharon Holm

III. Jiibayaaboozo

7. The Exceptional Power of the Dead in Heid E. Erdrich's *National Monuments*   149
     Deborah L. Madsen

8. Anishinaabe Being and the Fallen God of Sun-Worshiping Victorians   177
     Carter Meland

IV. Nanabozho

9. Beyond the Borders of Blood: An Anishinaaabe Tribalography of Identity   195
     Jill Doerfler

10. Enduring Critical Poses, Beyond Nation and History: The Legacy and Life of Anishinaabeg Literature and Letters   227
     Margaret Noodin

11. Enduring Cultural Poses: Memory, Resistance, and Symbolic Sculpture   249
     David Stirrup

Afterword   275
     Gordon Henry Jr. and Margaret Noodin

Contributors   281

Index   287

Acknowledgments

This book was made possible by the generations of storytellers and scholars before us and the colleagues who work alongside us at Michigan State University, the University of Wisconsin–Milwaukee, and the University of Kent. We thank Dawn Brill Duques and Matt Duques, sister and nephew of Susan Berry Brill de Ramírez, for working with us to ensure Susan's chapter was included after she left the world too soon on October 30, 2018. Many thanks are due to Amanda Lane-Camilli at State University of New York Press, who patiently assisted as we gathered versions and worked toward an ever-shifting deadline. We also owe a special debt of gratitude to Angela Mesic, whose brilliant work on the manuscript in the final stages was invaluable. We thank those who labored to bring this book into being, including our friends at SUNY Press, including Laura Poole, Ryan Morris, Amanda Lanne-Cammilli, and James Peltz; and our dedicated Nanaa'ibii'igekwe, Angela Mesic, who chased all the details across time and distance. *Gimiigwechwininin gakina gaa-naadamawiyaang!*

Introduction

GORDON HENRY JR., MARGARET NOODIN,
AND DAVID STIRRUP

Naanaagadawendam Anishinaabe:
Critical Poses of the Anishinaabe

Duration and endurance is Bergson's series of conscious states, Vizenor's trickster stories remembered, Cruikshank's subversion, and Rilke's trembling love. Anishinaabe storyteller Basil Johnston connected these characteristics, these enduring poses, to four brothers who represent ways of knowing honed by centuries of practice. The brothers were travelers and seekers of knowledge. Majikawiz, the eldest, became a historian who preserved events as history across time through sashes, scrolls, and teaching rocks; he was a leader and a warrior. Bakaawiz, who followed, created dances and dramas to transform memory into art through trickster transformations. The third brother, Jiibayaaboozo, continually asked questions, challenging and defining ways of thinking and being in the world. Nanabozho, the youngest, became a trickster. He once confronted his father and was met with a stream of arrows and a lesson in persistence and humility. He was rewarded with a pipe and went on to teach the Anishinaabeg by example, constantly making mistakes to be interpreted as guideposts by those paying attention.

This collection of critical thinking echoes the lessons of these brothers and focuses on Anishinaabe words, stories, and representations of endurance. Centered in the Great Lakes region of North America, the Anishinaabeg live in a space Johnston referred to as Maazikamikwe, a maternal source of sustainable life. They are a confederacy of communities organized across space and time by shared practices and entwined dialects. In this space, they have endured cultural distress and colonial oppression. What they were taught by the brothers of Johnston's living histories has been disrupted. Storytellers of the present must work to stabilize belief systems, ways of life, concepts of ethics, and practices of intercultural relations. The authors who write and are written about in this volume are a part of a network being revitalized. They are the Anishinaabeg who endure interpretive interventions, the critical imposition of external readings of their work, lives, cultures, and communities. Over the course of a long history of engagement with what is known to Euro-American literary and cultural studies as the "West," certain critical impositions from "outside" Anishinaabe culture have compromised but never fully suppressed the artistic and interpretive agency of Anishinaabe authors.

It is time for Anishinaabe creative and critical leanings, often transposed through the technics of Western letters and media, to re-mark the larger intellectual topography with Anishinaabe perspectives. In this space the "West" is the territory of the *manidoog*, the existential, spiritual, and philosophical, the home of Nanabozho's father, Epangishimog, and his brother, Jiibayaaboozo. The "East" is the place of dawn, a continually rotating point on the horizon, connected to the energy of the sun and the ability to endure and continue teaching. It is *gaagige-aadizooke*, a place of infinitely renewed stories. A legacy of critical engagement is being reframed as an advantage that speaks to the adaptive ability of the Anishinaabe.

Basil Johnston's life and literature provide us with important ways of discerning and extending the enduring elements of Anishinaabe culture that continue to inspire and influence Anishinaabe writers who remain connected to Anishinaabe communities, carrying on with work as scholars and tribal leaders. His book *The Manitous* imparts an understanding of life as an ongoing journey, of the multidimensional "spirit" of Anishinaabe culture. His work imparts a life and legacy that will continue as the *manitous* remain with us in his stories and writing. As you read these enduring poses in literary form, look for traces of the brothers and the spaces their memories still inhabit.

Baatayiinadoon Gaa-ezhi-zhiibendamaang Anishinaabeg: The Many Ways the Anishinaabe People Have Endured

Anishinaabe connection to place and community values and ethics have endured through the storytelling and maintaining collective memory.

According to traditional beliefs, Gizhemanidoo created the universe by activating perception, and creation infinitely recurs through cycles of vision and narration. The four Anishinaabe brothers are extensions of this belief as they represent various ways of knowing, branches of learning, and mediums for expression. *Baatayiinadoon Gaa-ezhi-zhiibendamaang Anishinaabeg.* There are many ways the Anishinaabe have endured.

The first teller was a stone, and the first story was of telling. As time passed, two branches of storytelling developed. The *dibaajimowinan*, classified as inanimate, are forms of accounting and communicating critical information through narration. Comedies, tragedies, poetry, novels, history, reports, legal treatises, ancient recipes, and digital game narratives are *dibaajimowinan*. They are not *aadizookanag*, which are classified as the animate branch of narration, simultaneously mutable and stable. Like a cell with a permeable but identifiable membrane and a central nucleus, *aadizookanag* are energy-based and evolving. These stories change and adapt to the needs of the teller, the audience, and the community. They are defined by language and collective memory, often merging with song and ceremony.

The Anishinaabe literary universe is vast and connects the past to the present. Stories of the four brothers are still widely exchanged and examined. In some ways they have remained the same, and in other ways they have developed distinct characteristics. In performance, practice, fiction, and nonfiction scholarship, the Anishinaabe voice has endured, not just as a tribally centric entity but as a mature voice in a global conversation.

Anishinaabe Writing in the Wider Native World

Since Simon Ortiz's (1981) claims for a nascent literary nationalism and Kimberly Blaeser's (1993) observation of the continued marginalization of Native literatures through the "colonizing" modes of Euro-Western discourses, discussions about the ethical response to Native literatures and literary criticism have proliferated. These considerations are crucial to the ethical response of literary criticism "after theory." Although there is still much heated debate about the means of defining an approach that is both tribally specific and capable of speaking to the broader common concerns of Native literatures, there is relatively clear consensus that these questions of ethics and responsibility shape the continued development of the field. Key considerations, beyond the larger questions of precisely what form such a criticism will take, include the sociopolitical relationship between a text and the world(s) in which it circulates and the ability of any tribal-centered criticism to take full account of the overlaps and border zones of the literary product and its markets. Tribal-centric approaches are establishing dialogues between various forms of criticism and modes of appreciation. These dialogues aid in the understanding of indigenous literatures and their relationships to the multiple contexts in which they circulate.

This volume of essays aims to explore the dimensions of this dialogue in the specific framework of writers of Anishinaabe (Ojibwe, Odawa, or Potawatomi) heritage. The contributors seek not to contain such writing but to use that framework as a form of methodology to encourage analysis of Anishinaabe-specific texts and contexts. We hope this tribal-centric framework will become a connection to the concerns of Native American literary studies and literary studies more widely—a means of ordering a set of questions rather than boxing up a set of assumptions. In "Splitting the Earth: First Utterances and Pluralist Separatism," Jace Weaver responds to Alan Velie's accusations of a pluralist separatism in conceptualizing American Indian literary nationalisms by embracing the term (46). He speaks to the distinctiveness and the diversity of Native American nationhood and Native American experience and to the acknowledgment of a common ground and core set of values that is not uniform but kaleidoscopic. To say simply that manifestations of culture, language, and religion; forms of survivance; and experiences of colonialism differ from nation to nation, however, is to utter a truism that should not need echoing. What is more significant—implicit in, yet occasionally submerged by responses to the literary nationalist project—is the range of diversity within tribal nations, which makes recognition of their heterogeneity an easier task than generating that type of homogeneous cultural and political community that Western historical forms of nationalism have tended to connote. That heterogeneity is writ large in the metaphorical fabric of Anishinaabewaking, in Anishinaabe writing, and in the wide range of critical responses to Anishinaabe cultural production. As Heidi Kiiwetinepinesiik Stark explains:

> Beyond recognizing a collective identity, the Anishinaabeg comprise distinct, separate nations (frequently referred to as bands) that span a vast geographic region from the Plains to the Great Lakes. They are historically and today a people who cross many political and geographical borders. Anishinaabe people share many beliefs and practices, yet individual nations

are influenced by their particular histories, geographic locations, political relations, and internal conflicts. (2012, 124)

In the most recent iteration of sustained Anishinaabe literary criticism—at least at the time of this writing—White Earth enrollee Adam Spry argues that earlier attempts to approach Ojibwe literature as manifestations of culture intrinsically fails to account for that diversity, imagining an homogeneous project rather than acknowledging the politically nimble, formally various purposes to which Anishinaabeg writers have put their literary outputs. Spry's *Our War-Paint Is Writer's Ink* is the first serious transnational-comparative work of Anishinaabeg and American literature, and it joins a significant and fast-growing body of literature and literary criticism by and about Anishinaabe writing. Margaret Noodin's *Bawaajimo*, the first monograph dedicated solely and explicitly to Anishinaabeg writing, addressed complex linguistic residues and crossovers between English and Anishinaabemowin, poetics, and more to work toward Anishinaabe-specific reading strategies in the work of four key Ojibwe authors. It appeared shortly after *Centering Anishinaabeg Studies*, a volume of essays edited by Jill Doerfler, Niigaanwewidam James Sinclair, and Heidi Kiiwetinepinesiik Stark, dedicated to the "cultural, political, and historical foundation" that stories and storytellers provide Anishinaabeg studies. We can add to these the range of monographs dedicated to individual Anishinaabeg writers, from the first, Kim Blaeser's *Gerald Vizenor: Writing in the Oral Tradition*, which sits alongside books on Vizenor by A. Robert Lee, Deborah L. Madsen, and Simone Pellerin; to the range of monographs and essay collections on Louise Erdrich's work by Frances Washburn, Connie A. Jacobs, P. Jane Hafen, Lorena Stookey, Hertha Dawn Wong, David Stirrup, Seema Kurup, Peter Beidler and Gay Barton, Deborah L. Madsen, and Allan Chavkin.

Just as Spry's dissertation lead to *Our War-Paint*, Niigaanwewidam James Sinclair's (St. Peter's/Little Peguis) dissertation *Nindoodemag Bagijiganan: a History of Anishinaabeg Narrative*, is eagerly anticipated in book form. Jill Doerfler's dissertation laid the basis for her book *Those Who Belong: Identity, Family, Blood, and Citizenship among the White Earth Anishinaabeg*, which followed publication of *White Earth Nation: Ratification of a Native Democratic Constitution* (coauthored with Gerald Vizenor). Heidi Kiiwetinepinesiik Stark's (Turtle Mountain) dissertation-based manuscript *Unsettled: Anishinaabe Treaty-Relations and U.S./Canada State-Formation* is slated for publication with the University of Minnesota

Press's First Peoples Series. We mention these as only a few of the Ojibwe scholars in Anishinaabeg studies, but we acknowledge there are now and will be other Anishinaabeg doctorates telling new critical stories and Anishinaabe scholarship continues to endure.

These scholars emerged in the "postnationalist" moment—by which we mean not the intellectual paradigm framed by transnationalism and globalization but the defining of the previously loose conversation around tribal nationhood and nation-specific literary studies by the "three W's"— Robert Warrior, Jace Weaver, and Craig S. Womack.[1] The story of Native literary studies' epic battle over the terms of the discourse have been much rehearsed elsewhere. It is a tale of good versus evil, of liberal multicultural values warding off the terrors of nationalist essentialism, of the rigor (and distance) of high theory versus the ethics of community-embedded attention to detail (lacking the authority of objectivity). In other words, it is much overblown. Marking a shift in Native literary studies from terms defined largely by non-Native scholars and approaches that combined an anthropological model of culture with a high-theoretical toolkit to the rise to prominence of a rank of largely Native (and Native-trained) field leaders armed with the tools of ideological and epistemological resistance, that moment—sometime around the turn of the millennium—saw a brief but perhaps necessary methodological tussle. In refusing to rehearse the minutiae of the debate again, it is perhaps best to turn to one of its archproponents/combatants (depending on which side of the canyon one chooses to stand): "Just as there are a number of realities that constitute Indian identity . . . there are also a number of legitimate approaches to analyzing Native literary production" (Womack 2). Ironically, perhaps, Craig Womack made that point on the second page of his book *Red on Red: Native American Literary Separatism*. *Red on Red* ended up at the center of that controversy as an example of what Kenneth Lincoln in "Red Stick Criticism" characterized as an "insider-only 'purge'" (quoted in Mackay 49), wherein Womack's next contestation—that some "I will argue . . . are more effective than others" represented, for some, the first in a chain of exclusionary pronouncements.

To return to the point, these scholars emerged in a changed environment, one where their Anishinaabeg-specific intellectual framing, while still needing explanation, required little justification. They added their voices to the exceptional scholarship of an older generation of Anishinaabeg scholars whose work, though still largely Ojibwe-focused, tended to break ground in a pan-Indian setting. In total, they demonstrate both the incredible value of this nation-specific work and the ways one can contribute regardless of whether one takes up "nationalist" or "Native cosmopolitanist" lenses.

In all cases, they and the many non-Native scholars who contribute to the conversation around Anishinaabe literary production respond to a rich and very diverse literary landscape. As Vizenor has long claimed, the Anishinaabeg have boasted the most authors—certainly literary authors—of any tribal nation.[2] In Jane Johnston Schoolcraft, or Bamewawagezhikaquay, they also boast the first Native poet to publish in her own language in North America. Early newspapers the *Progress* (1886–89) and later the *Tomahawk* (1903–26),[3] both published at White Earth by Gus and Theodor Beaulieu, provided syndicated national and then original local news for the White Earth population, with the latter in particular carrying a strong political focus. That journalistic tradition was later maintained by a Beaulieu descendant, Gerald Vizenor, who worked for the *Minneapolis Tribune* in the 1960s. As a teacher and editor, Vizenor has also long been a proponent of Anishinaabe-specific literary endeavors. His edited volume *Touchwood: A Collection of Ojibway Prose* drew together the work of four key Anishinaabe writers of the nineteenth and twentieth centuries, foregrounding the historical and formal depth of Anishinaabeg literature. His interviews, essays, criticism, and historical work (including *Everlasting Sky*, *Manifest Manners*, *The People Named the Chippewa*, to name just three of his most significant interventions) elaborate two clear strands: the broader, pan-Indian discussions of Native identity, particularly through lenses offered by poststructuralist theory as it intersects with Indigenous ways of seeing and knowing, and a more Anishinaabe-centric documentation of contemporary experience and endurance.

Vizenor's own creative work began in a mode of reclamation, working with older Anishinaabe forms and stories to recenter the relationship between voice and text. Among his earliest nonjournalistic works, *South of the Painted Stones* and *Summer in the Spring* delve into traditional stories published in locations like the *Tomahawk* and the dreamsongs recorded by Frances Densmore, retranslating and reinterpreting Anishinaabe narrative forms. Echoing a similar endeavor, the voluminous works of Basil Johnston take account of the Anishinaabe cosmological record, ceremonie,s and customs and of course the author's own story. Eddie Benton Banai, by no means as prolific, also embraced the task of putting Anishinaabe narrative in printed form, his children's book *The Mishomis Book* becoming a vital learning tool for children and adults alike.

The first novel-length story published in English by an Anishinaabe writer comes relatively late in this arc. Ignatia Broker's *Night Flying Woman: An Ojibway Narrative*, which recounted the life of Broker's great-great-grandmother, appeared in print only a year before Louise Erdrich's first edition of *Love Medicine*, but it tells of a world that is only just beginning to experience the ruptures that the nineteenth century wrought on the Anishinaabeg, the legacies of which are severely felt in the latter novel. Erdrich, as novelist, short story writer, poet, and memoirist, also embodies a key characteristic of the Anishinaabe (indeed, Native American more broadly) literati—the ability to inhabit form like a shapeshifter, refusing its constraints and adapting the container to fit the contents. Louise's sisters Heid and Lise, poets and prose writers both; Anton and David Treuer, linguists, historians, essayists, and the latter a novelist and memoirist; Gordon Henry Jr., novelist, poet, musician; Margaret Noodin, linguist, poet, translator, curriculum writer; Kimberly Blaeser, poet, short story writer, photographer; Leanne Betasamosake Simpson, poet, short story writer, essayist; Armand Garnet Ruffo, poet, biographer; Drew Hayden Taylor, playwright and essayist; Kateri Akiwenzi-Damm, poet, short story writer, editor; Jim Northrup, poet, essayist, reporter, basket maker; Winona LaDuke, novelist, essayist, politician; not to mention those who also impress as visual artists, such as poet and painter Leo Yerxa and playwright and painter Ruby Slipperjack—among many others, these creators exemplify the relative ease with which Anishinaabe writers cross genres and registers in pursuit of the story. This is by no means to belittle the achievements of those more commonly known in single genres, such as young adult novelists Lenore Keeshig-Tobias and Richard Wagamese, mystery author Carole LaFavor, or playwrights Alanis King and E. Donald Two-Rivers.

A brief glance at any and all of these is enough to confirm the highly selective nature of this volume. Some significant names are left out. In the nineteenth century, for instance, we have not covered Maungwudaus's fellow commentators, missionaries, speakers George Copway (Gaagigegaabaw), Peter Jones (Kahkewaquonaby), Joseph Sawyer (Nawahjegeshegwabe), Catherine Sutton (Nahnebahnwequay), Peter Jacobs (Pahtahsega), John Sunday (Shawundais), and Henry Bird Steinhauer (Shahwahnegezhik), Egerton Ryerson, and Robert Steinhauer (see Smith). Similarly, we neglect the wider array of non-Ojibwe Anishinaabe writers, such as Simon Pokagan (Bodéwadmi) or Andrew Blackbird (Odawa); writers of traditional stories such as Eliza Morrin Morrison and John Couchois Wright; autobiographers, advocates, sharers of Anishinaabeg environmental knowledge, such as John

Rogers, Keewaydinoquay Peschel, and Wub-e-ki-niew; other journalists like Waubgeshig Rice, Donna Smith, or Tanya Talage, to name a precious few; and the many other published poets, dramatists, short story writers, and scholars who do not feature in these pages.

When we began this project, we were interested in exploring how Anishinaabe literatures explore and assert the need for proactive rather than reactive agency, an issue central to the work of many indigenous writers. If Vizenor's concept of survivance is one such strategy, in what other ways do Anishinaabe writers explore this issue? How does Anishinaabe literature itself respond and contribute to this need? Scholars of Native literatures have long emphasized key ethical concerns, such as responsibility, community, and the relationship of praxis to theory. Anishinaabe writing does not merely represent but engages with and participates in critical cultural conversations. The "ethnocritical" demands of Western discourses have tended to divorce politics from aesthetics, for instance. How have the two been reimagined by Anishinaabe writers? How do Anishinaabe writers explore or assert the interrelationship of culture and aesthetics with sovereignty? The essays collected herein address these questions in various ways; in doing so, they raise myriad more.

Aadisookanan Onaagadawenimaawaan: Critical Commentary

This volume contains a mixture of Native and non-Native voices writing about Anishinaabe literary production. It is a celebration of Anishinaabeg diversity, not an attempt to limit or define a community. Through these essays run threads of continuity and endurance, often refracted in contrasting colors. Like Nanabozho and his brothers, the authors search for truth in many directions and find many different answers. This multilayered map of Anishinaabe storytelling, poem construction, visioning and revisioning of history reflects a landscape of survivance. The essays are gathered loosely around a structure based on the four brothers, reflecting a focus on the categories of history, transformation, critique, and challenge. These arrangements are not all-defining; the overlaps are considerable.

Majikawiz

As Chris LaLonde notes in chapter 1, "Louise Erdrich's *Books and Islands in Ojibwe Country*: Writing, Being, Healing, Place," Erdrich's second memoir confronts and navigates apprehensions of loss, in turn ruminating on the means of countering loss. At the heart, he notes, are writing and place. Exploring the journey with her daughter and the writing journey of the memoir, LaLonde explores how Erdrich rearticulates an Anishinaabe sense of place and "tacitly critiques" Euro-American and Euro-Canadian authority. "The island-books articulate the story of the island that is the Earth on Turtle's back," he explains while pointing to their enduring legacy: "With *Books and Islands in Ojibwe Country*, Louise Erdrich rearticulates that story."

Nichole Biber, meanwhile, writes about "The Old World Display and the New World Displaced" in a chapter focused on nineteenth-century Anishinaabe author Maungwudaus and his self-published account of travels intended to situate a cosmopolitan Anishinaabe perspective in the American public sphere. Her analysis with comparative commentary explains how Maungwudaus "favors adaptability over assimilation and the strategic intelligence of the realist over the default acquiescence of the victimized."

The last chapter in this first section, frankly appraising David Treuer's reception of both "great critical praise and pronounced censure," Padraig Kirwan's "An Indian's Journey and Tribal Memory" situates that critical rendering and Treuer's praxis as requisite context for a full reading of *Rez Life*. That memoir, he argues, "sets Treuer's literary production, and some of his more contrarian stances, in a wider and more fathomable context." Treuer's preoccupation with the power of the literary imagination certainly endures throughout those pages, but so do the social realities and historic legacies that give rise to "a direct consideration of many of the most pressing issues facing the communities [of Leech Lake and Red Lake]."

Bakaawiz

In "The Anishinaabe Eco-Poetics of Language, Life, and Place in the Poetry of Schoolcraft, Noodin, Blaeser, and Henry," Susan Berry Brill de Ramírez explores the ethics of language and place through the work of four Anishinaabe poets who connect various points of time and place. She finds in the poems of Jane Schoolcraft, Margaret Noodin, Kimberly Blaeser, and Gordon Henry "a language and grammar of connection that opens itself up across poetic worlds" as they co-creatively explore the possibilities of language and story.[4]

Focusing on just one poet—Gordon Henry Jr.—Stuart Rieke homes in on the motif of sight as a shorthand for perception in more nuanced and complex terms. "Ambiguity and Empathy in the Poetry of Gordon

Henry Jr." elaborates an ethical framework for reading a single poem by Henry. Rieke explores the significance of ambiguity and the openness to multiplicity of meaning in the poem that allow the reader to intuit specifically Anishinaabe ways of seeing.

Sharon Holm's chapter, "Justice *in absentia:* The Re-stor(y)ing of Native Legal Presence through Narratives of Survivance in Gerald Vizenor's 'Genocide Tribunals,'" shines light on the enduring qualities of ethics and justice in Vizenor's writing. Exploring the "intergenerational legacy of pain and loss" encapsulated by the suicide of Dane Michael White in the early 1970s, Holm's chapter navigates the multiple myopias in institutional and colonial discourses that are the stuff and substance of Vizenor's examination of how these Anishinaabe values endure and animate his post-Indian poetics, offering "counterstrategies and alternative interpretative vision(s) to the asymmetrical hierarchies of power enshrined in neoliberal settler-state legal regimes."

Jiibayaaboozo

In "The Exceptional Power of the Dead in Heid E. Erdrich's *National Monuments*," Deborah L. Madsen examines how Erdrich "deconstructs the settler narrative of American exceptionalism" through the poetic recontextualization of human remains and other artefacts removed from the landscape in the process of settler colonization. "Throughout [Erdrich's] volume," she asserts, "the settler claim to a national identity that arises from occupation of the land" and the erasure of Native presence is subverted. The poems, in a sense, become monuments to endurance.

In "Anishinaabe Being and the Fallen God of Sun-Worshiping Victorians" Carter Meland contemplates the complex critical and literary conception of Naanabozho "as an ever-shifting, never fully knowable but always known spirit who lives in stories as a means to teach Anishinaabe people how to live as Anishinaabe people." He invites readers to see the trickster's creative-destructive, subversive-transgressive life as enduring inspiration. Citing Gearald Vizenor, Paul Radin, Carl Jung, Daniel Brinton, and others, he reviews and revises critical trickster theory.

Nanabozho

This final section opens with Jill Doerfler's important "Beyond Borders of Blood: An Anishinaabe Tribalography of Identity." Doerfler practices

LeAnne Howe's method of tribalography as a method for connecting Anishinaabe stories. Her objective is to examine and narrate the stories of a community where collective and individual identity has been invented and maintained for centuries. She focuses on the White Earth reservation but speaks broadly of the Anishinaabeg. Through stories of individuals, she unmasks the manifestations of the group and calls for an end to terminal dominance.

Mixing Anishinaabe with English to practice Anishinaabe literary theory, Margaret Noodin recounts how Jim Northrup imagined new questions, teased critical interpretations, and shook the expectations of his audience. "Enduring Critical Poses, Beyond Nation and History" begins with a description of the storiverse, or *dibaajimo'akii*, and situates Northrup's work in Anishinaabe literary existentialism, irony, and comedy.

Finally, echoing the ambivalence toward monumentalization in Madsen's chapter, David Stirrup's chapter, "Enduring Cultural Poses: Memory, Resistance, and Symbolic Sculpture," turns to the monuments and memorialized spaces that settler colonialism sets aside for its relationship with Native peoples. Focusing on two plays—*Chili Corn* by E. Donald Two-Rivers and *Ishi and the Wood Ducks* by Gerald Vizenor—Stirrup examines the counterdiscursive strategies and straightforward protest these authors invoke in deconstructing and dismantling the enduring cultural poses through which the dominant society has rendered the image of the indigenous monolithic. In the course of this discussion, Stirrup examines recent artistic interventions into and for the removal of problematic sculptures that significantly complicate any too-easy narrative of resistance and subversion such removals suggest, pointing to the enduring effect of asymmetries of power that these removals ironically emphasize. A short afterword returns us to story and a rumination on the question of filiation and affiliation that runs throughout these discussions of Anishinaabe texts and contexts.

Giga-dibaajimomin apane: Always Storytelling

At the heart of Anishinaabe storytelling is endurance through the centering of creative, sustaining, healing energy. The first brother shaped that energy into history, and the second brother gave form to stories as dance. When the third brother added the gift of the drum, the fourth brother, the one most human, could express all the trials of life through story, song, and dance. As time has passed, the dances and stories have evolved. The chapters in this collection come from many directions but, like the Thirsty

Dance, are created to promote peace and unity. Individuals make their own offerings, in some cases sacrificing a bit of themselves in the process. To truly understand others, we sometimes need to give up a bit of ourselves and be willing to bear the scars of life. Our intent is not to leave readers confused or to reduce the power of ceremonies by comparing them to literary criticism. We hope you will let go of presumption, hierarchy, and the hold of the present to travel through various times and landscapes to better understand the stories of the Anishinaabeg and perhaps in the end better understand yourself.

Notes

1. The most prominent works in this debate were Womack's *Red on Red*, Robert Warrior's *Tribal Secrets: Recovering American Indian Intellectual Traditions*, Jace Weaver's *That the People Might Live: Native American Literatures and Native American Community*, the three W's of American Indian literary nationalism, and Elvira Pulitano's *Toward a Native American Critical Theory*. The debate broadly revolved around a theoretical tradition most closely associated with the likes of Vizenor, Louis Owens, and Arnold Krupat and a literary nationalism inspired and encapsulated by figures such as Simon Ortiz and Elizabeth Cook-Lynn.

2. Such claims are, of course, usually fairly nebulous. With the explosion in Native literary output in recent years, we are not sure how true this statement remains. This is not to detract from the continued healthy state of Anishinaabeg literary production.

3. The *Tomahawk* was sold, moved, and rebranded the *Callaway Tomahawk* in 1927, in which year it also folded.

4. In the process of putting this volume together, the very sad news arrived that Susan Berry Brill de Ramírez and her husband had been killed in October 2018.

References

Banai, Eddie Benton. *The Mishomis Book: The Voice of the Ojibway*. Minneapolis: University of Minnesota Press, 2010 (1979).

Blaeser, Kimberly M. "Native Literature: Seeking a Critical Center." In *Looking at the Words of Our People: First Nations Analysis of Literature*, edited by Jeanette Armstrong, 53–61. Penticton, BC: Theytus Books, 1993.

———. *Gerald Vizenor: Writing in the Oral Tradition*. Norman: University of Oklahoma Press, 1996.

Broker, Ignatia. *Night Flying Woman: An Ojibway Narrative*. St. Paul: Borealis Books, 2006 (1983).

Doerfler, Jill. *Those Who Belong: Identity, Family, Blood, and Citizenship among the White Earth Anishinaabeg*. East Lansing: Michigan State University Press, 2015.

Doerfler, Jill, Niigaanwewidam James Sinclair, and Heidi Kiiwetinepinesiik Start. *Centering Anishinaabeg Studies: Understanding the World through Stories*. East Lansing: Michigan State University Press, 2013.

Doerfler, Jill, and Gerald Vizenor. *The White Earth Nation: Ratification of a Native Democratic Constitution*. Lincoln: University of Nebraska Press, 2012.

Erdrich, Louise. *Love Medicine*. New York: HarperCollins, 1984.

Mackay, James. "Ethics and Axes: Insider-Outsider Approaches to Native American Literature." In *The Native American Renaissance: Literary Imagination and Achievement*, edited by Alan R. Velie and A. Robert Lee, 39–57. Norman: University of Oklahoma Press, 2013.

Noodin, Margaret. *Bawaajimo: A Dialect of Dreams in Anishinaabe Language and Literature*. East Lansing: Michigan State University Press, 2014.

Ortiz, Simon. "Towards a National Indian Literature: Cultural Authenticity in Nationalism." *MELUS* 8, no. 2 (1981): 7–12.

Pulitano, Elvira. *Toward a Native American Critical Theory*. Lincoln: University of Nebraska Press, 2003.

Sinclair, Niigaanwewidam James. *Nindoodemag Bagijiganan: A History of Anishinaabeg Narrative*. PhD diss., University of British Columbia, 2013.

Smith, Donald. *Mississauga Portraits: Ojibwe Voices from Nineteenth-Century Canada*. Toronto: University of Toronto Press, 2013.

Spry, Adam. *Our War-Paint Is Writer's Ink*. Albany: State University of New York Press, 2018.

Stark, Heidi Kiiwetinepinesiik. "Marked by Fire: Anishinaabe Articulations of Nationhood in Treaty Making with the United States and Canada." *American Indian Quarterly* 36, no. 2 (2012): 119–49.

Vizenor, Gerald. *South of the Painted Stones*. Minneapolis: Callimachus, 1963.

———. *Summer in the Spring: Anishinaabe Lyric Poems and Stories*. Norman: University of Oklahoma Press, 1993 (1965).

———. *Everlasting Sky: Voices of the Anishinabe People*. St. Paul: Minnesota Historical Society Press, 2001 [1972].

———. *The People Named the Chippewa: Narrative Histories*. Minneapolis: University of Minnesota Press, 1984.

———, ed. *Touchwood: A Collection of Ojibway Prose*. Minneapolis: New Rivers Press, 1987.

———. *Manifest Manners: Narratives on Postindian Survivance*. Lincoln: University of Nebraska Press, 1999.

Warrior, Robert Allen. *Tribal Secrets: Recovering American Indian Intellectual Traditions*. Minneapolis: University of Minnesota Press, 1995.

Weaver, Jace. *That the People Might Live: Native American Literatures and Native American Community.* New York: Oxford University Press, 1997.

———. "Splitting the Earth: First Utterances and Pluralist Separatism." In *American Indian Literary Nationalism*, edited by Jace Weaver, Craig S. Womack, and Robert Warrior, 1–90. Albuquerque: University of New Mexico Press, 2006.

Womack, Craig S. *Red on Red: Native American Literary Separatism.* Minneapolis: University of Minnesota Press, 1999.

I
Majikawiz

Chapter 1

Louise Erdrich's *Books and Islands in Ojibwe Country*

Writing, Being, Healing, Place

CHRIS LALONDE

In July 2002, acclaimed mixed-blood Anishinaabe writer Louise Erdrich left Minneapolis, Minnesota, bound for the Lake of the Woods (or, alternatively, the Lake of the Sand Hills) in and beyond the northernmost reaches of the state. There she was to rendezvous with her partner near his birthplace and ancestral home. She would also spend some time in a retreat at a most unusual island library on another border lake between the United States and Canada. Erdrich, an enrolled member of the Turtle Mountain Chippewa band, brought her eighteen-month-old daughter, Nenaa'ikiizhikok, and a question that had been with her, shaping and informing her life: in her words, "Books. Why?" (4). Her ruminations on that question, on the journey to the homeland of her youngest daughter's paternal grandmother, and on the various relationships she discovered and recovered along the way form the subject and substance of her 2003 memoir, *Books and Islands in Ojibwe Country*. Published by National Geographic in its Directions series, begun just two years earlier, *Books and Islands* is shaped by apprehensions of and regarding loss on one hand and by how to counter that—her apprehensions, if you will—on the other. Writing and place are at the heart of both.[1]

Given that *Books and Islands in Ojibwe Country* is full of rich, nuanced descriptions of the relationship between mother and child, it may strike one as odd, if not wrong-minded, to focus on Erdrich's apprehensions. After all, she writes of being dazzled at the prospect of pregnancy and childbirth at the age of forty-seven and the amazement she feels still at Kiizhikok's presence eighteen months after her birth (16–17). Nursing her baby in the water just off the Eternal Sands of Big Island in the Lake of the Woods, the occasional wave splashing them, Erdrich thinks, "I could sit here forever" (78). In the water off Ernest Oberholtzer's islands on Rainy Lake on a day marked by hot wind, Erdrich and Kiizhikok "float together, into the channel, sighing in dreamy relief. We bob along in our life jackets, talking part Ojibwe, part English, and part mother-baby nonsense. The world is perfect" (118). Relishing her relationship with her youngest daughter, it is perhaps no wonder that Erdrich goes to sleep at night holding the baby's foot. That physical connection helps her sleep with a comforting certainty: "The world is calm and clear. I wish for nothing. I am not nervous about the future. Her toes curl around my fingers. I could even stop writing books" (65). Nor is it surprising that in her daughter, asleep beside her near book's end after they have returned to Minneapolis, Erdrich sees a light that can counter the lightlessness she reads in W. G. Sebald's writing near the end of *Austerlitz* (135).

Nevertheless, Erdrich's apprehension is palpable, and it centers on her daughter in a way that is illuminating precisely because it goes beyond the concerns one might have for one's child and their safety and well-being. That is, beyond the worry about Kiizhikok putting rocks and wood ticks into her mouth and either choking on or swallowing them, of the child falling off an island into the water, beyond the odd and baseless fear that an adult *maang* (loon) will peck the little girl, there is the very real fact that both child and mother can be made subject to an authority that calls their relationship into question. Crossing the border from Canada back to the United States, worried only that she might be hassled about the eagle spikes she is bringing back from the Eternal Sands, Erdrich is asked by the border guard for proof that she is Kiizhikok's mother. Made to pull aside and suffer an interrogation that circles again and again back to the child, Erdrich is so shaken by the experience that she finds she craves a strong drink and a cigarette, things she had given up long ago, when finally they are allowed to go.

A lover of books, Erdrich takes a number with her on her journey, including Sebald's *Austerlitz*. She is struck by the image of lightlessness at the end of a text that tries to put into words the extraordinary loss suffered by the Jewish people: the abandoned open-pit mines are, for Erdrich, the "image of the vanished past of his family and his people which . . . can never be brought up from those depths again" (*Austerlitz* 297). For Erdrich, the light that is her daughter and what she represents is threatened by a similar lightlessness—the one produced by the agents of the dominant culture. Moreover, having all the power and authority in such situations, those agents can produce conditions and tests that are beyond apprehension by those subject to them. *Books and Islands* makes this clear when Erdrich writes, "We've passed some mother/daughter test" (101) without revealing what precisely that test is or what constitutes passing it. All she knows, all we know, is that the power she has been made subject to threatens to turn her into someone she is not.

Books and Islands in Ojibwe Country would have us see that what threatens Erdrich and her daughter, a separation that would lead to a loss of self and the loss of a light that can shine for this generation and beyond, threatens much more than them. Indeed, those agents and what they represent have taken so very much from the Natives of North America; this is a story no less painful because it is so familiar. Her baby's father, Tobasonakwut, suffered the loss of his community at Niiyaawaan-gashing on the shores of the Lake of the Sand Hills. In Erdrich's words, "It is his burden to have seen what survived of the Ojibwe world around him nearly demolished by death, removal, forced relocation, the poison of alcohol, and to have experienced what amounted to kidnapping and a brutal attempt at brainwashing" (33–34). What holds for Tobasonakwut and his people holds for others as well, *Books and Islands* tells us in no uncertain terms. Erdrich recognizes and would have us understand that when she looks into the past, she sees the lightlessness that comes from "nine of every ten native people [having] perished of European diseases, leaving only diminished and weakened people to encounter what came next—the aggressions of civilization including government policies and missionaries and residential schools" (134–35).

To be subject to authority, be one Native in North America or Jewish in Nazi Germany, is to be subject to death. This is what Erdrich apprehends. The knowledge haunts her memoir and makes her apprehensive. Books are one way to counter death, she realizes, one way "we can talk to you even though we are dead. Here we are, the writer and I, regarding each other" (55). A potential difficulty is that turning to books necessarily foregrounds loss. More to the point, *Books and Islands* explicitly links books, representation, and death with the image of the gravestone at the beginning of the Alcoholics Anonymous book that Tobasonakwut had not noticed for more than thirty-five years. The fact that he had missed it tacitly reveals the degree to which we tend to gloss over the fact that writing is necessarily about absence; it is a monument to loss. More to the point, writing can inscribe death, can mark the tomb of the Native inasmuch as it can be used to tell the same old story of loss and doom for the People.

The little white stone Kiizhikok innocently puts in her mouth, not knowing any better, could lead to her death; it is "a classic choking hazard" (Erdrich 29). Alcohol, cunning and deceptive (41), can lead to the same thing. The gravestone in the beginning of the AA book is a reminder of what awaits if the People either succumb to a curiosity or temptation offered first by white traders in the eighteenth century or are driven to it by contemporary agents of the dominant culture. Erdrich tells her readers that alcohol affects all Anishinaabeg, that "There are . . . [none], including mixed-bloods like me, whose lives have not been affected by the perplexing pains of addiction. The degrading longing and despair of alcoholism changes even the most intelligent among us" (41).

Erdrich has to get past her apprehension to reach an understanding. So does the reader. *Books and Islands in Ojibwe Country* opens with a standard device for apprehension, especially in travel writing: a map. Coming before page one, it is actually two maps. There is a relatively small representation of a portion of North America with the United States both dominant and tellingly made to stand out by being highlighted in white. The nation is labeled, but only the state of Minnesota is rendered in outline. Canada is also labeled, although we do not see the whole of the country, and three provinces are outlined (at least in part). Two of them are named with abbreviations. There is a scale. This simple map purports to help the reader get a handle on place by locating it in space and orienting it in relation to nations and borders. We have known for some time the relationship between cartography and authority, between maps and ideology. A map can be, in Thongchai Winichakul's words, "a model for, rather than a model of, what it purported to represent" (quoted in Anderson 173). Here, the logo-map erases geographical specificity in favor of national identity and separation.

A section of this small map is boxed and enlarged to its immediate left and above. In effect, we move from logo-map toward a map of place as we move from smaller to larger map. In the latter, the reader is offered a scale for distance as well; there are also lines of longitude and latitude to degree and minute, state and province names, the international border, major highways, towns, lakes, rivers, reservation, and reserve. The specificity of the larger map does not necessarily mean that it is any less problematic, of course. Writing on the relation between cultural imperialism and the writings of big game hunters to British North America in the mid-nineteenth century, for instance, Greg Gillespie reminds us that the selectivity of map-making is bound up in how "a culture imposes itself on space" (570). Such imposition is frequently imposed on the earlier inhabitants of that space, as new place names are deployed to make the space over into that which is recognizable by the dominant culture and its agents (Gillespie 570). In the larger map, the most telling instances of such naming concern the body of water, seventy miles long and wide, that covers nearly the whole of the northwest angle of Minnesota, the town identified on its shore, and the reservations and reserves on either side of the international border.

The large lake is labeled Lake of the Woods. Erdrich quotes John Tanner on the inappropriateness of that name, on there being precious little forest around the lake, and on the Anishinaabe name for the lake: Pub-be-kwaw-waung-gaw Sau-gi-e-gun, or Lake of the Sand Hills. An 1897 presentation at the annual meeting of the Historical and Scientific Society of Manitoba reveals that the name the lake is now known by is a mistranslation of one of the two names given by the French explorer Verendrye in 1731. One wonders if the initial and continued identification of the lake with woods is connected to the fur trade and the logging industry. The lake was the route Voyageurs took into the northwest territory, and it was a key location once logging came to that part of Canada and Minnesota. In any case, the act of translation and naming is indicative of the desire of the dominant culture to make the place its own.

According to Alan Rayburn, the township and thus the community of Morson, the place on the eastern shore of Lake of the Woods from which Erdrich departs to get to her island lodge base camp, was named for Frederick Montye Morson, a county of York, Ontario, judge who served from 1891 until 1931. The Law Society of Upper Canada notes in its anniversary reminiscence of Morson that he was the last judicial appointment made by the first prime minister of Canada, John A. Macdonald. The name of the township and town stands as an example of how naming can be linked to nationalism and the appropriation of place. This also holds for the reservations and reserves, those spaces determined and set aside by the Canadian and US governments.

The reach of the Macdonald government and the desire to forge a nation that motivated it were contested by the Métis rebellion, led by Louis Riel. Riel enters *Books and Islands in Ojibwe Country* via a young Anishinaabe guide at the fishing lodge who is named after the nineteenth-century Métis leader. In effect, the twentieth-century native links present and past and, I suggest, Erdrich's text with rebellion against authority and its desire to name and take ownership of place. Such rebellion begins with the map itself. Even before she engages in an act of renaming (or rather returning to name) concerning the body of water we know of as Lake of the Woods, Erdrich locates on her larger map the place where Tobasonakwut was born and spent his childhood, identifies it with its Anishinaabemowin name, and labels the whole area Ojibwe Country. Tobasonakwut's dream is to return the traditional healing practices of the Midewewin to Niyaawaangashing, to take back what has been lost when the government and the church cleaved the People from their land, their language, and their spiritual practices.

In labeling the larger map Ojibwe Country, *Books and Islands* produces a supplement to the nation, be it the United States or Canada, and thus calls the identity of and their authority and power into question. Of perhaps greater import is the fact that the effort at apprehension and orientation at the heart of all maps is immediately supplemented in Erdrich's narrative by a certain disorientation and reorientation. The narrative begins with the declaration: "My travels have become so focused on books and islands that the two have merged for me. Books, islands. Islands, books. Lake of the Woods in Ontario and Minnesota has 14,000 islands" (3). In merging books and islands, in blurring the boundaries between them, the opening calls into question boundaries, arbitrary and otherwise, and begins to produce another map and mapping, one from an Anishinaabe perspective rooted in Ojibwe Country. This other perspective, and what it reveals about relations and relationships, runs counter to the border, its guards, and what we might consider an ideology based on separation and the process of Othering.

Early on, Erdrich writes that once settled in on the Lake of the Woods island lodge that serves as their base camp, she gives herself over to "*doing what the baby wants*" (28; emphasis in original). She notes that there is a certain lack of distinction and sharpness as a result, a certain dream-like quality to place and time, but she also notes that this is a time "of great complexity and learning" (28). What she describes is strikingly similar to what fellow Anishinaabe author Winona LaDuke tells us is the fundamental character of the Anishinaabe world. In *All Our Relations*, LaDuke writes,

> The Anishinaabeg world undulated between material and spiritual shadows, never clear which was more prominent at any time. It was as if the world rested in those periods rather than in the light of day. Dawn and dusk, *biidaabin* and *oshkidibikad*. The gray of sky and earth just the same, the distinctions between the worlds barely discernible. (*All Our Relations* 115)

Theresa S. Smith also notes the "fluidity" of the Anishinaabe world and worldview (46). In the borderlands and in a border state, fully immersed in the world and worldview of the People, Erdrich is in a position to do more than simply recognize the depth and complexity of her relationship with her daughter; she is able to see and articulate the same thing regarding the place, the People, and their language.

The Anishinaabe worldview recognizes the interplay of change and constancy as well as the fluidity and interconnectedness between people and place. Basil Johnston, whose tapes of Anishinaabemowin Erdrich listens to when she begins to learn the language, tells us that the vision of Gitche Manitou that led to the first creation of the world revealed to the Creator the constancy that ran through the change he beheld (Johnston 12). In Erdrich's text, bogs serve as the image of this tenet of the People's understanding and apprehension of the world. As lake levels rise, a portion of *mashkii* pulls loose from the bottom and drifts with currents and wind until bumping into either the mainland or an island. There it can stay until picked up again by the wind or until it breaks apart. Shorelines can change; in the case of an island, bogs "can change its shape instantly" (Erdrich 58) by attaching to it.

Bogs may be rooted to the lake bottom or floating, attached to shorelines or adrift, and this mutability is a telling reminder of the change at the heart of Gitche Manitou's vision and Ojibwe Country. At the same time, the nature of *mashkii* as the place of *mashkikii*, medicine from the bog, remains constant. Erdrich writes of the various uses of bog plants. She becomes very happy when she sees the great bog between the Red Lake Reservation and the Lake of the Woods on her drive north because she recognizes that the rich ecosystem is full of medicine that helps the People heal. It also tells her she is in Ojibwe Country, for as Tobasonakwut says, "'Where there is wiikenh [a bog plant with myriad medicinal uses], there are Anishinaabeg'" (59).

For Erdrich, Anishinaabemowin, or Ojibewemowin, the language of the People, is connected to the "ineffable and compassionate spirit residing in all that lives" (85). That language is "especially good at describing intellectual and dream states" (84). Given that the Creator, Gitche Manitou, gave humans the power to dream, the relationship between language and dreaming speaks to the nature of Anishinaabe identity. Tobasonakwut cherishes the language which agents of the dominant culture tried to beat out of him, and he especially likes the phrase *andopawatchigan*, or "seek your dream" (84). If realized, that phrase means that the dreamer first identifies and then apprehends the dream; they then carry out over and over what the dream tells them to do. This leads to the dreamer "gradually com[ing] into a balanced relationship with all of life" (84). That relationship is articulated, LaDuke tells us, in the phrase *minobimaatisiiwin*, or "good life" (*All Our Relations* 132).

Books and Islands in Ojibwe Country makes clear that there is also a direct and intimate relationship between language and place. Erdrich tells us that Anishinaabemowin "is adapted to the land as no other language can possibly be. Its philosophy is bound up in northern earth, lakes, rivers, forests, and plains" (85). Erdrich is not alone in recognizing the connection between language and place. In *The People Named the Chippewa*, Gerald Vizenor tells us that "The words the woodland tribes spoke were connected to the place the words were spoken. The poetic images were held, for some tribal families, in song pictures and in the rhythms of visions and dreams in music: timeless and natural patterns of seeing and knowing the energies of the earth" (24–26). Biologist Michael Wassegijig Price noted that Anishinaabe naming of plants is contingent and place-based more so than systematic. Language and naming, then, is part of and indicative of, in his words, "a very . . . fluid system."

There is also, of course, a direct and intimate relationship between the Anishinaabeg and place. *Books and Islands* offers us Tobasonakwut and his people as an example of this. Prior to contact, the ravages of economics and disease, removal, and relocation, the Big George family lived a life linked to the lake. There they found the Creator's gifts, sustenance and medicine, for which they offered thanks. "Literally cell by cell composed of the lake and the lake's islands," the People were the "waves on the lake" that is the creator (Erdrich 34). Moreover, the big water dotted with islands is a complex system that necessitates that one read carefully, pay attention to context, and not be blindly taken in by appearance. This attention to contingency and context is at the heart of the Anishinaabe way of seeing and knowing the world. The image of this complexity in *Books and Islands in Ojibwe Country*, for Erdrich and for readers, is the waves, counterwaves, underwaves, and crosswaves produced by wind, water, and islands. The waves are the product of yesterday's wind from one direction and today's wind from another. Thus, seeing and feeling only today's wind would be to misapprehend the lake. Erdrich links the People to the lake and recognizes that the "image of complexity and shifting mutability" (77) of the former is also true of the latter.

In Anishinaabe cosmology, lakes in the north country are linked by "watery tunnels" (Erdrich 72) that enable the underwater Manitouk to travel between bodies of water and continue their struggle with the Thunderers. Theirs is a dynamic relationship that helps keep the world balanced while emphasizing to the People the need to pay attention and take care. One does not want to be on the water when a Thunderer comes; one shows respect for the Thunderers and Mishebeshu. The underground waterways that stretch throughout northern Minnesota and Ontario give the lie to the border, making it of little consequence, by emphasizing connections that are bound up in a different way of knowing and being in the world.

Erdrich's rendering of place from an Anishinaabe perspective constitutes an alternate map to that offered by and from the West. In effect, she is at once following and departing from the lead of Ernest Oberholtzer, the man whose Rainy Lake island library she goes to after leaving the Lake of the Woods and weathering the international border crossing. In 1912, Oberholtzer and Anishinaabe Taytahpaswaywitong, or Billy McGee, set out by canoe to explore the largely poorly mapped and (from the white perspective at least) unknown area of Canada known as the Barrens. Oberholtzer mapped the streams, rivers, and lakes they paddled and the terrain they passed. In Erdrich's phrasing, Oberholtzer "filled in the blanks on the maps" (105). Erdrich does the same. The difference is that her dreamlike time in Ojibwe Country leads to an articulation of a path to healing rooted in language and place. Oberholtzer's journey, on the other hand, comes to be marked by desperation, hallucination, and a sense of foreboding. This is understandable, given that Oberholtzer and Taytahpaswaywitong were racing against time as they struggled to find their way through the Barrens and on to Hudson Bay, only to be too late for the last steamer out, and then to Lake Winnipeg before winter locked them in. More must be said, however; Erdrich writes that "Loneliness, anxiety, and the strangeness of the lake" (105) called Nueltin or Sleeping Island Lake, contributed to Oberholtzer's mental state and sense at one point that he would die in the wild. He goes so far as to pen and leave his last words atop an esker.

Erdrich recognizes and would have us know that Oberholtzer was a champion of the natural world, instrumental in the creation of the Quetico-Superior wilderness, and a friend to and lover of the Anishinaabeg and their culture. He asked them to tell him stories so often that the Anishinaabeg gave him the name Atisokan, which means "story" (Erdrich 125). He never fashioned the stories he heard and the things he learned about the People into books, however. He never wrote a book recounting his extraordinary journey with Taytahpaswaywitong. In short, the island or islands remained sleeping, and with them slumbered any articulation of place that might have been, as was the case of John Tanner's memoir of the lakes country, informed by an Anishinaabe perspective. Contra Oberholtzer beset by loneliness in the far reaches of the Barrens, Erdrich turns to books, the last words of *Books and Islands in Ojibwe Country* tell us, "So that I will never be alone" (141). This is true, I think, for both reading them and writing them.

Erdrich favors the word *Ojibwe* for the People rather than the original form, Anishinaabe, because she pictures that the former is derived from the verb which means "to write": *Ozhibii'ige* (Erdrich 11). She would have her reader see, then, that the identity of the People is connected not merely to place and to language but to writing. Tracing the root *mazina*, Erdrich shows us it is shared by the Anishinaabemowin words for books and for pictographs, along with a host of other words that name constructed images and the "substances upon which the images are put" (5). The rock paintings on the islands, hundreds to thousands of years old, are examples of the centrality of writing and representation to the People. The pictographs that she describes articulate the nature of the world and the worldview of the Anishinaabe. The wild rice spirit pictograph, for instance, reminds us that there is a spirit in all things. It is also a reminder of the importance of gifts and reciprocity, for *manoomin* was and is a gift from the Creator, and one has to be sure to give thanks, often with tobacco, in return. The horned figure and water drum picture the vitality of ceremony in general and the practices of the Midewiwin society in particular. Erdrich asks that we pay particular attention to the "lines drawn between things" in the pictographs "for they express relationships" (56). The rock painting of the journey to the spirit world and the pictograph of the Thunderbird with a line linking it to another figure are reminders of the connections between things and between persons.

Leaving Oberholtzer's islands to return home, Erdrich's mobile phone finds a signal and she is able to call family, friends, and her bookstore from the road. She proclaims, "All of a sudden I am back in the web of connection" and fancies that she is "off the islands," but she qualifies herself immediately with "Or so I think" (130). Arriving home tells us why she was mistaken and reinforces that she must stay on the islands, figuratively if not literally, and that she has in effect not left them. The arrival brings a sign of impending death and loss. The great elm in the front yard, bigger than any other tree in the neighborhood, has contracted Dutch elm disease and is slated for removal in an effort to slow its spread. Erdrich feels the shock of its passing as it is first limbed and then felled. She finishes *Books and Islands in Ojibwe Country* as the city stump grinder reduces the last of the tree to chips and sawdust. Here we see in no uncertain terms that Erdrich turns to writing in the face of loss and thus returns to the connections that are articulated in the writings she finds especially on Painted Rock Island.

The elm Erdrich named Old Stalwart is marked with the letter A and a red ring, "sign of doom" (Erdrich 131). Because they are alive, because they are evidence that the material and symbolic practices of the Anishinaabe are alive (50), the rock paintings counter the story of doom foretold in the bright red circled A. The first pictograph she visits on Painted Rock Island, of a great sturgeon floating above a divining tent, links place, people, the material and the spiritual. It reminds her and us of the need to recognize, honor, and learn from those connections and put them and what is to be learned from them into writing, into books. It reminds us of what the Anishinaabeg have known for generations. The sturgeon is an especially rich example for Erdrich and the reader. Because its life span is so long, females can live upward of 100 years, and because it ranges widely, reintroduced individuals at the southern limit of its range have been found hundreds of miles away, the lake sturgeon is, in LaDuke's words, "a great teacher of interconnectivity" (*Recovering the Sacred* 234). Listening to the sturgeon, paying attention to what it has to teach us about relationships, teaches us much about our responsibility to the other inhabitants of Earth and to each other. The island-books articulate the story of the island that is the Earth on Turtle's back. With

Books and Islands in Ojibwe Country, Erdrich rearticulates that story. In so doing, she offers an answer to her opening question, and ours.

Books. Why?
Because they are wealth, sobriety, and hope. (99)

Notes

1. In his 2006 article on *Books and Islands in Ojibwe Country*, David T. McNab focuses on place and indigenous knowledge. My analysis differs from McNab's in attending to the fundamental role death and loss play in Erdrich's text and its shaping; in taking the measure of representations in and of the text, especially as they are connected to what I read as a tacit critique of Euro-American and Euro-Canadian authority, and rooting Erdrich's memoir in Anishinaabe cosmology and worldview. Quotations from *Books and Islands in Ojibwe Country* are from the 2003 hardcover edition published by the National Geographic Society.

References

Anderson, Benedict. *Imagined Communities*. Rev. ed. London: Verso, 1991.
Erdrich, Louise. *Books and Islands in Ojibwe Country*. Washington, DC: National Geographic Society, 2003.
Gillespie, Greg. "'I Was Well Pleased with Our Sport Among the Buffalo': Big-Game Hunters, Travel Writing, and Cultural Imperialism in the British North American West, 1847–72." *Canadian Historical Review* 83, no. 4 (December 2002): 555–84.
Johnston, Basil. *Ojibway Heritage*. Lincoln: University of Nebraska Press, 1976.
LaDuke, Winona. *All Our Relations: Native Struggles for Land and Life*. Boston: South End Press, 1999.
———. *Recovering the Sacred: The Power of Naming and Claiming*. Boston: South End Press, 2005.
McNab, David T. "The Significance of Place and Indigenous Knowledge in Louise Erdrich's *Books and Islands in Ojibwe Country*." *European Journal of American Culture* 25, no. 3 (2006): 205–19.
Price, Michael Wassegijig. "Ojibwe Plant Names." Public lecture, Bemidji State University, Bemidji Minnesota, February 20, 2006.
Rayburn, Alan. *Place Names of Ontario*. Toronto: University of Toronto Press, 1997.
Sebald, Winfried Georg. *Austerlitz*. Translated by Anthea Bell. New York: Random House, 2001.

Smith, Theresa S. *Island of the Anishinaabeg*. Moscow: University of Idaho Press, 1995.
Vizenor, Gerald. *The People Named the Chippewa*. Minneapolis: University of Minnesota Press, 1983.
"York County Court Judge F. Montye Morson, 1853–1944." Time Capsule, Winter 2004. Law Society of Upper Canada. http://www.lsuc.on.ca/about/a/history/time-capsule/winter04.

Chapter 2

The Old World Display and the New World Displaced

NICHOLE BIBER

On the cover of the slim volume published by nineteenth-century Anishinaabek author Maungwudaus, an ink drawing of an indigenous man dressed in full regalia likely was sufficient to pique the interest of a nineteenth-century public alternately fascinated and repulsed by North American Indians. The man pictured wears a headdress of feathers, what appears to be a bear-claw necklace, and furs, and he holds a long bow while looking off into the distance. Above him appears a straightforward title: "An Account of the Chippewa Indians." Below his feet, potential readers may find the "Price: 12 ½ cents," and the information "Boston; Published By The Author, 1848." Though naming a specific tribe may or may not have made a difference to those seeking to satisfy their curiosity or preconceptions about North America's original inhabitants, the provided detail indicates an author who prioritized accuracy. In this self-published work, a subtle story of motivations unfolds. Maunguwudaus exposes the decided peculiarity of the English-speaking world through his perspective as an independent-minded Chippewa Indian well aware of his perceptual captivity in the self-professed norms of the dominant culture. The sheer catharsis and intrinsic social activism of voicing his singular experience and insights hinge on a tribal point of view that continues to operate in the confines of the English language and culture.

This concise, rich account offers important insights into the question of what exactly is meant when one speaks of a tribal point of view—a concept fraught with potential oversimplification and pat sentimentalization. As an indigenous person born and raised in an urban, English-speaking world, Maungwudaus provided a way for me to unpack whether and why and how contemporary Indians might still consider our perspectives as distinctly tribal. In essence, I understand the tribal perspective as the accumulation of values dependent on deference to the natural world and then expressed through clear observation of how the present moment does and does not acquiesce to that central truth. Maungwudaus, equipped with Anishinaabemowin as his first language and his lived experience in both traditional forest life and urban centers, provides contemporary readers to access what D'Arcy McNickle calls the "conditions and consequences" of identification.

In *Native American Tribalism: Indian Survival and Renewals*, McNickle's survey of contact history rests on a foundation that views the "covert, inner life of the people" as an underconsidered aspect of the ongoing contact narrative that is at least as important as legal quotes and dates of significant treaties or legislation. McNickle supports a "more rational modern thesis" that "proposes a correlation between basic personality structure and cultural persistence." Interior, indigenous identifications that remain intact despite external circumstances that would denigrate or remove these alignments suggest that there is something about indigenous inner life that proves particularly adept at retaining tribal identifications and loyalties. The massive changes wrought by contact entails an inescapable reckoning with the dominant culture. What factors determine whether that adaptation is underscored by the desire to retain the dignity of autonomous definitions of community and self? McNickle's reckoning of tribal identity is based largely on the question of what "agreement or conformity existed between observable acculturated behavior and the covert, inner life of the people" (8), indicating an intrinsic value system that underlays every observation and interaction. The contact narrative provided by Maungwudaus shows how key influential aspects of indigenous identity are not necessarily named as such, but nevertheless infuse every interaction and iteration. Foremost, the centrality of present-moment accretions of meaning that characterize the Anishinaabek language operate alongside the elder brother status of the animal and plant worlds and together provide covertly tribal observations.

This view favors adaptability over assimilation and the strategic intelligence of the realist over the default acquiescence of the victimized.

In response to arguments that suggest the loss of traditional industries and languages as equivalent to cultural loss, McNickle points to the simple fact that tribal peoples continue to self-identify as such, making it difficult to entirely dismiss the possibility that tribal alignments remain viable. More concretely, the retention of certain lands, a unique legal status, and against-the-odds increases in population underscore the unique position that existing tribal peoples maintain. Concerning the "survival of fragments out of the past," McNickle offers that the "function of culture is always to reconstitute the fragments into an operational system. The Indians, for all that has been lost or rendered useless out of their ancient experience, remain a continuing ethnic and cultural enclave with a stake in the future" (9). This offers a template for exploring the dual psychological and social acumen of an author like Maungwudaus. Faced with displays of largess and poverty at the center of the cosmopolitan world of the mid-nineteenth century, Maungwudaus responds with critical insight, subtle humor, and a confidential tone that indicates a steady foundation of the values born of his cultural alignments.

For those drawn in enough to read further, the title page of "An Account of the Chippewa Indians" supplies the following details:

> An Account of the Chippewa Indians, Who have been Traveling Among the Whites, in the United States, England, Ireland, Scotland, France and Belgium: with very interesting incidents in relation to the general characteristics of the English, Irish, Scotch, French, and Americans, with regard to their hospitality, peculiarities, etc. Written by Maungwudaus, The Self-Taught Indian of the Chippewa Nation, for the benefit of his youngest Son, called Noodinokay, whose Mother died in England. Price 12 1/2 cents. Boston: Published By The Author. 1848.

It is notable that Maungwudaus supplies only his and his son's Anishinaabek names, free of translation and unaccompanied by any Anglicized aliases that would otherwise compromise this decision to self-identify so strictly. He is certain to proclaim that he is both self-taught and self-published, taking full responsibility for his literacy in English and stressing the independent thinking behind his project. McNickle proposes that the "perceptual screen" of particularly indigenous psychological traits determine what "the group accepts and what it rejects among the choices made possible" (11). Considering the care he takes to underscore the independent nature of his learning, it follows that Maungwudaus's pursuit of literacy was in accord with his self-identification as a Chippewa with something to say, rather that any urge toward assimilation (11). The phrase "for the benefit of his youngest Son" potentially links his English literacy to the desire to benefit his family—notably a young son, who represents the continuity of future generations.

Maungwudaus's title page provides further clues to the process and motivations behind his writing. The specification that he is of the "Chippewa Nation," as opposed to simply a Chippewa, indicates that his politics tend toward the assertion of tribal nationhood and sovereignty. Considering the ongoing legislative efforts to undermine tribal affiliations and encourage assimilation, his wording roundly rejects the conditional renunciation of tribal loyalties as the road to the implied benefits of US citizenship. Even before he delves into the larger communication of his perspectives, this deceptively brief listing of particulars initiates the careful reader into a key facet of the writer's narrative style—a depth of interrelated issues made apparent through an economy of words. The complexity of influences that are apparent in seemingly small decisions—the dedication to his son, the clarification that he is of the Chippewa Nation—offer a sense of how his writing process is an example of a "universal psychological trait" that McNickle and others strive to prove a viable concept.

In *Red on Red: Native American Literary Separatism*, contemporary Creek scholar Craig Womack examines how "structural categories become problematic—they separate the stories from their political context" (17). In other words, the critical voice is limited by the conviction that stories are spoken about in one manner, politics another, and personal reflection yet another. (The genre-related breakdown of courses offered by myriad English departments proves his point. Perhaps the current movement toward interdisciplinary studies indicates burgeoning awareness of the limits of the category.) Womack's efforts to "demonstrate the interdependency of politics and literature" (17) find a champion in this late nineteenth-century Anishinaabek author. Maungwudaus seamlessly blends social, psychological, cultural, and political commentary into a highly accessible work that proves to be both unapologetically critical and richly entertaining.

As a matter of praxis, accomplished storytellers craft narratives that are accessible, entertaining, and instructive to a variety of ages and interests. Basil Johnston prefaces *Ojibway Heritage* with the reminder that "The stories recorded are not to be interpreted literally; but freely, yet rationally according to the Ojibway views of life. Readers and listeners are expected to draw their own inferences, conclusions, and meanings according to their intellectual capacities" (8). Stories with abundant layers of meaning within a concisely phrased commonality invite the audience to respond according to individual associations that reflect the culture's views of life. Gerald Vizenor considers the characteristic flexibility of storytelling in the following terms:

> The woodland creation stories are told from visual memories and ecstatic strategies, not scriptures. In the oral tradition, the mythic origins of tribal people are creative expressions, original eruptions in time, not a mere recitation or a recorded narrative in grammatical time. The teller of stories is an artist, a person of wit and imagination, who relumes the diverse memories of the visual past into the experiences and metaphors of the present. (7)

Vizenor conjures a social context hinging on the vastness of the present moment. Preordained forms reliant on convention and authority prove inadequate for matching traditional storytelling as a creative act born of context. Interpretation or criticism on the part of the narrator would be superfluous and out of keeping with the moral capacity of storytelling. Moral lessons are certainly there, to be picked up on or missed by those more or less acquainted with the societies in question. It is not the teller but the interaction that leads to the insight. These dynamics reflect the composition of traditional stories and language, wherein individuated communal experience determines accurate expression. In other words, what is happening houses the richest significance. Definitions attached after the fact only limit the depth and scope of a moment's inherent gauging of cultural morality and values, which in turn limits the freedom of interpretation for any particular reader or listener. It takes "wit and imagination" to express how current thought exists in tandem with the remembered. The quest to understand their simultaneity requires "ecstatic strategies" that offer liberation from the categorization (and thus limitation) of experience. Expressing the living moment as the constant forging of reality is a group effort involving the speaker, listener, relatives, spirits, and undergirding ideologies.

Prioritizing shared experience invites the clear expression of this inclusivity. Narrative success is measured by the diverse sensory, emotional, intellectual, and visceral responses inspired by the story. The vast interweaving of possibility and influence that makes up each moment of a narrative reflects that same phenomena in life. Spiritual, generational, historical, ecological, and psychological influences are ongoing and of uncanny depth. An artist storyteller can concisely expose the inadequacy of categories and roles that wash out and limit the awareness of this whole. In this spirit, Maungwudaus offers direct observations, stated clearly and thus able to access the richest stores of insight. Like the "teller of stories" in Vizenor's explanation, Maungwudaus is an experiential artist whose talents are an example of McNickle's vision of a specifically indigenous perspective. His "Account" offers a deep understanding of his tribal identity by way of a clear explanation of the decidedly foreign context in which he finds himself. His frame of reference proves unmistakably Chippewa and thus reveals the key flexibility and adaptability of his ultimately traditional narrative sense.

One avowed purpose of "Account" is to inform his son of the "peculiarities" of the whites. Presenting the whites as subjects of an almost ethnographic curiosity establishes a far different tone than that found in nineteenth-century works by Native authors who are careful to cite sympathetic whites as their model reading audience, while also courting them for entrance into the world of publishing. Though Maungwudaus does include "pleasing testimony" from the likes of George Catlin and Joseph John Gurney, these character sketches and appeals for kindness are relegated to the back pages (12). This makes for a distinctly different set of priorities in comparison with the conspicuous namedrop that begins George Copway's *Traditional History*, which on the very first page informs the reader that the contents are dedicated "TO AMOS LAWRENCE, ESQ, OF Boston, Massachusetts, THIS VOLUME WITH FEELINGS OF DEEP GRATITUDE, AND SENTIMENTS OF THE HIGHEST RESPECT, IS AFFECTIONATELY INSCRIBED BY THE AUTHOR" (1). In writing for his son, Maungwudaus grants his narrative a foundation of intimacy and unedited reflection. This "Account" promises to be something different from those penned by Copway, Andrew Blackbird, and even William Warren, whose avowed wishes to prove beneficial to their nations read as vague and general in comparison with Maungwudaus's filial motivations. Furthermore, the death in England of Noodinokay's mother, Maungwudaus's wife, firmly establishes the personal nature of his writing, assuring that what follows is going to be candid and answer to no one but himself, his son, and the memory of the departed. In other words, this is an Anishinaabek text for an Anishinaabek audience, that also happens to be written in English.

That this is a self-published work attests to the likely small distribution and notice it received. Maungwudaus probably did not expect to garner great interest among the majority of readers. (I also mention how this resonates with my own difficulty in locating and procuring a copy of his work in the twenty-first century.) Still, the fact that he wrote it in English and took the trouble to have it published in Boston attests that although he only promises the contents will be beneficial to Noodinokay, outside readers were still desirable. Indeed, he begins with the statement, "I will not ask the reader for pardon. The short notice of me on another page will induce him to excuse me for using improperly the English language" (3). The unseen, potential audience of the public sphere is acknowledged at the outset, providing an additional layer of intent to whatever effect the "Account" might have. His attitude is not one of self-belittlement or the appeasement of superiors; rather, he bluntly states the conditions of this literary relationship by saying what he won't do and what the reader will. This suggests a subtle difference between pardon and excuse: he is not asking to be indulged or tolerated so much as justified and exempted. By the same token, he is not so much invoking as dismissing or speaking apart from the conventional English muse. Far from being an apologist for his forays into the literate sphere, he takes command of his efforts and demands to be read on his own terms.

Throughout the narrative, the cultural basis of Maungwudaus's perspective invites the reader to ascribe exoticism to European behaviors. Through his careful selection of details and understated reportage, Maungwudaus deftly casts provocative social judgment on the highest of European society. He was not a passive curiosity to be ogled; he constantly forged his own assessments of the Europeans by observing how they displayed themselves as they displayed the Chippewa. What the Europeans choose to show the visitors speaks volumes about their self-conception and affords Maungwudaus an important outlet for the inherent autonomy of his critical perspective.

This brief account—not twenty pages in length—is replete with provocative social commentary concerning the cultures he came in contact with. The fact that he and the rest of the company of Anishinaabek were traveling partly under the dubious auspices of "Catlin's Indian Curiousities" is indicative of the spirit in which they were received—exotic specimens tailored to civilized amusement. This is well illustrated by a scene in which "Our war-chief shot a buck in the Park, through the heart, and it fell down dead three hundred yards before four thousand ladies and gentlemen. This was done to amuse them" (4–5). The understated tone and keen word choice showcase Maungwudaus's facility with the impact of concise phrasing. Straightforward imagery underscores the stark reality of this carefully staged and constructed death scene, wherein the Chippewa actors and British observers engage in a playacted hunt.

The unadorned description of the scene evokes a sense of disconnect that is diametrically different from the preparations, songs, and rituals that characterize the Anishinaabek way of procuring game. In this foreign land, all involved are merely props to a forced version of authentic Indian doings—a showcase of stereotyped exoticism. In the end, there is only a real dead buck alongside the intrinsically abstract and ethically questionable sense of amusement gained in witnessing such a kill. The appellation "ladies and gentleman" highlights the disparity of this thinly veiled bloodlust, in which 4,000 dignitaries and citizens of a civilized nation gather for the chance to witness a buck "fall down dead" by the hand of a "war-chief." The difference between this and the hunting patterns at home hinge on the spirit and circumstances under which such killing is undertaken. One death is attended to through rituals that detail sustainable survival in a specific ecosystem, the other is a curiosity designed to "amuse" those present in the manufactured confines of the park.

In France, where they stayed five months with the Catlin show, the company of Chippewa "Shook hands with Louis Phillipe and all his family in the Park, called St. Cloud; gave them little war dance, shooting with bows and arrows at a target, ball play; also rowed our birch bark canoe in the artificial lake, amongst swans and geese. There were about four thousand French ladies and gentlemen with them" (6). The poignant imagery of Chippewa, swans, and geese on display on an artificial lake is again written with a descriptively concise air. The quality of restraint in his selection of adjectives grants the embedded social criticism a crisp subtlety. The "little war dance" takes on an air of absurdity, a trifling affair that has nothing to do with the intense ritual it is meant to represent. The specific mention of "our birch bark canoe" evokes the long hours of gathering and careful craftsmanship that lay behind its construction. The following account is provided in Frances Densmore's 1928 publication *Uses of Plants by the Chippewa Indian*:

> In old times the procuring of birch and cedar bark was an event in which all participated. A number of families went to the vicinity of these trees and made a camp. A gathering was held,

at which a venerable man, speaking for the entire company, expressed gratitude to the spirit of the trees and of the woods, saying they had come to gather a supply which they needed, and asking permission to do this together with protection and strength for their work. He also asked the protection and good will of the thunderbirds so that no harm would come from them. The reason he asked the protection of the spirit of the woods was that sometimes people were careless and cut trees thoughtlessly, and the trees fell and hurt them. The speaker then offered tobacco to the cardinal points, the sky, and the earth, murmuring petitions as he did so. He then put the tobacco on the ground at the foot of the tree. Filling a pipe, he offered it as he had offered the tobacco, again murmuring petitions. He then lit and smoked the pipe while tobacco was distributed among the company, who smoked for a time. This simple ceremony was followed by a feast. The next day the company divided into small groups and proceeded to cut the trees and remove the bark. (*How the Indians Use Plants* 386)

This underlying process has distinctly cultural implications. It requires the commitment and work of many to create a birch bark canoe. The offerings and petitions made to the trees a full day before harvest is considered not a delay but a necessity. In *Recovering the Sacred: The Power of Naming and Claiming*, Winona LaDuke highlights how "Native American rituals are frequently based on the reaffirmation of the relationship of humans to the Creation" (12). She succinctly states the sincerity of intent behind such acts as offering tobacco to the birch trees and insists that "understanding the complexity of these belief systems is central to understanding the societies built on those spiritual foundations—the relationship of peoples to their sacred lands, to relatives with fins or hooves, to the plant and animal foods that anchor a way of life" (12). In this view, the Chippewa way of life is anchored to the birch trees at a foundational level of spiritual kinship. The canoes and other implements made from their bark depend on the rituals that underscore the people's dual dependency and responsibility.

In contrast, the presence of the artificial lake assigns a different set of priorities to the French. Ostensibly, many hands must have been required to construct a place that is ultimately a testament to the carefully manicured aesthetics of the privileged. St. Cloud Park reflects a lifestyle of manufactured ease, wherein the bows and arrows the Chippewa might have used for hunting or warfare are suitable only for target practice. In tandem with the "little war dance" and "ball play," the royals and "four thousand French ladies and gentlemen" find themselves in a place removed of any reality of danger yet well suited to the application of whatever imaginative details might make the show more thrilling. The pat degeneracy ascribed by Europeans to indigenous populations is not just a form of ignorance, it is a reason to feast minds and eyes on the dark sexuality, unbridled passions, and sleek physique of Indians imagined and imported. The show put on for the French, as described by Maungwudaus, fails to satisfy any macabre thirst for shocking displays of barbarism. By highlighting the phoniness of the setting, this self-identifying Chippewa also defuses the fantasy of stereotypes intended to flesh out the scene.

Upon first landing in the Old World at Portsmouth, the Chippewa are taken to see "Lord Nelson's war-ship" and the "navy yard where there were many war ships. Another war chief invited us and showed us all his warriors under him in the barracks" (Maungwudaus 3). In what may have been a matter of either convenient logistics or purposeful initiation, these paragons of military might provide the Chippewa with their first impressions of Europe. Maungwudaus's mention of the "warriors under him in the barracks" suggests that he was more focused on the men as visual proof of hierarchical subjugation, rather than being impressed by the man who was over them. Thoughts of resistance or escape seem patently defused by the implied power of the scene and situation. It is a place befitting the world's mightiest nation, whose material history reflects the success of its empirical intent. Still, Maungwudaus distills the pomp into a readily available referent: the men in charge of the soldiers and the fleet are simply war chiefs. The designation indicates a role and an occupation. The scope of the display does not overshadow the straightforward function of its substance. Maungwudaus does not allow European self-concepts and ideologies an unquestioned existence. In this, he denies his hosts the luxury of an intact self-identity, using the very medium of words long employed in co-opting his people's identities in favor of the imagined Other. The difference here is that Maungwudaus sticks to reporting the details of his observations with few flourishes or damning judgments. He lets his hosts speak for themselves through the medium of their class structures and politics, permitting their works to define their character.

The scope of the Portsmouth military complex seems designed to overwhelm all who encounter it, outsiders from a woodlands upbringing in particular. Yet Maungwudaus maintains a tone of curious composure, subverting intentions to intimidate him with the decidedly journalistic air of his travel documentation. In *The Transatlantic Indian, 1776–1930*, Kate Flint explores "the degree to which those Indians who visited Britain in this period possessed agency when it came to determining the impression that they made, and the degree to which this offset the ways in which they were manipulated by others for ideological and commercial purposes" (9). These cleanly expressed impressions shows how agency can be a function of perspective. Any untoward manipulations on the part of the Europeans are offset by a firmly Chippewa point of view and frame of reference that Maungwudaus does not forsake.

Even when directly insulted by a group of boys, his straightforward telling of the interaction is allowed to convey any accompanying social commentary, deep history, or moral judgment. While the company was visiting England, the following incident occurred:

> Riding through a town in our native costume, we saw a monkey performing in the street upon a music box, about fifty young men looking at him. He was dressed like a man. When the young men saw us, they began to make fun of us, and made use of very insulting language, making a very great noise;—at the same time when the monkey saw us he forgot his performances, and while we were looking at him, he took off his red cap and made a bow at us. A gentleman standing by, said to the audience, "Look at the monkey take off his cap and make a bow in saluting those strangers; which of the two the strangers will think are most civilized, you or the monkey? You ought to be ashamed of yourselves. You may consider yourselves better and wiser than those strangers, but you are very much mistaken. Your treatment to them tells them that you are not, and you are so foolish and ignorant, you know nothing about it. I have been traveling five years amongst these people in their own country, and I never, not once, was insulted, but I was always kindly treated and respected by every one of them. Their little children have far better manners than you. Young men, the monkey pays you well for all the pennies you have given him; he is worthy to become your teacher." (Maungwudaus 9)

Maungwudaus defers to the rejoinder offered by the boys' fellow Brit, who directly condemns the boys' behavior and offers the contrasting habits of hospitality the British gentleman directly experienced among the Anishinaabek.

In the *Ojibwa Texts* collected by William Jones in the early twentieth century, the word "strangers" is provided as the translation for *piiwiitaa*. A footnote informs the reader that "The usual meaning of this word is 'visitor' or 'guest;' i.e., one to whom one renders hospitality" (311). This collection also features a cycle of stories in which Nanabusu repeatedly and strategically visits his more canny animal spirit neighbors during times of famine for his family. He knows he will be fed by them, using whatever means are at their disposal. Indeed, "Once he was addressed by his wife saying: 'How are we going to live? Never a thing do you kill.'" To this, Nanabusu responds, "Therefore always will I go a-visiting" (341). Further underscoring that this provisional relationship between guest and host is a social norm, when Nanabusu enters a family's wigwam that is replete with covetable bear tallow, the man asks, "What shall we give the guest to eat?" The woman replies: "Why the same as you generally do when we want to eat, is what you should do when providing your gift" (343). Another footnote informs us that the term *Kaagiigaa'a'nk*, translated as "What shall we give (to eat)?," as an "expression occurs in such connections as here. Where food is the thing given; and so it has come to be a synonym for 'to feed,' but its real sense is in the giving of a present" (343).

The English gentleman who spoke in defense of the Chippewa company surely received the fulsome welcoming among the tribes he claims he did. Indeed, such behavior is considered a cultural priority, as indicated by his assessment of the Anishinaabek children's manners, who at several points in Densmore's text are told "that they must not laugh at anything unusual nor show disrespect to older people" (*Chippewa Customs* 58). Combined with the fact that a boy's first kill and a girl's first efforts at food preparation were offered to neighbors, it becomes clear that hospitality functions as a core value among a people who credit the animals with providing them food and a selfless tendency to share the bounty.

Whether the gentleman was aware of stories like those in the Jones collection, he rightly names the monkey as a fitting teacher of wayward humans. Certainly, Maungwudaus and his son Noodinokay would see no conflict in the roles. In *Ojibway Heritage*, Johnston offers a succinct summation of the proper ordering of creation, when Epingishmook (West Wind) informs his son Nanabush that "From last to first, each order must abide by the laws that govern the universe and the world. Man is constrained by this law to live by and learn from the animals and the plants, as the animals are dependent upon plants which draw their sustenance and existence from the earth and sun" (21). The hospitality enjoyed by the English gentleman is in direct relation to the Anishinaabek's gratitude toward the animals that have sustained them physically and through the moral example of a natural provisioning understood as generosity.

Maungwudaus does not state these matters directly. The deeper implications inherent to the scene are foremost conveyed by a faithful reproduction of the observed occurrence. Muangwudaus's reticence to directly censure the boy's behavior is reminiscent of the community crier, whom Densmore notes "spoke impersonally of the conduct of the young people, describing incidents in such a manner that those concerned in them would know to what he referred" (*Chippeway Customs* 60). Free from static impositions of meaning, narrative can reveal the symbiotic moral relationship between original experience and associative memory.

The Chippewa company is invited to a host of dinners with various dignitaries and lords, confirming that the visitors caused a sensation throughout the populace. Far from being treated as a sideshow designed to assuage the vulgar curiosity of the common people, Catlin's Indian Curiousities drew the notice of Europe's most privileged. Regarding the British empire's associations with America in particular, Kate Flint makes the point that "the Indian is a touchstone for a whole range of British perceptions concerning America during the long nineteenth century and plays a pivotal role in the understanding and imagining of cultural difference" (2). This conjures the familiar connection between nationalist ideology and notions of exoticism, the dually reflective and repellent Other able to support self-conceptions of exceptionalism. But as Flint's book and Maungwudaus's example go on to point out, the visiting Indians provided "living proof that, in their capacity to react and respond to modern life, they refused to be consigned to that role of the mythical and prehistorical that was so frequently assigned them" (Flint 24). The facility with which Maungwudaus gleans the most socially suggestive details of his encounters attests to the flexibility of a critical eye firmly rooted in Anishinaabek understandings.

Maungwudaus and his fellow Anishinaabek are taken to meet the queen of England in her palace. Maungwudaus remarks that "Her house is large, quiet country inside of it. We got tired before we went through all the rooms in it. Great many warriors with their swords and guns stand outside watching for the enemy. We have been told that she has three or four other houses in other places as large. The one we saw they say is too small for her, and they are building a much larger one on the side of it" (4). His hosts are clearly invested in displaying their martial strength and riches, but his autonomous analysis consistently takes especial note of unintended revelations. Why does a "small woman" require so much property when what she has is enough to grow tired walking through? How much manpower and how many resources are allocated to the presence of the "great many warriors'" who will in all likelihood never be called on to defend the palace from an enemy? What happens in the "three or four other houses in other places just as large" when she is not there but the expectation that such opulence is at the ready remains? Maungwudaus's straightforward descriptions highlight the clarity of the folly and do not require any spirited judgment or condemnation. The sheer waste that lay behind the queen's vast holdings is there to behold. Allowing the scene to speak for itself, his unveiled vision allows access to the ironic and sociopolitically suggestive notes of the composed scene. What was intended to impress is instead laid bare as a study in excess and nonsensical privilege. What does it say that in London, the apex of her glittering realm, "Most of the houses are rather dark in color on account of too much smoke" (4)?

Cross-cultural revelations gain further depth considered in specific relation to the influence of Anishinaabemowin. The social insights already shown to be parcel to "An Account of the Chippewa" are profoundly enriched by a process of reverse translation that applies Anishinaabemowin equivalencies. In Maria Tymoczko's contribution to the collection *Changing the Terms*, "Translations of Themselves: The Contours of Postcolonial Fiction," she observes how "One advantage of multilinguistic literary writing is the possibility of evoking multiple layers of thematic meaning simultaneously by invoking meanings in more than one language simultaneously" (151). In her project, she focuses on the work of James Joyce in relation to the indigenous Irish language. In this, a certain equivalency of circumstances is partly supported by Maunwudaus's comment that "The Irish are very kind-hearted people. The country people make fire of turf; many of them are very poor; the British government is over them" (8).

Concerning the matter of the conventional translation equivalents (CTEs, such as "hello" for *bonjour* even though it's more specifically "good day"), Tymoczko writes that "Rather than merely being peppered with a few overt borrowings from Irish as signs of cultural otherness, Joyce's texts are pregnant with CTEs that carry a double cultural load and that actively construct the complex double meanings of his text" (156). The fact that the "Account" is written in English underscores the function of double meanings, insofar as the presence of Anishinaabemowin can only be deciphered by those familiar enough with the language to understand how certain English words and phrases are stand-ins for the richer sense evoked by Maungwudaus's first language.

My efforts to access illustrative CTEs were significantly aided and supported by my teacher Helen Roy, a first-language Anishinaabemowin speaker also fluent in her second language of English. In deference to my limitations with the language, I offer just two examples in Maungwudaus's text that I believe accomplish what Tymoczko refers to as "carrying a double referential load that communicates differently to its readers, depending on their ability to decipher veiled linguistic code, and their familiarity with the indigenous culture underlying the postcolonial text" (155). About the population of London, Maungwudaus observes how "Like musketoes in America in the summer season, so are the people in this city, in their numbers, and biting one another to get a living. Many very rich, and many very poor" (3). Whereas the English usage of "musketoe" is derived from the Spanish diminutive of *mosca*, meaning fly, the term for the insect in Anishinaabemowin is *zagimenh*. *Zagi* refers to a state of being attached on, which containing the sound *igi* is further refined to mean he (an animate being) takes a part of you. The *menh* makes it understood that it's just what he does. A being that attaches on and takes a part of you as a function of essence. This provides a significantly richer and provocative comparative metaphor than the already suggestive swarm of small, biting flies. Numerous references can be found attesting to a purposeful distribution of resources in the traditional Anishinaabek polity to ensure that no person or family was destitute or hungry as long as there was any sustenance available among the people. That the people of London are likened to *zagimenh-ag* supplies commentary on the relationship between the rich and the poor—such attachments as involve taking a part of one's being are simply a matter of course in the midst of such inequity.

Accompanying his more ironic observations, "An Account of the Chippewa" is also characterized by Maungwudaus's understated sense of humor, often employed when providing physical descriptions of the native Europeans. Of the English men, he notes that "They do not shave the upper part of their mouths, but let the beards grow long, and this makes them look fierce and savage like our American dogs when carrying black squirrels in their mouths" (4). Later he mentions of the French men that "others wear beards only on the upper part of their mouths, which makes them look as if they had black squirrel's tails sticking on each side of their mouths" (6). This descriptive phrasing is distinct to Anishinaabemowin patterns of speech, wherein the subject at hand can take on as many specifying details as one cares to set to the task. The Anishinaabemowin translation of the comment about the French men could be stated as: "Aanind misshi'odoniwag eta ishimidoning miidash mkade'ajidamoon-azaw e-njigingi edawayiing odooniwaang zhinaagwaziwaad." A rough English breakdown of this might look like the following:

> aanind—others
> miishi—fuzz, as on a peach, velvet, a mustache, a beard
> odooniwag—mouths
> eta—only
> ishpimi(ng)—upper direction
> dooning—on/at the mouth
> miidash—and so
> mkade—black
> ajidamoon—squirrel
> azaw—tail
> e-njigingi—the source from which it grows to a shape
> edawayiing—coming from both sides
> zhinaagwaziwaad—they look as if.

As any fluent speaker would realize, translations based on CTEs are troublesome in their superficiality. To indicate one such limitation, and also give more accurate testament to Maungwudaus's brand of humor, we can consider the word *azaw*, used to refer to a tail. More accurately, it refers to the place where feces comes out—a nuance that speaks volumes in the contextual location that places *azaw* at both sides of the mouth. It seems safe to assume that such subtleties abound throughout the "Account," lacing what is written with covert signs of Maungwudaus's Anishinaabek understandings, ready to be ascertained by his son and anyone able to trace the English back to the first language from which it was filtered.

This is a much more personal enterprise of self-identification than the sort of universal linguistic archeology that, in "Nature," Ralph Waldo Emerson proposes will lead to "the working of the Original Cause" (37). What is original to Maungwudaus's language and imagery is parcel to his particular experience and expression. The cause lurking behind his doubly loaded word choice is just as much the modern cities he visits as it is the woodland scenes from which his indigenous language and thought patterns arose. Rather than depending on an Emersonian "simplicity of his character," Maungwudaus demonstrates that the "power to connect his thought with its proper symbol" (36) requires keen observation of the situation he is in. The ogling crowds, insults, exploitative treatment, and deaths of his wife, three of his children, and several of his countrymen from smallpox while abroad essentially amount to a reverse captivity narrative. That he responds with a document of such rich insight, humor, and stark ethical judgment gives moving evidence of Tymoczko's assertion that "for a colonized people subjected to oppression, such covert communication is a powerful means of subversion and emancipation" (155). Having survived in the midst of so much loss, this man is able to use his self-taught English in service to an inquiring Anishinaabek eye and ear. In so doing, he exposes the dark realities of a modern age that Emerson would separate him from as chiefly symbolic. Unwilling to be neither mere symbol nor amusing curiosity, Maungwudaus boldly asserts the specificity and complexity of his awareness. He thus allows contemporary readers a route to understanding how indigenous identity remains rooted in clear observation of the natural world. We continue the struggle to express the reality of our dual exile from and dependency on the living Earth.

References

Copway, George. *The Traditional History and Characteristic Sketches of the Ojibway Nation*. London: Gilpin, Hatchrad, 1850.
Densmore, Frances. *Chippewa Customs*. Washington: US Government Printing Office, 1929.
———. *How the Indians Use Plants for Food, Medicine, and Crafts*. New York: Dover, 1974. (Formerly published as *Uses of Plants by the Chippewa Indians*, 1928.)
Emerson, Ralph Waldo. "Nature." In *Emerson's Prose and Poetry: A Norton Critical Edition*, edited by Joel Porte and Saundra Morris. New York: Norton, 2001.
Flint, Kate. *The Transatlantic Indian, 1776–1930*. Princeton, NJ: Princeton University Press, 2009.
Johnston, Basil. *Ojibway Heritage*. New York: Columbia University Press, 1976.
Jones, William, coll. *Ojibwa Texts*, edited by Truman Michaelson. Leiden: Brill, 1917.
LaDuke, Winona. *Recovering the Sacred: The Power of Naming and Claiming*. Cambridge, MA: South End Press, 2005.
Maungwudaus. "An Account of the Chippewa Indians." Boston: Author, 1848.
McNickle, D'Arcy. *Native American Tribalism: Indian Survival and Renewals*. Oxford: Oxford University Press, 1973.

Tymoczko, Maria. "Translations of Themselves: The Contours of Postcolonial Fiction." In *Changing the Terms: Translating in the Postcolonial Era*, edited by Sherry Simon and Paul St-Pierre, 147–63. Ottawa: University of Ottawa Press, 2000.

Vizenor, Gerald. *The People Named the Chippewa: Narrative Histories*. Minneapolis: University of Minnesota Press, 1984.

Womack, Craig. *Red on Red: Native American Literary Separatism*. Minneapolis: University of Minnesota Press, 1999.

Chapter 3

An Indian's Journey and Tribal Memory

David Treuer's *Rez Life*

Padraig Kirwan

With a historian's attention to detail, a documentarian's keen eye, a novelist's wit, and a son's love, Treuer takes readers home to northern Minnesota.

—Sarah O'Connell

He wrote a book to show off for white folks, and we Indians are giggling at him.[1]

—Sherman Alexie speaking to Jon Lurie

Readers familiar with Sherman Alexie's directorial debut, *The Business of Fancydancing*, will undoubtedly recall the "reviews" that appear in that movie's opening scene and may well find an echo of them in the copious and ongoing commentary that has accompanied the career of David Treuer. In Alexie's movie, Seymour Polatkin, the central protagonist, is momentarily heralded as the future of Native American literature. The *New York Literature Quarterly*, the fictitious organ conjured by Alexie, describes Polatkin's work as "funny, angry, authentic, and ultimately redemptive." With those mainstream, refined, and learned accolades duly paid and noted, the words of an unnamed reviewer, putatively writing for the website Indianz.com, appear on the screen and declare, more forthrightly, "Seymour Polatkin is full of shit." Like the *Business of Fancydancing*'s young, gay poet from Spokane, Treuer has been the recipient of both great critical praise and pronounced censure.[2]

Much of the latter was generated after the publication of Treuer's 2006 collection of essays, *Native American Fiction: A User's Manual*. The central thesis of this extremely forthright, controversial, and some would say slightly reckless volume rested on the notion that it is necessary to make "a distinction between reading books *as* culture and seeing books as [being] capable of *suggesting* culture" (*Native American Fiction* 5). That notion, in and of itself, is not especially contentious. However, Treuer's insistence that "the study of Native American fiction should be the study of style" (*Native American Fiction* 4), unsurprisingly did create ripples within Native American literary studies. Gerald Vizenor saw fit to issue readers with a timely reminder that Anishinaabeg lifeways, cultural animation, and tribal continuance do, quite necessarily, inform tribal literatures and thereby sought to complicate *Native American Fiction*'s thesis. "[If] there is *only* literature by some dubious discovery of the 'true value' of the cold, white pages of style," Vizenor reckoned, "then there is no sense of native presence and survivance" (17). Christopher Taylor, similarly unconvinced by *Native American Fiction*'s rationale, argues that "Treuer leaps to the conclusion that all criticism interested in cultural origins is flawed" and is capable, as a result, of "conceiv[ing] of contemporary Native culture *only as absence*" (33).

It was not just the collection's analytic approach that garnered stinging rebukes. Instead, Treuer's glib and altogether unfortunate—not to mention slightly inflammatory—allusions to "so-called Native American fiction (if there is such a thing)," was conjoined with an intentionally "harsh" style of literary analysis (*Native American Fiction* 3). Although I have argued elsewhere that some of the main tenets of Treuer's thesis are possibly defensible—or simply engaging and generative insofar as they force us to reconsider would-be suppositions concerning the definition of tribal literature—it must be said that Taylor has a point. With that, many of Treuer's personalized attacks and criticisms are often unwarranted; his treatment of the creative skills of indigenous writers who are quite rightly celebrated and revered is often wrongheaded and unfounded. Treuer's overall approach and his individual readings of works such as *Ceremony*, *Love Medicine*, and *Fools Crow* resulted in many readers believing that the young writer was mean-spirited or, worse, misguided and imprecise, Arnold Krupat was at one of the first to criticize the collection on exactly these grounds in his essay "Culturalism and Its Discontents." Indeed, Krupat's response and that of other scholars would suggest that Treuer's scathing critique of acclaimed writers and *Native American Fiction*'s various inaccuracies could have been avoided. It is likely that neither would have appeared in a peer-reviewed book published by a large academic press with experience of publishing in the field. At one point, in terms of the book's reception, it seemed that the only thing missing was the pithy summation that can be found in Alexie's fictionalized Indianz.com.

At the same time, Treuer has received considerable acclaim. John D. Kalb referred to Treuer's novel, *Little* (1995), as an "astonishing first novel," and later noted that his second novel, *The Hiawatha* (1999), was an "even superior accomplishment" (Kalb 113). Toni Morrison—Treuer's creative writing instructor at Princeton—provided her name and her approval on no fewer than two occasions: first by endorsing *Little*, and then by penning a testimonial for his novel *Prudence* (2015). Like Seymour Polatkin, the Ojibwe author is capable of dividing opinion, it seems. Intriguingly, commendations and condemnations for Treuer have even come from the same pen at times. Despite his appreciation of Treuer's first two novels (which he compares favorably with the work of William Faulkner and the American modernists), Kalb offers an unforgiving assessment of *Native American Fiction* and pointed to what he felt were some rather "egregious errors and substantial [critical] misreadings" in that book (114).[3] Although the reviewer agrees with "Treuer's observation that much is lost 'when we interpret Native American fiction with more stress placed on "Native" than on "fiction"'" (114), Kalb finds himself at odds with the general argument made in *Native American Fiction*. He even concludes that Treuer's contention is "that the entire canon of Native American/American Indian literature is ostensibly an illusion, and those who produce, teach, or critique it are merely faking or, worse, perpetrating a falsehood" (114).

The fact that certain scholars have felt compelled to heap scorn as well as praise on Treuer's fiction and nonfiction gives rise, in my opinion, to a particular intertwined and complex set of considerations. In the first instance, it might well be that Treuer's temptation to court controversy did, rather inevitably, lead to the storm that followed the publication of *Native American Fiction*. Second, alternatively, it could be argued that Treuer has suffered from drastic slumps in form and that *Native American Fiction* and *The Translation of Dr Apelles* (Kalb described the latter as a "preposterous" and "overblown fantasy of beauty and love") could be read as misfires from the author's pen. In that context, those works might be taken as literary experiments and perhaps failures; ultimately, this might reflect jaggedness in Treuer's art and criticism. A third, more sophisticated, and, I would argue, more useful appraisal of matters has been provided by Daniel Heath Justice. He allows that *Native American Fiction*'s greatest value lies specifically in its rather contrarian take on the interpretation of indigenous literatures. In that vein, Heath Justice has suggested that: "Treuer's work—both fiction and nonfiction—is a challenge to all of us to be more carefully attentive to the work *as literature* and for us to bring to bear more of our specific skills as literary and textual interpreters, translators, and, even more generally, embodied readers" (345; emphasis in original). This summation, along with Kalb's passing reference to the "personal narratives" that intersperse the critical readings in *Native American Fiction*, suggest that Treuer is quite intentionally—and necessarily—provoking us to reconsider both our position as readers, the generic categorizations currently applied to forms of Native American writing, including fiction, criticism, and life writing, and the stance taken by individual Native writers. Accordingly, his nonfiction (and possibly much of his fiction) proposes that we might think not only about the relationship between the embodied reader and the writing itself but also about the relationship between the indigenous author's lived realities and the various fictional and nonfictional worlds and works they create. The purpose of this chapter, then, is to consider the extent to which Treuer's work invites us to reconsider the edges of the space in which the reader/author/critic dynamic is shaped and how his melding of genres possibly underscores not only the need to devise new readerly practices as "embodied reader[s]" but also the need to consider the part played—and the position taken by—the embodied author. It is intriguing, then, to consider what Treuer's turn to and inclusion of "personal narratives" in a work such as *Native American Fiction* might say about his bid to challenge extant definitions of Native American literature and criticism. In many respects, the intermingling of personal narratives alongside attempts at literary and scholarly interpretation is a means of not only "reconfiguring subjectivity as diverse, provisional and intersubjective" in Native American literary studies, but also of "expanding the object of study from putatively literary [and scholarly] texts to life narratives as they might be most broadly understood: testimony; autoethnography; . . . and so on" (Kalb 114; McCooey 277).[4]

It seems entirely fitting that Heath Justice has suggested that Treuer's genre-crossing work ultimately reminds us of the need to stretch our concept of the readerly space that we inhabit as an audience and as critics, thereby accepting the challenge to track and grapple with Treuer's bid to "reconfigure" and "expand" the genres he works in. Accordingly, it might be worth considering much of Treuer's recent work in the context of Philippe Lejeune's mission to concentrate on "mode[s] of reading" throughout his study of literature and auto/biography. Lejeune's specific understanding of "the relationship between autobiographer and reader as a 'pact' (a formal agreement of limitations)"—as well as his gesture toward the "limits of proposing limits"—are almost a tidy summation of Treuer's own meditations on "the limits between literary and factual writing; between narrative as a literary device and narrative as lived experience; and between autobiography and fiction" (McCooey 277). Indeed, during an interview I conducted with him in 2009, Treuer explained that his writing presents the reader with stories from Leech Lake even as he seeks to "'subvert stereotypes in order to gain the type artistic freedom guaranteed non-Native writers by virtue of their whiteness,' . . . [while also permitting] his characters to 'shield themselves from the kinds of scrutiny people are used to bringing to bear on Native American fiction'" (Kirwan, "Language and Signs" 82). Treuer was referring specifically to *Little* and *Native American Fiction* when he made those comments. Nevertheless, his remarks might be said to reflect on the kind of "pact" that Lejeune once identified. In Treuer's case, that pact is between the indigenous author and the (often non-Native) reader who recognizes the boundaries of their understanding and access to tribal worlds. This line of reasoning might lead us to think more deeply about the limits and the opportunities made possible by what McCooey calls "conceptual play" (277); Treuer would appear to engage in such play when he interweaves fiction and real stories, scholarly work and personal narratives. For this reason, it seems entirely possible that his book *Rez Life: An Indian's Journey through Reservation Life* has even more to tell us about the writer's approach to writing, about literature, and about criticism's relationship to Anishinaabeg lifeways, literary and cultural sovereignties, and more broadly the field of study itself.

Using *A User's Manual*: How To

In fall 1999, the earliest reviews of *The Hiawatha* were confirming the belief that *Little* had marked the beginning of an illustrious literary career. Treuer had begun to interrogate the methodological tools that were ordinarily pressed into action during the assessment and interpretation of tribal literatures.[5] He has long been interested in the current state of the Ojibwemowin, politics on the Leech Lake reserve, life in the northern reaches of the American Midwest, and many other topics. The *Translation of Dr Apelles* also posed something of a challenge to what Treuer has described as the dominant modes of literary discourse in Native American literary studies.[6] Arrestingly, in that novel—as in his earlier work *The Hiawatha*—Treuer made use of strategies that may well have arisen out of his conviction that "the world [should] reach a little closer and push a little harder, dig a little deeper," toward an understanding of his tribe and their beliefs (Kirwan, "Language and Signs" 86). He does so by including paragraphs and sentences in Anishinaabemowin—portions of prose that he then refuses to translate these for non-Ojibwe readers.[7] It was difficult, then, to predict or fully appreciate the level of disagreement that *Native American Fiction* would cause, or the backlash that would ensue once it had been published. This was partly because the unashamedly strident tone that Treuer had adopted while directly attacking tribal authors and commentators was not readily apparent in his earlier work. Moreover, the howls of incredulity that greeted Treuer's critique of the creative and interpretive practices in Native American literary studies might have been somewhat unanticipated, given that others had also called for and been in receipt of harsh criticism. As well as suggesting that "[Native writers] have been far too nice to each other for too long," Alexie even suggested that Native writers were "not going to get any better unless [they] really start hammering on each other" (Purdy and Alexie 7).[8] What might strike many readers as somewhat difficult to reconcile with *Native American Fiction*'s speculative line of argument is Treuer's keenness, in interview, to reflect on the realities of life for the Anishinaabeg at Leech Lake, and his insistence that readers and commentators gain some degree of insight into the complexity of the tribe's lived experiences. Outside of his fiction and *Native American Fiction*, he refers to the cultural, spiritual, and historical materiality that Ojibwemowin produces, protects, and projects out into the world. Longer exchanges with the author reveal his depth of appreciation for the tribal and intellectual traditions.[9] Despite, or rather because of, that grounding, Treuer is resolute that his fictional work can never explain, reflect, or (for want of better word) capture the collective wealth of Anishinaabeg experience, knowledge, and practices. To his mind, the textual worlds he can produce do not provide an instinctive or effortless account of tribal life. Instead, they are highly mediated versions or accounts of human existence; versions that are broadly inferred into an international literary marketplace. Of course, Treuer often adds during conversation, and when read alongside some of the finer scholarly analyses of indigenous literature from the 1990s and the early years of the 2000s, the arguments made in *Native American Fiction* may seem a little anachronistic, if not entirely unnecessary.[10]

Why, then, have I and others sought to tentatively welcome Treuer's attempt to generate new and necessary dialogue about fiction and form? We have done so mainly because it is necessary to applaud his bid to "provoke important discussions about the place of the *literary* in the field [of Native American studies]," despite *Native American Fiction*'s methodology, critical oversights, and general crankiness (Heath Justice 355). As Heath Justice suggests, it is necessary to appreciate the extent to which *Native American Fiction* is in direct conversation with recent scholarship and consider the role that creative fiction might play in various forms of social, cultural, and political praxis. He proposes, thereafter, that the collection's contrarian stance amplifies and restates vital questions concerning literature's capacity to reflect cultural presences—although by focusing on a particular set of novels' inability to reflect contemporary realities, languages, traditions, and cultures as fully as the authors in question might claim their books did.[11] In that context, it does appear to be the case that Treuer seeks to challenge the assumption that novels written by Native writers *innately* or *automatically* comment on a very specific set of tribal contexts, regardless of setting, genre, form, or other characteristics. Subsequently, even though Treuer's countervailing argument appears to risk becoming an overcorrection of sorts, whereby a supposed imbalanced attention to the contextual and tribal experience gives way to the preponderance of the literary, the creative, and the imaginary, it would be a bit of stretch to suggest that *Native American Fiction* insists on or seeks to prioritize one interpretive approach to Native American fiction. Nor does Treuer argue that "*all* criticism interested in cultural origins is flawed," which is the charge that Christopher Taylor makes of *Native American Fiction* (Taylor 33; emphasis added).[12] Instead, it poses a crucial question about "what is gained and what is lost when we interpret Native American fiction with *more stress* placed on 'Native' than on 'fiction'" (*Native American Fiction* 5; emphasis added). It is essential that we note the phrasing "more stress," because even though Treuer's assertions are often anything but moderate, *Native American Fiction* may yet add a degree of steadiness to our readings of the fiction. There is a vital corollary to that point, insofar as it suggests that a form of writing other than fiction might be better suited to the articulation and consideration of indigenous lifeways and the nuances of Native life. *Rez Life*, Treuer's first book-length foray into creative nonfiction, may be a fine working example of this.

"An Indian's Journey"

In *Rez Life*, Treuer avails himself of a number of genres and styles, blending memoir and autobiography, journalism, scholarly prose, and direct storytelling. Using journalistic and artistic techniques, Treuer meanders through an assortment of seemingly disparate yet thoroughly interconnected subjects: tribal sovereignty, federal Indian policy, Ojibwemowin language revival, Indian gaming, identity, childhood memories, kinship networks, and his relationship with his home place, Leech Lake. Described by *Kirkus Reviews* as "a book that is part memoir, part journalistic exposé and part cultural history" ("Powerful, Important Reading"), and by *Dallas News*'s Steve Weinberg as "part family memoir, part American history, part contemporary cultural journey," the book has earned significant praise for dexterously melding the poetic and the reportorial. Featuring as an observer and at times a participant in the narrative, Treuer draws attention to the dynamic association between the personal and the social and documents various forms of Indian presence and experience as he does so. On this level, the book exhibits many of the tendencies that Paul John Eakin finds in autobiography; what Sidonie Smith and Julia Watson describe as the "referentiality to a historical and material world" that Eakin studied is evident in *Rez Life* (Smith and Watson 141). So is the question of how "we create identity in narrative," which is central to Eakin's later work *How Our Lives Become Stories: Making Selves* (Smith and Watson 141). The point that Treuer has spoken about how he "felt like [he] was in school for seven years" and claims to have learned a huge amount about reservation life while scribing the book, coheres with Eakin's notion of an autofictional mediation between the self and the world (Rall).

It is important to note that there are details that some critics might cite to align the book more closely with the generic conventions of memoir rather than autobiography, however. The "I" that Treuer uses does not appear to "share . . . with confessional discourse an assumed interiority and an ethical mandate to interrogate that interiority," as autobiographical works usually do (Quinby 274). Instead, Treuer's "externalized . . . and dialogical"

"I" more closely resembles the memoirist's "I" and is perhaps typical of that genres engagement with a wider field of protagonists (Quinby 274). It might be wisest to describe *Rez Life* as autofiction, or a fine example of periautography, the latter of which is James Olney's preferred term for this type of writing. Loosely translatable as "writing about or around the self," periautography is a term that, to Olney's mind, is attractive because of its "indefinition and lack of generic rigor" as well as its "comfortably loose fit and general adaptability" (Olney xv).[13] The adaptability of the word might be useful if we are to parse Treuer's words with greater understanding and success and appreciate the gambit behind the project. *Rez Life* does adhere to what is often seen as creative nonfiction's most important organizing principle, that is, "writing from in-between and overlapping spaces" and exploring "many identities, multiple perspectives, and layers of locations" ("Nonfiction Reading Series"). Through the plurality of voices and the profuse richness of the stories told, writer and reader find their positionality and subjectivity challenged. *Rez Life* produces a powerful sense of crowdedness, fragmentation, and general narrative dissonance or messiness by bringing many strands of the master narrative of settlement, colonization, and modernity into contact with Anishinaabeg narratives from the North American heartland. "I want people to recognize what to me is the beautiful, complicated and sometimes confusing, complexity of reservations," Treuer explains, continuing to say that "the popular accounting of [Indian] lives needed a fuller, richer complex look" (Rall). Rather than simply embracing the "confessional age, in which memoirs and personal revelations tumble out in unprecedented abundance" or merely controlling the story by mobilizing strong stylistic conventions (the poetic turn of phrase, the empathetic move from the personal to the tribal, the introduction of formidable and fantastic characters), Treuer seems to engage with what William Lowell Randall calls the "poetics of learning" (Mendelsohn; Randall 7–8). Defining poetics in modern times as the "analysis and evaluation of literature in general, including kinds of literature as diverse as the autobiography and the novel," and learning as the attempt to 'make meaning' out of our existence, and 'make something' out of our lives," Randall describes the "poetics of learning" as the literary act through which we continually "organize and re-organize . . . story and re-story—both ourselves *and* our world" (7–8; emphasis in original). As such, *Rez Life* is much more than a memoir, an oral historiography, an ethnographical meditation on indigenous lifeways, or a piece of narrative journalism, even though it surely contains characteristics of found in each of those genres. David Ulin took stock of this while considering Treuer's process as a creative nonfictionist, noting that the book "is not, for all its intimacy, a memoir, just as it is not exactly a work of reportage or a work of history." "It is," he concluded, "a nuanced hybrid" (Ulin.[14]

"Where. I. Come From"

The intermingling of narrative journalism, which is a publicly regulated form of literary production, and memoir, often seen as a more private affair, is intriguing. An extra layer of critical and creative energy is added to the terms of this latest move when one considers how Treuer's earlier work—specifically *Native American Fiction* and *The Translation of Dr Apelles*—raise key questions concerning authorial position, fictional spaces, and indigenous presence. In the former, Treuer asks that the reader place the emphasis on the novel itself, rather than the contextual or geographical markers that are often cited during the analysis of Native American literature: "Instead of basing our analysis on the first four words of [the] phrase ["where I come from, stories . . .], we should take a close look at the fifth. Stories" ("Reading Culture" 52). In the *Translation of Dr Apelles*, he riffs beautifully (and sarcastically) on the position of the Native author and storyteller. In the novel, the central protagonist, Apelles, is a professional writer and is busily translating the story told in a manuscript he found in a forlorn and forgotten library. The story of two Ojibwe lovers, Bimaadiz and Eta, this book is, for Apelles, "*the most amazing tale [he's] ever heard—full of Indians beautiful to look at and also Indians who were treacherous, full also of hunting episodes, of capture and recapture*" ("Translator's Introduction" 1; emphasis in original). Lost in that world, he is able to sublimate a deep-seated fear about the telling or release of personal stories. In short, Apelles is terrified at the prospect of revealing his inner narrative, or in any way linking his own story to matters of ancestry, culture, reservation life, or, broadly speaking, "the past." As such, Treuer's fictional scholar is achingly conscious of the fact that disclosures about the private life can carry a huge risk, for an Indian, and he believes that storying his life will result in a form of personal displacement that not only diminishes his individual interiority but might erase his individualism altogether:

> his life was real to him, [. . .] but] if he told it in the wrong way or for the wrong reasons it would cease to be real, it would no longer be his life because it would become a story like all

the other stories about his people, and if he told it he would only become a character in that story and would be only the Indian they knew and the Indian they told their friends about. (*Translation* 203)

Like Little, the enigmatic, selectively mute child at the heart of Treuer's first novel, Apelles withdraws, often stymieing his own narrative. Not wishing for certain stories about his Indian self to be told, he adopts a self-imposed silence and subsequently has "no language for [him]self" (*Translation* 312). Rather than express himself, he wishes, as David Yost observes, to "break free of the text that Euroamerican culture has already written for him" (68). It is only toward the end of the novel, Yost explains, that Apelles escapes "what he calls the 'mere fairy tale'" that he is translating and is able to "translate himself . . . [thereby finding] a 'much better,' more genuine love" (Yost 71–72). Here, the writer is free to tell his own tale once he disregards the conventions regulating "Indian" stories.

On the face of it, this plea for imaginative freedom certainly accords with the central thesis expounded in *Native American Fiction*, and there seems to be reason to blithely suggest that Apelles is a characterization of Treuer's creative and professional principles. Both men seem to specialize in appearing as culturally distanced attachés dramatically lost in humanity, and Apelles's particular form of self-inflicted deracination and deculturalization appears to align with his creator's distaste for culturally informed and tribally specific readings of Native literatures. For many readers, it may seem as though Treuer wants to hold on to what Apelles describes as "the sovereign part of himself" to be a writer and a citizen on the world stage. There is, then, a grain of truth about the representation of Apelles's experience as a writer. More specifically, there is a grain of what Treuer sees as the truth in his account of the author's life. In that manner, Kalb describes the move as possibly being "Treuer's way of breaking himself from the limiting chains of being identified as a Native American novelist," but then immediately questions the author's "ability as an artist to visualize and recreate a world beyond our experience yet keep that world anchored in a seeming reality" (116).

There is a slightly more complicated and arresting set of dynamics at play in this particular Frankensteinian relationship. Aside from highlighting the authorial reflexivity and creative distancing that is a vital part of Treuer's characterization of his lonely protagonist—a distancing undercuts and preempts the notion that Apelles is a Freudian self-revelation of sorts—the decision to write about an author in the space of the novel reinforces the simple truth that Apelles is a literary character that operates in a fictional space; he is a fabrication, a composite. Although this account of the life of a contemporary author struggling with the question of how to best protect or shield his identity as an Anishinaabe man in the contemporary world certainly faintly echoes Treuer's own experiences, Apelles's rather comical and slightly bumbling responses to his circumstances and tribulations are ultimately a fabrication. His silence is not Treuer's per se, and the latter's production of that silence certainly does not mean that the "real" author (as opposed to the implied author or the fictional Apelles) is similarly at a loss for words. On the contrary, Apelles's final epiphany, in which he realizes that he "needs no . . . readers" other than himself, is certainly not one that Treuer has had (*Translation* 315). In fact, rather than seeing himself as being personally damaged by a form of involuntary silencing or a suppression of voice, Treuer had availed himself once again of the opportunity to consider the relationship between indigenous fiction and cultural contexts. As Yost explains, this move readily demonstrates the reality that fiction, in its purer form, never reveals much about contextual realities or the lives of the people (65). Rather than proving to be a weakness of Treuer's third novel, the fact that the story of Apelles's life is as "implausible" as the "preposterous" tale of Bimaadiz and Eta's love is in fact the point (Kalb 116). In this moment, the reader might acknowledge that Treuer is parodying the belief that fictional forms disclose biographical or cultural detail. This in itself is an entirely serious comment about the *hors-texte* concerns facing indigenous authors. Just as telling is the fact that Treuer was plotting a whole new literary endeavor at the very moment he was providing his fictional character with as happy an ending as a lonely scholar can hope to achieve: *Rez Life*. Fundamentally, this move crystallizes the line of reasoning which suggests that he distinguishes between fictional writing as an artistic pursuit and other forms of writing. More important, the decision to turn to creative nonfiction reiterates Treuer's conviction that the complexities and richnesses of the tribal world are best reflected in literary work that is collectively formed and factually informed.[15]

"None of It Is Dead"

Rez Life deals directly with historical, cultural, and tribal perspectives, and unlike Treuer's fiction, the author believed that it "had to be useful" (Ulin). That sense of praxis is one of the more striking elements of the book. The essays thread a series of stories told by contemporary residents of several reservations along with Treuer's commentary on familial experiences, Anishinaabeg culture, and the history of tribal nations' sovereign relationship with the US government. Whether it is remembering the attacks that accompanied the enforcement of fishing rights in the 1980s, the trials of language preservation, or the hardships facing teenagers today, Treuer's narrative structure relies heavily on the stories found in Leech Lake, Red Lake, and White Earth, and he relies on tribal voices to frame his narrative. Across the space of the book the reader is introduced to (among others) Ogimaa-giihig, known also as Officer Charley Grolla, a Red Lake conservation officer; Helen (Bryan) Johnson, the housewife who won a landmark court case over taxes and land rights; Shalah Tibbetts, a young woman who lost her father, Warren, to an act of mindless violence on Tract 33, beside Cass Lake, Minnesota; and his mother, Margaret, the first women to become a tribal judge. A large proportion of the book consists of the author's recounting of the wonderfully animated and extremely informative conversations he has with these protagonists. In several cases, like that of Sean Fahrlander, a former US Navy air traffic controller from Mille Lacs, Treuer transcribes huge swaths of his interviewee's dialogue, thereby allowing that person to drive the narrative forward and explain yet another dimension of life on the reservations today. Frequently, those voices reveal something of their private lives. At times, the speakers recount sites of personal and collective traumas, many of which arise out of racism and deprivation. Just as often, their disclosures underscore powerful signs of Anishinaabeg resolve and endurance, as well as the continuing growth of tribal communities throughout North America.

"Native Americans were supposed to die off, as endangered species do, a century ago," Treuer writes at the opening of *Rez Life*'s final chapter, before simply stating: "but I am not dead after all" (259). The cataloging of census numbers detailing the growth of the Native American population nationally and the chapter's subsequent consideration of language and culture are typical of Treuer's movement from personal perspectives, opinions, and reveries to the historic and public record. This sense of personal testimony and historical record is one of the work's defining aspects. *Rez Life* does far more than locate the point at which the individually private and the collectively public—whether tribal or national—intersect or intertwine, however. It excavates (to steal a metaphor from Treuer) and celebrates stories and lives from Ojibwe country. In this regard, his recounting of the suicide and later the funeral of his grandfather Eugene

Seelye sets the tone for the book on many levels. Having glossed Seelye's crabbiness and his idiosyncrasies in a familial context, Treuer limns the story of his maternal grandfather's military service in World War II, his complete refusal to live anywhere except Leech Lake on his return, and the extent to which the facts of the older man's life might easily confound non-Native ideas about "typical Indian lives." In the closing paragraphs of the book, Treuer recalls pondering the Ojibwe past as he stood at his grandfather's graveside, regarding the land where the tribe's dead are buried, and wondering to himself, "how much more crowded with story and personality and life can the ground get?" (*Rez Life* 319). As is so often the case with this writer, his question is rhetorical, and even though he allows that there are "always more" lives to be cut short, he acclaims:

> None of the people are dead, none of the sense they made of their lives is dead, and on the reservation at least, none of the whims, acts, and actions of presidents, Indian agents, congressional reformers, tribal leaders, and tribal citizens are dead. Or if any of this is dead, it is certainly not buried: nowhere more than in reservation life can we see, can we feel, the past shaping the present. On the reservation the past is hardly past at all. (*Rez Life* 319)

It is virtually impossible, when reading these words, not to think of LeAnne Howe's vision of tribalography, or the critical definition and the material application of that term by scholars like Joseph Bauerkamper and Jill Doerfler.[16] In an important essay written in 1999, Howe outlined the "rhetorical space" of tribalography. According to the Choctaw author and artist, this was the site where "Native people create narratives that [are] histories and stories with the power to transform" ("Tribalography" 118). On a fundamental level, Treuer's narrative sweep and his journey across the rhetorical landscapes of the Anishinaabeg world certainly appear to mesh with the tribal foundations of Howe's theory and the type of literary and material practices that she identifies in her essay. The relationship between various forms of narrative, cultural, and physical presence outlined in *Rez Life* also, to my mind, suggests the type of connectedness and continuance that Bauerkamper finds in tribalography, which, he says, "gifts us with innovative and exceptionally productive ways to encounter and understand Native story, writing, and performance of the entangled past, present, and future" (Bauerkamper 4).

Some key facts regarding style and effect are thrown into stark relief when *Rez Life* is read against tribalography in this way. In the first instance, the book layers personal, tribal, intertribal, and national narratives together and melds a number of genres together in a rather distinctive, tribally informed manner. This is an important point, not least because Howe notes that Native writers do not write "strictly autobiographical stories" and are given to intermingling genres, rhetorical structures, and stylistic conventions ("The Story of America" 42). Rather than simply being influenced by broader artistic and cultural developments—namely, contemporary culture's fascination with self-exposure and creative nonfiction's blurring of "memoir . . . history . . . fiction"—Treuer could be said to be working in tribally informed mode and making use of culturally specific techniques. Like so many of the books that Howe mentions, *Rez Life* might also be deemed "a kind of story that includes collaboration" ("The Story of America" 4). In the second case, there is the matter of the book's efficacy and its contribution in terms of a literature of survivance (to borrow a phrase from Vizenor, one of Treuer's earlier detractors). Treuer's framing of affecting stories from the reservation against wider political, social, and historical events, and the fact that he is both a professional writer and a tenured professor, surely cause us to consider what Doerfler calls "the relationship between scholarship and the real life experiences of Natives" (65). The sense that *Rez Life*, like other books written by those working in American Indian studies, can act as a vital form of tribal advocacy, thereby buttressing developments in the area of law, health care, and economics, is both incredibly enlivening and terribly exciting. Here, writing appears as a powerful medium through which to affect change within Native American communities, and the polyphonic structure of *Rez Life* demonstrates how indigenous lifeways and identities are shaped, enacted, and expanded locally. As a result, Treuer's literary act corroborates Doerfler's conviction that "Stories create us as individuals, families, communities, and nations; they help us formulate understandings of who we were, are, and will become" (67–68). Contextually informed and collectively shared, the tales in *Rez Life* are ultimately moored in the tribal real just as much as they aim to inspire the tribal imagination.

On another level, *Rez Life* can surely be a part of a wider set of writing that alters perceptions of tribal communities, their experiences, their sovereignties, and their narratives outside of the reservation's borders. Fundamentally, this book has some important and necessary teachings to impart to non-Natives, as mainstream reviewers have noted. A. K.

Mayhew describes Treuer's project as being "as much a mind-opening act for non-Minnesotans as it is for those who have already heard of the Ojibwe," while Sarah O'Connell and Pamela Miller conclude that this is a that "belongs on the shelves of serious scholars and avid readers alike" (O'Connell) and is "one you'll want to read if you're at all curious about contemporary American Indians" (Miller). Accordingly, *Rez Life*, and texts like it, enable a deeper consideration of the discrete spaces in which processes of decolonization are possible, and in which "reciprocal obligations" are both acknowledge and honored (Doerfler 68). As such, those stories sit nicely in a burgeoning collection of texts that act as death knell to the worst excesses of the overly active non-Native imagination, even if this is not their primary goal. Although remaining aware of his position as an individual writer working inside the culture, Treuer appears keen to search for a broader and collective transformation through this particular literary endeavor. "This book will show our face to the rest of the world," he explained to Patt Rall of the *Red Lake Nation News*. Moreover, by working through the dynamics of sovereign-to-sovereign relationships, Treuer locates and explains various points of law, historic flashpoints, and ongoing challenges that influence intertribal and intratribal relationships, as well as the tribes' relationships with the federal government. In so doing, he signals the tensions and the values that emerge out of various states—and degrees—of cultural, spiritual, legal, and political separation.

In light of the arguments expounded in *Native American Fiction*, it is entirely understandable that puzzled expressions might greet the suggestion that Treuer shares any great deal of common creative or critical ground with Howe, or any other writer who believes that ancestry, community, and indigenous identity shapes the art of Native peoples. After all, as outlined already, he is known to most as the author who has singularly and forcefully sought to outline why the novel as a form and an entity should be treated as a separate and discrete thing and why interpretive practices must distinguish between literature and tribal lifeways and traditions. He has sharply criticized fellow artists for the constructedness of essays, stories, and novels that begin with a single premise: "Where. I. Come. From." An ornery reader might even wonder if Treuer is now doing exactly what he has criticized others for in the past. What we are we to make of Treuer's recent authorial foray into tribal life and the apparent division of life and art that occurred in his earlier work? Might this clear departure from his earlier authorial practice and his comments on the nature of fiction, imagination, and artistry be taken as a form of slippage, insofar as his recent reveries about Leech Lake and Ojibwe country often demonstrates the extent to which his fiction is informed and inspired by physical and perceptible realities? Should we note the fact that Treuer has written about a handicapped childhood fishing buddy, Patrick Morgan, who bears resemblance to the eponymous character in *Little*? Might we suggest that his commentary on the tracts/"tracks" around Leech Lake, the history of logging in Ojibwe territory, and discussion of American Indian movement activists—who later populated several scenes on *The Hiawatha*'s Franklin Avenue—all serve to suggest that his novels are "anchored in . . . reality" in a way that *Native American Fiction* possibly aims to deny or disown (*Rez Life* 163, 170–71, 179, 265; Kalb 116)?[17]

"Welcome to the Leech Lake Indian Reservation"

If anything, Treuer's creative nonfiction compliments, rather than contradicts, his work as a creative writer and his controversial stance as a critic. By presenting the reader with layers and types of complexity that are factually instead of than interpretively derived, Treuer suggests the intricacy of this book arises out of his experiences among the Anishinaabeg and the community's affinity for story, transformation, and resilience. This is a joint story, not merely a David Treuer story. With that, readers do not require literary interpretation or scholarly conjecture to acknowledge the narrative range found in *Rez Life*. Like Howe, Vizenor, Heath Justice, Louis Owens, Craig Womack, and many others, Treuer is consciously performing the shift from the personal "I" of the author to a broader sense of the tribal self. Furthermore, by writing a book that one reviewer has described as "exposé . . . [that] sheds light on aspects of Indian culture closed to most non-Natives," and which another calls "gritty, raw," Treuer has divulged various pieces of information and explained certain aspects of Native life that he would never do in his fiction ("Powerful, Important Reading"; Sides). That is, he undertakes an analysis of the lives and culture of the Anishinaabeg in the space of *Rez Life*'s six chapters that he has never attempted and would never attempt elsewhere. This seems to be partly because Treuer feels that a fictional treatment of the culture would be a disservice to the culture's intricacy, even if he were to write to Joycean length. It also seems to be because he would find it restrictive, as an artist working in a creative medium, to produce fiction that "truth tell[s]" (Kirwan, "Language and Signs" 77). That point, coupled with the fact that Treuer is extraordinarily mindful of readers' predisposition to expect Native fiction to operate in a certain manner and perform Indianness seems to have informed his preference to approach creative fiction and creative nonfiction with a slightly different authorial perspective. While Howe and more recently Womack might have reveled in the freedom to meld culturally discursive, critical and creative energies in the space of a single story or book, Treuer has, until now, chosen to write only novels and scholarly works.[18] However, it is most certainly the case that *Rez Life* connects with many of the energies that are evident in those earlier works, and the most recent book marks an important stage in what appears to be a progressive and incremental journey; Treuer's publications, when read collectively, can help curious readers decipher between the fictionist's narrative, tribal stories, and cultural continuance. They also demonstrate how those spaces are central to and overlap in the Native American writer's sense of herself as an artist and a member of a community and wider family. It is hardly any wonder, then, that one of the more interesting assertions emerging from Ulin's conversation with Treuer is the newspaper man's appreciation and celebration of the writer's bid to discover "a locus where fiction and nonfiction come together, [and] where both add up to literature" (Ulin).

In light of all of this, it is difficult not to consider *Rez Life* as a book that sets Treuer's literary production, and some of his more contrarian stances, in a wider and more fathomable context. The book appears to navigate the tension between the relative solipsism of the fictionist and critic on one hand—whatever solipsism can be said to exist in the indigenous writer, that is—and the expansive nature of communally formed and collectively shared narrative strands on the other. It does so in part because it forces us to think about the differences between fiction and creative nonfiction and then scrutinizes those distinctions closely and rigorously, and in part because the publication of the more recent work reflects Treuer's investment in producing a literary form that accommodates a far greater sense of narrative plurality. It is as though the latest book proves earlier critical points and responds to the criticism that the author is being willfully self-regarding—even though *Native American Fiction* had not been published when Treuer received a contract to write *Rez Life*. Moreover, instead of producing a form of "creative writing that use[s] fictional and poetic techniques to capture *self-experience*, including physical and emotional experience, personal memories, and present and past relations with others" (Hunt ix; emphasis added), Treuer seeks to highlight the originality and innovation found in several Anishinaabeg communities. If *Rez Life* is transformative (and I would suggest that it is), it is because of its relationship to the people and its investment in the exact type of embodiment that Heath Justice refers to. What must be noted, then, is the fact that Treuer has referred in several interviews to the book's potential role in the process of making Anishinaabeg visible and reminding us of the material aspects of the culture (Rall; Ulin; Weinburg). In considering that possibility, he appears to have put a great deal of thought into the same set of questions that Doerfler raises about the constructed nature of writing: "What story do we want to tell? What work do we want that story to do? What kind of future does the story construct" (Doerfler 67). He seems to have found that in this instance, creative nonfiction was the genre best suited to this particular story and the task in hand.

Rez Life is therefore another leg of the writer's journey through the spaces inhabited by the Leech Lake and Red Lake Bands of the Anishinaabe and the other nations around the United States. Although he is as concerned with romanticization and imagination as ever he was—both the troubling presence of the "Indian" in the non-Native imagination and the power of the Native author's imagination—Treuer has seized the opportunity to examine actual circumstance instead of working through metaphor or symbol. It seems that such directness is well suited to a direct consideration of many of the most pressing issues facing the communities. *Rez Life*'s consideration of matters such as the complex nature of sovereignty, which means the tribes "can determine [their] own lives . . . [but] also have the latitude to destroy them" and "the intricacies of a language tailored for [the tribe's] space in the world" are fine examples of this (*Rez Life* 45, 305). At the same time, it must be said that the intricate nature of the fictional worlds that Treuer produces during his creative practice also call into play many of the same questions, although implicitly and amorphously, in what is a thoroughly suggestible manner. It may be the case that his creative nonfiction speaks with greater certainty, intent, and candor, but the basic premise remains the same: Native literature is more than a simple record of Native life, and the whole of Native life is not recorded in Native literature. *Rez Life*, then, is part of a continuum, and its publication has done much to clarify Treuer's personal engagement with broader sets of historical, cultural, political, social, and personal affairs that may never make their way into fiction, even though they may certainly influence his writing and our readings of it.

Notes

1. This was Alexie's cavalier assessment of the situation after David Treuer published *Native American Fiction: A User's Manual* in 2006. Although Treuer's book certainly has many flaws, several of which are cited in this essay, Alexie unfairly and presumptuously purports to speak for the entire Native community in his rather snide comment. Moreover, as Kathleen Washburn notes, Treuer is not alone in his treatment of Alexie's work; other critics—most notably Elizabeth Cook-Lynn and Gloria Bird—"have charged Alexie with hyperbolically negative portrayals of reservation life, or what David Treuer decries as the damaging cultural shorthand of 'Indian tears'" (111).

2. It is surely fair to say that the rhetorical jostling that has taken place between Alexie and Treuer (as well as other prominent Native authors) has, more often than not, arisen from the Alexie's wish to court and generate controversy. Sadly, as readers now know, it appears that Alexie's public—and often petty—bid for professional dominance may have masked far more upsetting and damaging attempts to personally control or exercise power over others. I have chosen not to omit the exchange from my essay, which was in preparation prior the revelation about Alexie's alleged abuse of a number of women. I have done so to remind readers not only of the troubling tone of Alexie's rhetorical assaults but also of the apparent risks when a single author is deemed to speak for everyone or is deemed to offer a public critique that represents the convictions of the entire cohort—which Alexie does when referring to "we Indians."

3. Treuer's third novel, *The Translation of Dr Apelles* (2006), was also heavily criticized in Kalb's review, and he accused the author of presenting the reader with rather stereotypical, highly fantasized Native protagonists.

4. I am greatly indebted to one of the peer reviewers of this collection and to the editors for their willingness to share some great insights into Treuer's collection of essays and his propensity to cross the boundaries that often separate various genres of writing. These observations were extremely useful and offered in a generous spirit. Any remaining deficiencies in the argument are entirely my own doing.

5. Many of these topics are covered in Kirwan, "Language and Signs," which I published after having met Treuer in Minneapolis.

6. David Yost has written about a potential "war of texts" that takes place in *Translation of Dr Appeles*, and argues convincingly that the novel also shows "the text that Euroamerican culture has already created for its Indian characters: an idyllic pastoral romance" (59).

7. The editors of this volume have also pointed out that at least some point of connection can be made between the plot of *Apelles* and events that are glossed in *Rez Life*. That is to say, there is an uncanny echo between the recollections of Apelles, who feels lost when he has "no language" for himself, and those of Treuer as he begins to examine his own family and community. In

particular, there seems to be something of a reverberation or connection between the moment the fictional character is taken by his father to view the body of a Caucasian hunter who has committed suicide, and Treuer's description of the scene that he finds after the suicide of his maternal grandfather, Eugene Seelye. In working through the facts and by cataloging the experience in prose, Dr Apelles and the author achieve what Yost (paraphrasing Vizenor) describes as a form of "narrative recreation" (71).

8. His personal life aside, Alexie has been on the receiving end of some ruthless analysis by tribal writers and colleagues. Alexie's comments came a full nine years before the publication of *Native American Fiction*, and two years after Gloria Bird published a stinging rebuke of some of Alexie's literary tactics. Notably, Treuer chimes on several techniques and observations that Bird found fault with, and his discussion of Alexie's use of "hyperbole [and] sanctioned exaggeration" in *Reservation Blues* (1995) certainly owes a debt to Bird's review. Of course, these assessments of Alexie's work were far from being the only or earliest moment when one Native writer expressed some rather strident opinions about the work of another. At the time of writing, it has been twenty-nine years since Susan Castillo wrote about one of the more high-profile cases.

9. In an interview with Virginia Kennedy, Treuer refers to "the real cultures that we try to live" (51).

10. At the end of his short review of *Native American Fiction* James Ruppert concludes, quite simply: "this book is one long complaint against writers, readers, and critics who think literature is a window on culture and therefore judge Native texts on the basis of authenticity. He takes very little time, however, to show that this even exists in contemporary writing and criticism" (Ruppert 81).

11. Similar concerns and commentaries are found in the work of countless critics and authors, not all of whom can be cited here. I am thinking especially of publications by Sean Teuton, Craig Womack, LeAnne Howe, Michelle H. Raheja, Dean Rader, Scott Lyons, Gordon Henry Jr., and Meg Noodin, among others. Of course, Treuer would have done well to engage with that work, just as he might have placed his own thesis among his peers' investigations into the connection between fiction, interpretive practices, and cultural centers. In fact, one need only quickly consult the Association for the Study of American Indian Literatures notes to get a quick overview of the developing conversation that *Native American Fiction* could have been a part of during the late 1990s and early 2000s. In 1998, Dean Rader chaired a session at the MLA titled "Born into Memory: Refiguring Language in Contemporary American Indian Poetry." In 1995, the MLA session "Native American Voices in the Midwest" also included readings by Betty Louise Bell, Kim Blaeser, William Penn, Roberta Hill Whiteman, and Carter Revard; the "Native American Literature: Seeking a Critical Center" panel heard papers from Kate Shanley, Gordon Henry Jr., Robert Warrior and Craig Womack. That said, the early twenty-first century witnessed a new and burgeoning approach to the

interstices of literature and culture. Accordingly, it could be argued (as I am sure Treuer might), that many of the more influential texts examining the relationship between contemporary fiction and tribal contexts were published around the same time that *Native American Fiction* appeared (2006). Foremost among those works are Womack, Heath Justice, and Teuton; Weaver, Womack, and Warrior; and Teuton.

12. It is understandable that Taylor should take it that *Native American Fiction*'s central argument is that any form of cultural reading is misguided and misdirected. In many ways, he is right to do so given the stridency—and occasional heavy-handedness—of Treuer's critical prose. In many ways, *Native American Fiction* underscores the extent to which the reader can interpret the novel in any way they choose to.

14. It is also important and only fair to note—as Meg Noodin wisely did while reading an earlier draft of this essay—that Treuer is following in the footsteps of several gifted and generous Ojibwe writers and storytellers. The voices that resonate most clearly in *Rez Life* include that of Jim Northrup, Brenda Child, Gerald Vizenor, and Linda LeGarde Grover. Treuer once wrote, "Jim Northrup makes me proud to be Ojibwe and grateful I can read about it," and the style and structure of works such as *The Rez Road Follies: Canoes, Casinos, Computers, and Birch Bark Baskets* surely informed the younger man's art ("Praise"). By the same token, the stunning ability of authors like Brenda Child to organize a history of Ojibwe people around her personal remembrances and familial experiences also underscores the fact that the skill and dexterity that Treuer demonstrates is evident in the writing and scholarship of several other writers.

15. In Kirwan, *Sovereign Stories*, I point out that tribal authors' approaches to fictional and critical writing vary significantly. For instance, Elizabeth Cook-Lynn's particular brand of realism—or didacticism, if you heed her critics—has a seriousness that is obviously very different from LeAnne Howe's outrageous humor. Yet both women construct fictional narratives that force the reader to consider indigenous presences, beliefs, experiences, and futures.

16. I am naming just two out of the many scholars interested in the material and theoretical efficacy of the term *tribalography* here. A recent special edition of *Studies in American Indian Literatures* (26, no. 2, Special Issue: Tribalography [2014]) examines this term in full and features contributions from Chanette Romero, Carter Meland, Patrice Hollrah, Jodi A. Byrd, and Howe. In his introduction to the edition, Bauerkemper lists an even wider range of critics who have written about the theory (5-6).

17. I am not for a second suggesting that, having encountered *Rez Life*, the reader is suddenly made aware of a possibility that she had previously been blind to (namely, that *Little*, *The Hiawatha*, or *The Translation of Dr Apelles* narrativize certain real-life events in the space of the novel). That was already self-evident. What I am interested in is the way Treuer's decision to revisit a specific set of personal stories, most especially those about Patrick Morgan and the poverty suffered by many of those living in tract housing on the reservation, serves to

remind us of the fictionality of a novel such as *Little*—which hugely conflates and dramatizes the boy's physical deformity and his position in the community—and underscores the extent to which the real-life contexts have shaped Treuer's career. What is most interesting is the fact that this nod to the connection between the fictional and the real is likely to cause the reader to revisit and reconsider the relationship between them and the possible efficacy and limitations of both forms. As well as being in keeping with Treuer's own project, this move echoes the work of scholars such as Catherine Gallagher and Richard Walsh, who believe that we must carefully examine fictionality as a particular characteristic of the novel form and appreciate the complexities revealed through a comparative analysis of fictionality and other forms of narrativizing. One of Walsh's best examples is Salman Rushdie's *Midnight's Children*, readings of which, he argues, "somewhat recklessly pass over the possibility that Rushdie might be more interestingly engaged with India and the experience of Partition in particular" (112). According to Walsh, Rushdie's "means of [engaging with India] are integral to the novel's rhetoric of fictionality, which encompasses and inflects its narrative self-consciousness as well as its story" (112). For Walsh, what is lost in readings that possibly overlook what Manfred Naumann once called "the relational structure" within literary production is the "sense [that] the specifically fictional nature of the novel's engagement" is a comment on the book's historical and cultural contexts (Walsh 112). In short, Walsh argues that by paying insufficient attention to Rushdie's interest in Partition, we might fail to acknowledge the richness and dexterity of his fictionalization of that particular historical moment and might also overlook that moment's place in the production of the fiction. To do so would be to overlook interdependence. Naumann warns against "neglecting the connection that holds between the prehistory of a work, its subsequent history, and its current standing" (Naumann and Heath 107). I would argue that similar energies are at play in *Little* and *Dr Apelles*, through which Treuer draws our attention to the issues of "fictionality" and "narrative self-consciousness" in Native American fiction. See Gallagher and Walsh.

18. See my discussion of Womack's *Art as Performance, Story as Criticism: Reflections on Native Literary Aesthetics* (Norman: University of Oklahoma Press, 2010) in Kirwan, *Sovereign Stories*.

References

Alexie, Sherman (dir.). *The Business of Fancydancing*. Outrider Pictures, 2002.
Bauerkemper, Joseph. "Introduction: Assessing and Advancing Tribalography." *Studies in American Indian Literatures* 26, no. 2 (2014): 3–12.
Bird, Gloria. "The Exaggeration of Despair in Sherman Alexie's *Reservation Blues*." *Wicazo Sa Review* 11, no. 2 (1995): 47–52.
Castillo, Susan. "Postmodernism, Native American Literature and the Real: The Silko-Erdrich Controversy." *Massachusetts Review* 32, no. 2 (1991): 285–94.

Doerfler, Jill. "Making it Work: A Model of Tribalography as Methodology." *Studies in American Indian Literatures* 26, no. 2 (2014): 65–74.

Eakin, Paul J. *Touching the World: Reference in Autobiography*. Princeton, NJ: Princeton University Press, 2001.

Gallagher, Catherine. "The Rise of Fictionality." In *The Novel, Volume 1: History, Geography, and Culture*, ed. Franco Moretti, 336–63. Princeton, NJ: Princeton University Press, 2006.

Heath Justice, Daniel. "Currents of Trans/National Criticism in Indigenous Literary Studies." *American Indian Quarterly* 35, no. 3 (2011): 334–52.

Howe, LeAnne. "Tribalography: The Power of Native Stories." *Journal of Dramatic Theory and Criticism* 14 (1999): 117–25.

———. "The Story of America: A Tribalography." In *Clearing a Path: Theorizing the Past in Native American Studies*, edited by Nancy Shoemaker, 29–48. New York: Routledge, 2002.

Hunt, Celia. *Transformative Learning through Creative Life Writing: Exploring the Self in the Learning Process*. Abingdon: Routledge, 2013.

Kalb, John D. Review of *Native American Fiction: A User's Manual* by David Treuer; *The Translation of Dr. Apelles: A Love Story* by David Treuer. *Studies in American Indian Literatures* 20, no. 2 (2008): 113–16.

Kennedy, Virginia. "A Conversation with David Treuer." *Studies in American Indian Literatures* 20, no. 2 (2008): 47–63.

Kirwan, Padraig. "Language and Signs: An Interview with Ojibwe Novelist David Treuer." *Journal of American Studies* 43, no. 1 (2009): 71–88.

———. *Sovereign Stories: Aesthetics, Autonomy and Contemporary Native American Writing*. Oxford: Peter Lang, 2013.

Krupat, Arnold. "Culturalism and Its Discontents: David Treuer's 'Native American Fiction: A User's Manual.'" *American Indian Quarterly* 33, no. 1 (2009): 131–60.

Mayhew, A. K. "Book Review: *Rez Life: An Indian's Journey through Reservation Life*." *Specter Magazine*, February 6, 2020. http://www.spectermagazine.com/six/rez-life/.

McCooey, David. "The Limits of Life Writing." *Life Writing* 14, no. 3 (2017): 277–80.

Mendelsohn, Daniel. "But Enough about Me: What Does the Popularity of Memoirs Tell Us about Ourselves?" *New Yorker*, January 25, 2010. https://www.newyorker.com/magazine/2010/01/25/but-enough-about-me-2.

Miller, Pamela. "Nonfiction: 'Rez Life,' by David Treuer." *Star Tribune*, February 18, 2020. https://www.startribune.com/nonfiction-rez-life-by-david-treuer/139474453/.

Naumann, Manfred, and Peter Heath. "Literary Production and Reception." *New Literary History* 8, no. 1 (1976): 107–26.

"Nonfiction Reading Series." Syracuse University, n.d. https://thecollege.syr.edu/writing-studies-rhetoric-and-composition/nfrs/ (accessed June 10, 2019).

O'Connell, Sarah J. "Rez Life: An Indian's Journey through Reservation Life by David Treuer." *World Literature Today* 86, no. 5 (2012): 79.

Olney, James. *Memory and Narrative: The Weave of Life-Writing.* Chicago: University of Chicago Press, 1998.

"Powerful, Important Reading." *Kirkus Review*, November 7, 2011. https://www.kirkusreviews.com/book-reviews/david-treuer/rez-life/.

Purdy, John, and Sherman Alexie. "Crossroads: A Conversation with Sherman Alexie." *Studies in American Indian Literatures* 9, no. 4 (1997): 1–18.

Quinby, Lee. "The Subject of Memoirs: The Woman Warriors' Technology of Ideographic Selfhood." In *De/Colonizing the Subject: The Politics of Gender in Women's Autobiography*, edited by Sidonie Smith and Julia Watson, 297–320. Minneapolis: University of Minnesota Press, 1992.

Rall, Patt. "Author David Treuer Describes Reservation Life." *Red Lake Nation News*, February 22, 2012. https://www.redlakenationnews.com/story/2012/02/22/features/author-david-treuer-describes-reservation-life/022220120656119736305.html.

Randall, William Lowell. *The Stories We Are: An Essay on Self-Creation.* Toronto: University of Toronto Press, 1995.

Ruppert, James, "Review of *Native American Fiction: A User's Manual* by David Treuer." *Great Plains Quarterly* 1164 (2009). https://digitalcommons.unl.edu/greatplainsquarterly/1164.

Sides, Hampton. "Praise for *Rez Life*." Grove Atlantic, n.d. https://groveatlantic.com/book/rez-life/ (accessed June 10, 2019.

Smith, Sidonie, and Julia Watson. *Reading Autobiography: A Guide for Interpreting Life Narratives*, 2nd ed. Minneapolis: University of Minnesota Press, 2010.

Taylor, Christopher. "North America as Contact Zone: Native American Literary Nationalism and the Cross-Cultural Dilemma." *Studies in American Indian Literatures* 22, no. 3 (2010): 26–44.

Teuton, Sean. *Red Land, Red Power: Grounding Knowledge in the American Indian Novel.* Durham, NC: Duke University Press, 2008.

Treuer, David. "Reading Culture." *Studies in American Indian Literatures* 14, no. 1 (2002): 51–64.

———. *Native American Fiction: A User's Manual.* St. Paul, MN: Graywolf Press, 2006.

———. *The Translation of Dr Apelles: A Love Story.* St. Paul, MN: Graywolf Press, 2006.

———. *Rez Life: An Indian's Journey through Reservation Life.* New York: Grove Press, 2012.

———. "Praise for *Anishinabe Syndicated*." Minnesota Historical Society, n.d. https://shop.mnhs.org/products/anishinaabe-syndicated (accessed August 11, 2019).

Ulin, David. "The Writing Life: David Treuer Mines His Family's 'Rez Life.'" *Los Angeles Times*, April 15, 2012. https://www.latimes.com/entertainment/la-xpm-2012-apr-15-la-ca-david-treuer-20120415-story.html.

Vizenor, Gerald R. *Survivance: Narratives of Native Presence*. Lincoln: University of Nebraska Press, 2009.

Walsh, Richard. "Fictionality and Mimesis: Between Narrativity and Fictional Worlds." *Narrative* 11, no. 1 (2003): 110–21.

Washburn, Kathleen. "*Conversations with Sherman Alexie* Edited by Nancy J. Peterson (Review)." *American Indian Quarterly* 38, no. 1 (2014): 110–13.

Weaver, Jace, Craig S. Womack, and Robert Warrior. *American Indian Literary Nationalism*. Albuquerque: University of New Mexico Press, 2006.

Weinberg, Steve. "Book Review: *Rez Life: An Indian's Journey through Reservation Life*, by David Treuer." *Dallas Morning News*, February 24, 2012. https://www.dallasnews.com/arts-entertainment/books/2012/02/25/book-review-rez-life-an-indians-journey-through-reservation-life-by-david-treuer/.

Womack, Craig S., Daniel Heath Justice, and Christopher B. Teuton (eds.). *Reasoning Together: The Native Critics Collection*. Norman: University of Oklahoma Press, 2008.

Yost, David. "Apelles's War: Transcending Stereotypes of American Indigenous Peoples in David Treuer's *The Translation of Dr. Apelles*." *Studies in American Indian Literatures* 22, no. 2 (2010): 59–74.

II
Bakaawiz

Chapter 4

The Anishinaabe Eco-Poetics of Language, Life, and Place in the Poetry of Schoolcraft, Noodin, Blaeser, and Henry

Susan Berry Brill de Ramírez

There is a language and grammar of connection that opens itself up across poetic worlds. It can be accessed by imaginative readers who are open to becoming part of experiential worlds that are linguistically lived. Meaningfulness in life comes from connection. We can interpret signs from a distance, but hermeneutical meanings require deeper and closer contact. We can interpret aspects of literature from an objective distance, and we can analyze information and data, but if we want to gain a deep sense of meaning, that is achieved relationally, inter-subjectively, affiliatively. Linguistic beauty and harmony present sonorous rhythms that are emotionally, passionately, and spiritually moving. It is in the intersections of mind and heart, of body and soul, that poetic language elicits reader responses that co-creatively bring story to life, to re-membered experience even when that experience is linguistically and imaginatively experienced. Through close attention to four journey poems by three contemporary Anishinaabe poets, Kimberly Blaeser, Margaret Noodin, and Gordon Henry Jr., and the earlier Jane Johnston Schoolcraft, we see poetic evocations of distinctively Anishinaabe worlds, words, and affiliative relations for their readers' co-creative response. In this way, the poetic craft of connection is manifested in its presence (and absence) in the poems' parallel literary structures and referents as the larger story of motion, journey, change, and "transmotion" emerges in the texts and interstices of Anishinaabe poetic articulation (Vizenor, *Fugitive Poses* 197, 199). As Anishinaabe language scholar Noodin explains, "Events and imaginings best reflect a culture when transmitted with the full benefit of both the sound and structure of the language developed by the community through centuries of use" ("Megwa" 9).

Describing the pictorial creations of his people, tribal member Gerald Vizenor writes, "Clearly, anishinaabe visual stories, totemic creations, and other pictures are mappery, the virtual cartography of native survivance and sovereignty" (*Fugitive Poses* 178). What Vizenor describes about the Anishinaabe visual realm is also true of the literary work of Anishinaabe writers. There is a veritable cartography of the processes of struggle and survivance that manifests itself in Anishinaabe poetry. Following Vizenor's assertion that "Motion is the originary" (*Fugitive Poses* 55) and Niigonwedom James Sinclair's affirmation that "transmotion" is "a complex, powerful message based in Anishinaabeg consciousness and intellectualism" regarding "how Anishinaabeg survivance is actualized and assured" (129), I seek to demonstrate as much. I have chosen journey poems by four different Anishinaabe poets as a means of exploring distinctive commonalities in Anishinaabe poetics. Two poems are in the Anishinaabe language, and two are in English. In notably telling "family resemblances" of repetition, parallelism, metrical rhythmics, and emphatic pauses (e.g., caesura, line and stanza breaks), as well as tribally geographic and historical referents, the voices of the Anishinaabeg resonate across the centuries and in the poetic voices of four otherwise very different poets. My hope is that this beginning delineation of select aspects of Schoolcraft's, Noodin's, Blaeser's, and Henry's poetics will be helpful for future studies of their poetry and prose, the craft of other Anishinaabe poets and writers, and perhaps also the rhythms, language, and form of traditional and contemporary Anishinaabe song, story, and poetry.

Blaeser and Henry are contemporaries; both are from White Earth and are academics and scholars as well as creative writers. Similarities in their poetry would point us in valuable directions, but it is not clear to what extent such a small and similar sample of two Anishinaabe poets would help in elucidating distinctively Anishinaabe rhythms and poetic patterns. There are indeed certain rhythms that pervade the work of these writers, but are these rhythms specifically Anishinaabe rhythms? Of course they are, but poetic and literary rhythms cannot be wholly defined by the limits of ancestry, tribe, and land. As is the case for any writer, literary craft is the product of the fullness of one's life, one's study, one's practice, and one's personal proclivities (literary and otherwise): idiosyncrasy, the respective history of a person's life, tribal affiliation and legacy, national and regional cultures, landscapes and geographies of belonging, placefulness and movement, change and growth, juvenilia and the maturation of craft. These coalesce and cohere in varying ways that reflect the ebbs and flows of any writer's work. What does all this mean for the distinctive influence of tribal ancestry, culture, history, language, and lands? Can Shakespeare be read outside of the context of the landscapes, histories, cultures, languages, and peoples that are England? Yes, but at great cost, for even *Othello*, *Julius Caesar*, and *The Tempest* are distinctly English plays. Even within the complex literary legacies of diverse Jewish American writers can we read the poetry of Emma Lazarus, Gertrude Stein, Allen Ginsberg, Jerome Rothenberg, Adrienne Rich, or Bob Perelman wholly outside the boundaries of diaspora and the historical connections to and disconnections from ancestral place, tribal language, and religion? While the specificity of the literary extends beyond the bounds of ethnicity, ancestry, history, and geography, these integrally inform the directions and meaningfulness of any writer's work. So must tribe inform Schoolcraft's, Noodin's, Blaeser's, and Henry's poetic cartographies in distinctly Anishinaabe directions.

The twentieth century's critically formal turns through the New Criticism, the Chicago School, and psychoanalytic, linguistic, feminist, and Marxist criticisms as well as the later poststructurally semiotic, deconstructive, and Lacanian orientations all indicated that the specificities of ancestry and origin were unnecessary for critical insight. Notwithstanding Matthew Arnold's and T. S. Eliot's calls for a disinterested criticism, there is an ancestrally genetic (originative) memory that endures throughout time, across the distances of diasporic divides and Holocaust ovens, and beyond the genocidal legacies of conquests, broken treaties, relocations, and boarding schools. To ground Blaeser's and Henry's English-language poetry in distinctively Anishinaabeg lexical, rhythmic, and rhetorical registers, we can turn back two centuries to the Anishinaabe poetry of Schoolcraft and then forward to the contemporary Anishinaabe poetry of Noodin to see the ancestrally and linguistically genetic literary foundation on which to consider the resonances of a tribally informed poetics and aesthetic. Whereas genetic literary study generally focuses on a writer's own prior originative manuscripts, here I use the word "genetic" more broadly to extend diachronically and synchronically across diverse Anishinaabe poets, trolling for traces that will help map the literary cartography of Anishinaabe letters in the systems of the literature as a whole and in its discrete alphabetic signs.

One well-known poem of Schoolcraft's and one contemporary poem of Noodin's provide sufficient intricacy to open up significant elements of Anishinaabeg poetry and song. Schoolcraft's poem "On leaving my children John and Jane at School, in the Atlantic states, and preparing to return to the interior" is particularly interesting in that the English title provides a clear context for a poem that is nonetheless written in Anishinaabe. This introduction establishes the poem's orientation on the "journey" movement of Schoolcraft, the mother who is leaving her children: "leaving" in that she is going away and "leaving" in that she is the subject who has taken and is now leaving her children at the school. The poem as it appears below includes Schoolcraft's original version on the left along with a contemporary and standardized Anishinaabeg spelling and an English translation, both provided by Margaret Noodin.[1] Schoolcraft has left her children and is preparing herself to journey home in a departure or leaving that is focused upon arrival—to home, to homeland, to an integral interiority of self that is made possible within the grounds of ancestry and home. Written in 1839, the poem is poignantly prescient of Schoolcraft's own spirit journey beyond this world with her death a mere three years later.

On leaving my children John and Jane at School, in the
   Atlantic states,
and preparing to return to the interior

Nyau nin de nain dum	Nyaah nindinendam	Oh I am thinking
May kow e yaun in	Mekawiyaanin	I am reminded
Ain dah nuk ki yaun	Endanakiiyaan	Of my homeland
Waus sa wa kom eg	Waasawekamig	A faraway place
Ain dah nuk ki yaun	Endanakiiyaan	My homeland
Ne dau nis ainse e	Nindaanisens e	
Ne gwis is ainse e	Nigwizisens e	My little daughter
Ishe nau gun ug wau	Ishe naganagwaa	My little son
Waus sa wa kom eg	Waasawekamig	I leave them far behind
She gwau go sha ween	Zhigwa gosha wiin	A faraway place

Ba sho waud e we	Beshowad e we	
Nin zhe ka we yea	Ninizhike we ya	Now
Ishe ez hau jau yaun	Ishe izhayaan	It is near
Ain dah nuk ke yaun	Endanakiiyaan	I am alone
Ain dah nuk ke yaun	Endanakiiyaan	As I go
Nin zhe ke we yea	Ninizhike we ya	My homeland
Ishe ke way aun e	Ishe giiweyaan e	
Nyau ne gush kain dum	Nyaa nigashkendam	My homeland
		I am alone
		I am going home
		Oh I am sad

In addition, Noodin provides a sonorous and prosodic guide to the Schoolcraft poem with her audio reading.[2]

Schoolcraft's lyrical poem is poetically interesting for many reasons. The poem is emphatically framed by the speaker's thoughts and feelings with the poignantly sad repetition of "Nyau" in the first and last lines, which Noodin explains "is the first person prefix to a verb that is being used in a reduplicative fashion to emphasize her experience" (personal communication, March 8, 2013). "Nyaah nindinendam" and "Nyaa nigashkendam" parallel each other in their ending rhymes, grammatical construction, and metrical rhythm (/ u/u/). In this way, the poem draws special attention to the profound sadness of a mother's separation from her children, her genetic and most beloved lineage—a separation that reminds her, too, of her (and their) distance from their people, culture, and tribal homelands (distinguished in the poem from the "home" with her Euro-American husband). By leaving her children at school, Schoolcraft returns to a home that in the absence of her children becomes more Euro-American. The increasing distance from the school and children increases her felt distance and desired return for a clear sense of self, ancestry, culture, and homelands. In the third stanza, Schoolcraft utters her loneliness, her aloneness, immediately before writing "Ishe ez hau jau yaun" ("As I go"). She repeats this in the final stanza, "Nin zhe ka we yea / Ishe ke way aun e" ("I am alone / I am going home"). Home should be a place of felt belonging, of love and comfort, yet in this poem Schoolcraft conveys her utter loneliness in going "home" without her children. The tribal, genetic, maternal, and geographic pull of her disassociated self is oriented in the emphatic repetition of "Ain dah nuk ke yaun" ("My homeland") with the added emphatic pause of the stanza break.

Although the poem ostensibly focuses on Schoolcraft's felt loss of and for her children as they are left at school, the larger loss that circumscribes the sense of solitary disconnection in the poem is the expressed distance from tribe and homeland. She begins her poem with its contextualizing English title, but the fact that the poem is in her native language underscores the desired connection to tribal ancestry, culture, language, and place while closing off this version of the poem and its speaker to non-Anishinaabe readers. Schoolcraft uses her Anishinaabeg language to filiative and connective ends, speaking her love and relationships to daughter, son, and homeland in the language that stitches them together ancestrally and forward into the future. The connection to homeland is made explicit four times in the poem. No other part of the poem is repeated with the geographic wholeness of the four directions and four seasons. Other repetitions come in pairs or triads. The reference to "My homeland" is given even greater weight as the final line in stanzas one and three, lengthening them to five lines. In addition, the utterances, assertions, affirmations, and laments of "My homeland" are made that much more emphatically understood as the lines repeat in pairs with one line between them. In the first stanza, the assertions of distanced homeland are separated and contrasted by the line "Waus sa wa kom eg" ("A faraway place"), which is brought into parallel comparison with the comparably felt distance of the children's school, also "Waus sa wa kom eg." Schoolcraft gives the second pairing of "Ain dah nuk ke yaun" ("My homeland") great emphatic weight as the affiliative references to homeland are separated by the silence of the pausal line and stanza break, including the doubled emphatic of the referents serving as the final and first lines of their third and fourth stanzas.

Schoolcraft, or Bamewawagezhikoquay (the sound the stars make rushing through the sky), powerfully articulates her felt belonging to her Anishinaabeg homelands. The ties of any person to his or her childhood landscapes are often fondly remembered and sorely missed. In central Illinois, Edgar Lee Masters crafted poignant poems about the people and lands of his early years around Petersburg.[3] So it is not merely the fondness a writer holds for the world and place of their childhood years that distinguishes the writing. We must look further to understand those elements of Schoolcraft's (and Noodin's, Blaeser's, and Henry's) poetry that makes it distinctively Anishinaabe.[4] Analysis of these journey poems identifies four elements in the poetics of these writers that cohere as part of a distinctively Anishinaabe poetics: the central grounding of an indigenous Anishinaabe homeland, the rhythms and sounds of tribal language (including resonances in traditional metrics and other Anishinaabe prosodic traces), the emphasis on movement and change, and the specificity of Anishinaabe survivance through colonization, Western education, and modernization with their concomitant stresses of distance, disorientation, and disconnection that are powerfully balanced with an underlying thematic of connection, place, and identity.

Before moving to the contemporary poems, we need to turn to the metrical rhythms of Anishinaabe lyric. There are rhythmic models common in many Anishinaabe songs that exemplify linguistic and semantic patterns evident in the poetry of these creative writers. Noodin's Anishinaabe-language website at the University of Michigan provides a number of helpful examples of traditional Anishinaabe songs that demonstrate the iambic rhythms of the drum and human heartbeat.[5] These songs have one other rhythmic pattern that is especially interesting; there is a common pattern such that the rhythm of individual lines followed by pausal breaks concludes with accented beats. There is an important semantic difference between line endings that are accented and those that are not. Accented line endings point strongly forward in more connective ways toward that which follows, whereas unaccented endings (as in a trochee /u) provide a stronger and disconnected stop. A contemporary Anishinaabe band from Canada, appropriately named Anishnabe, has Anishinaabe and French lyrics that manifest this same rhythmic patterning with the strongly connective accenting on the ends of lines.[6] This pattern is consistent regardless of whether the songs have a more traditional Anishinaabe tune or a more contemporary country and Western tune.

Turning to the Schoolcraft poem as recited/sung by Noodin, the poem can be scanned as follows:

Nyaah nindinendam	/ u/u/	Oh I am thinking / /u/u
Mekawiyaanin	/u/u/	I am reminded /u u/u
Endanakiiyaan	u/u/u/	Of my homeland /u/u
Waasawekamig	/ u/u/	A faraway place u/u//
Endanakiiyaan	-/u/u/	My homeland u/u
Nindaanisens e		
Nigwizisens e	u/ /u/	My little daughter u/u/u
Ishe naganagwaa	u/u/u/	My little son u/u/
Waasawekamig	u/ u/u/	I leave them far behind u/u/u/
Zhigwa gosha wiin	/ u/u/	A faraway place u/u//

Beshowad e we		
Ninizhike we ya	u/ u/u/	Now /
Ishe izhayaan	/u /u/	It is near /u/
Endanakiiyaan	u/u /u/	I am alone u/u/
Endanakiiyaan	u/ u/u/	As I go /u/
Ninizhike we ya	-/u/u/	My homeland u/u
Ishe giiweyaan e		
Nyaa nigashkendam	-/u/u/	My homeland u/u
	u/u /u/	I am alone u/u/
	u/ u/u/	I am going home u//u/
	/ u/u/	Oh I am sad / /u/

The self-referentiality in the poem is counterbalanced by its connective semantics, syntax, and rhythmics that reflect her deeply felt and lived Anishinaabe heritage, culture, language, and life. Homeland is "my homeland," expressed in her language as *Endanakiiyaan* with its accented and lengthened final syllabic beat that is both emphatic and elongated, pointing toward connection and return—a place that is far away but brought near through her creative force of poesis and Native language. In the Anishinaabe version of the poem, every line demonstrates Anishinaabe rhythms, including the strongly connective and forward-pointing emphatic line breaks with their accented final beats. This contrasts with the English version in which the first part of the poem has the harder stops of unaccented line endings, but as the poem shifts focus to Schoolcraft's return, the rhythm in the English version shifts to a more Anishinaabe rhythmic.

Noodin's contemporary Anishinaabe poem "Waanimazinbiigananke / Writing Images in Circles" honors Canadian First Nations artist Daphne Odjig (1919–2016). The poem is in many ways a journey poem about the powers of art and language to bring persons, times, and worlds together, as Odjig did in her art and as Noodin does in her poem:

Waanimazinbiigananke / Writing Images in Circles
For Daphne Odjig

Maajamigad maage maajtaamigad
It is leaving   or   it is beginning

ezhi-dibaajimoying name giizis miinwa dibikigiizis?
the way we tell stories under the sun and the night sun?

Ezhinaagwaziyaang ina n'mishomisinanig miinwa nokomisinanig?
Do we look like our grandfathers and grandmothers?

Nd'shkitoomi waabmaa'angidwa ezhi waabmaa'awad
Can we see them the way they saw them

anzhenii gii miinigoig kina enaandeg ziigidiwiigwaas,
  waasawaaskone, miskopskidoskine biinojinsing?
the angels who gave us the colors of wrinkled birchbark,
  far lit flowers and pink elbows of babies?

Nd'shkitoomi waabmaa'angidwa ina
Can we see them the way they saw them

niizh-ochaakanag niimiiwag dibishko baapaaseog bakadewaad
  deakogewaad?
two spirits dancing like woodpeckers hungry and knocking?

Giisphin maamwi-sagajigaaboying oshki niizhing aakiiong.
If we walk together in these two new worlds

mii sa gonemaa ingoding wii depsiniying.
perhaps then we will be satisfied.

Nd'aawmi miigisag negwikeong, migiziag mitigwaking,
  anongansag giizhigong.
We are shells in the sand, eagles in the forest, stars in the sky.

Maajaayaang pane maajtaayaang pane.
We are always leaving, we are always starting.

Here art (look, see) and poetry (tell stories) are shown to be ways "we walk together in these two new worlds" ("Giisphin maamwi-sagajigaaboying oshki niizhing aakiiong" /u /u/ | /uu/u/ | /u u/ | /u/). Noodin's poem is very interesting in that virtually every pause within lines and at line breaks ends with accented beats that strongly point forward in connection and relation. Demonstrating Vizenor's and Sinclair's emphases on Anishinaabe transmotion, Noodin's journey poem speaks of traveling in life and art. It concludes: "Maajaayaang pane maajtaayaang pane. (//u/

u/ | /uu/ u/) We are always leaving, we are always starting." Canadian Anishinaabe scholar Sinclair expressly points to the thematic of motion and transmotion as central to Anishinaabe lives and stories in his essay, "A Sovereignty of Transmotion: Imagination and the 'Real,' Gerald Vizenor, and Native Literary Nationalism." He explains that the Anishinabeg are a people for whom movement has defined their individual lives, as well as their cultural and political lives in both pre-conquest and post-conquest times, and that this has been a crucial feature in their survivance:

> The idea that Anishinaabeg peoples have always been on the move, on their own imaginative and narrative terms, is a sovereign concept. It is a principle inherent in Anishinaabeg notions of lands, maps, histories. It is the way material existence is perceived and the way bodies travel, live, and die in this life. It is also the way change is provoked and tribal selves and communities are maintained, as well as how both are brought forth into reality. (148)

Schoolcraft's powerful poem speaks the desire for such survivance in the midst of loss and catastrophic change. She speaks her frailty during the traumatic post–War of 1812 America in which attacks against tribes, tribal cultures, and languages were becoming even more severe, leading to "trails of tears" and genocidal relocations. In the dominant Euro-American world, change did not proffer strength and forward motion for Native peoples, but loss and death. Almost two centuries later, Noodin's early twenty-first-century poem speaks of a categorically different time such that Odjig is honored with Canadian postal service stamps (among many other awards) that depict her artwork. Regardless of the historical differences across time, Noodin and Schoolcraft speak strong Anishinaabe words and rhythms that give meaningful and relational life to their poetic words. Similar to Schoolcraft, Noodin uses repetition and parallelism evident in virtually every line. The beginning and ending lines of the poem are especially interesting: "Maajamigad maage maajtaamigad" ("It is leaving or it is beginning") and "Maajaayaang pane maajtaayaang pane" ("We are always leaving, we are always starting") as the final line points back to the beginning in a backward and yet forward circular motion that emphasizes the "transmotion" inherent in life and made explicit in Anishinaabe poetry and art. There are many significant parallels in the Anishinaabe-language poetry of Schoolcraft and Noodin, but are these tribal poetics limited to poetry that is written in the tribal language, or are there distinctively

Anishinaabe poetic traces that transcend the indigenous language and are evident in the English poetry of Anishinaabe poets Blaeser and Henry?

Much like Noodin's poem that is focused through visual and lexical lenses, Blaeser's first collection of poetry *Trailing You* begins with a photo collage of family and home at White Earth. This visual grounding orients the collection via the Twin Lakes of White Earth. As Blaeser writes in the preface to the volume, "Much of my life and my writing searches out the connections of self, family, community, place and history. Like many Indian people, I write partly to remember, because remembering, we recover; remembering, we survive" (*Trailing You* ix). Here Blaeser articulates the very process of transmotive journeying in which Anishinaabe poem as story is deeply connective, transformative, and healing. Blaeser's English poem "On the Way to the Chicago Pow-Wow" parallels the Schoolcraft poem in remarkable ways, but this is not to say that Blaeser had the Schoolcraft poem in mind at all when she wrote her poem. The differences between an early nineteenth-century Anishinaabe poem about an Anishinaabe woman leaving her children at an Indian boarding school and a late twentieth-century poem about an Anishinaabe woman driving to a pow-wow in Chicago are sufficient that the similarities are that much more striking. Noodin, Blaeser, and Schoolcraft are all pioneering intellectual women, creative writers, and scholars deeply proud of their ancestry, but Schoolcraft's life was painfully defined and deformed by her times and the Calvinist strictures of her husband's Presbyterianism compounded by the racism that surrounded her adult life, eventually succumbing to the depressive degradation of laudanum and an early death in 1842. Here Schoolcraft contrasts radically with Noodin and Blaeser, both leading scholars, poets, and mothers whose work emerged in a different time for Native women in the latter half of the twentieth century and whose scholarship and creative production continue to progress forward well into the twenty-first century.

It is helpful to review Blaeser's poem in its entirety as a reference for the prosodic, lexical, and syntactic elements that meaningfully resonate with Schoolcraft's poetics.

On the Way to the Chicago Pow-Wow

On the way to the Chicago pow-wow, //
Weaving through four-lanes of traffic, /u
   going into the heart of Carl Sandburg's hog-butcher to the
     world, u/
   ironic, I think, landing at Navy Pier for a pow-wow. //

> I think of what Roberta said: "Indian people across the
>   country are working on a puzzle, trying to figure out
>   what I call—the abyss." u/
> Driving into the abyss. Going to a pow-wow. //
>
> On the way to the Chicago pow-wow, //
> Laugh when I look down at my hands. u/
> Trying to tell you, needing to hear you laugh out loud u/
>   because the puzzle was made by madmen who want us all
>   lost in the rotating maze. u/
> I think my hands have stepped out of Linda Hogan's poem: u/
> One wears silver and tourquoise [sic], a Zuni bracelet and a
>   Navaho [sic] ring. //
> One wears gold and diamonds, an Elgin watch and a
>   Simonson's half-carat; /u
> The madman's classic mixedblood, a cliché. u/
> Together, laughing out loud at the madness. Going to a
>   pow-wow. //
>
> On the way to the Chicago pow-wow, //
> Thinking of home, I know we are driving the wrong way. //
> It's not Lake Michigan I want to see. u/
> It's not Wriggly [sic] Field. u/
> But there is no exit here to 113, no cut-across. u/
> I think of Helen's cabin, sitting by the fire drying my hair,
>   and Collin talking: /u
>   "Sometimes you have to go in the wrong direction to get
>   where you're heading." /u
> Driving southeast, heading northwest. Heading home, u/
>   to White Earth Lake, u/
>   to Indian ball diamonds, //
>   to open air pow-wows. //
> Taking the Eden's, going to the Chicago pow-wow, //
>   on the way back home. // (*Trailing You* 12–13)

In the Schoolcraft and Blaeser poems, we have Anishinaabe women speakers who articulate the extent to which their travels eastward bring them back home, either in painful memory in Schoolcraft's poem or in remembered actuality in the Blaeser poem. The former poem bespeaks the absence of connection and the distance felt in that absence—in her longing to return home and her sadness in her children's distance from mother and homeland. The latter poem expresses distance but in the more joyful frame of unquestioned connection and affiliative bonds. Schoolcraft uses her native language to express her utter loneliness as she speaks her sadness forward into the linguistic abyss of nineteenth-century English poetry readers who would not be able to read the Anishinaabe of her poem and the majority of her contemporary tribal members whose illiteracy would distance them from her poetry regardless of its language—even the bilingual Native people in the missionary communities whose literacy would be predominantly in English. The very idea of any written language bereft of readers speaks volumes about the extent of Schoolcraft's solitude as expressed in her tribally relational and affiliative choice to use Anishinaabe as the primary language of her poem. Indeed, it was not until the twenty-first century with the publication of Robert Dale Parker's edited collection with much of Schoolcraft's poetry that her work has gained its well-deserved readership.

One hundred sixty years later, Blaeser's eminently accessible poem communicates much about belonging, the importance of placefulness and a sense of home, and how a person can achieve a balanced sense of connection in different circumstances, different times, and different places. As Blaeser writes in her poem "Y2K Indian," "Another absentee Indian / *calling myself home.* / Do I begin with the songs / whose words I've lost / . . . / *One finds the way by heart* / . . . / the university and the pow-wow circuit / the church pew and the cedar smoke circle. / . . . / I become comfortable / with the story of doubleness / learn *survival this way.* / Another Y2K Indian / *writing the circle* / of return" (*Absentee Indians* 129–31). Blaeser is echoed in Noodin's lines "Maajaayaang pane maajtaayaang pane. We are always leaving, we are always starting," as ends are also beginnings and what appear to be reversals are actually continuances in the transmotive connectiveness of life cycles and language.

In "On the way to the Chicago pow-wow," the speaker of the poem articulates just this sense of malleable connectedness, that even when "driving the wrong way," one can be going the right way, "Heading home, / to White Earth Lake, / to Indian ball diamonds, / to open air pow-wows." A sense of grounding, a geography of belonging can extend far beyond the limits of tribal origination, ancestral homelands, and childhood homes. Like Schoolcraft, Blaeser effects the sense of her poem in tightly-crafted lines that creatively interweave prose statements in the poem. In this way, she literally and conversively brings other persons and voices into the world of the poem, dialogically infusing it with an oral sense of community. "I think of what Roberta said: . . . ," "I think my hands have stepped out of Linda Hogan's poem: . . . ," "I think of . . . Collin talking: . . ." The poem's three stanzas include one of these dialogic shifts in its center, thereby demonstrating the interpersonal and intersubjective relations that make it possible to be "home" in a place far from one's natal and tribal ancestral homelands. Like Schoolcraft and Noodin, throughout her poem Blaeser makes effective and strategic use of parallel constructions (gerund phrases, prepositional phrases, negations, series), repetition (words, phrases, clauses), geographic referents (Chicago pow-wow [four times], a pow-wow [three times], open air pow-wows, the world, the country, the abyss [two times], home [three times], Lake Michigan, Wriggly Field, Helen's cabin, White Earth Lake, Indian ball diamonds), present-tense verbs that give a sense of movement and change (weaving, going [three times], landing, driving [three times], laughing, sitting, drying, heading [three times], taking), assertions of thought and remembrance ("I think of," "Thinking of home," "I know"), emphatic pauses (including caesura and line and stanza breaks), and metrical rhythms that fluctuate the pacing of the poem.

Blaeser and Schoolcraft end their journey poems asserting that they are going home ("Ishe ke way aun e" and "Heading home / . . . / on the way back home"). For Schoolcraft, in her return to her northwestern home and homelands, her deep sense of tribal and geographic belonging is fractured because of her children's absence from her and her expressed sadness. In contrast, Blaeser's contemporary poem is much more upbeat, ending on the affirmation that "driving southeast" is, in fact, "heading northwest" with a deeply articulated sense of joyous affiliative "home." The home indicated in the poem is White Earth, reservation land, homeland, so referenced three times by Blaeser: "Thinking of home," "Heading home," "on the way back home"—all of which occur in the final stanza, underscoring the poem's concluding sense of tribal, familial, and ancestral belonging even in an urban metropolis far from White Earth. The metrical rhythms of the "home" phrases give their accented weight to home ("Thinking of home": a trochee followed by an iamb, "Heading home": the long-short-long rhythm of an amphimacer, and "on the way back home": an amphimacer followed by the double long accentuation of the emphatic spondee). For Blaeser, the inter- and pan-tribal experiences of late twentieth-century pow-wows provide indigenous expressions of culture, community, and continuance in ways that make a trip to Chicago a homecoming. Such opportunities were not available for Schoolcraft, and she became increasingly alienated due to the distancing strictures of her husband's judgmental strand of Christianity compounded by her physical removal from her tribal community, her biological family (children and others), and her homeland. Her deep anomie is manifest in the self-referentiality that pervades her poem in the speaker's loss, the speaker's sadness, and the speaker's isolation. The self-referentiality of Schoolcraft's poem draws attention to the distressed condition of Native people (then and now) isolated from their tribal communities and their traditional communal worldviews because of the anguished traumas of conquest, colonization, relocation, and racism.

"On the Way to the Chicago Pow-Wow" depicts a very different reality in which the poem's speaker expresses the continuance of community and belonging as evidenced in the diverse persons who populate the world of the poem and the indigenous community of the pan-tribal Chicago pow-wow. Here, self-referentiality in no way refracts back on the poem's speaker or its author, Blaeser; rather, the self-referentiality is merely the originating orientation that communally embraces diverse geographies of belonging that all coalesce in their "hominess" as absence and physical distance from White Earth actually facilitate tribally felt connection. Indeed, the Blaeser poem opens itself up to the reader in its familiarization (in the converse sense of Viktor Shklovsky's defamiliarization), which brings the reality of the mixed-blood Anishinaabe speaker into the world of the reader through the rhetorical informality of the poem that speaks conversively to the reader. Voice shifts to second-person direct address ("Trying to tell you, needing to hear you laugh"), the first-person plural inclusive "we," and commonly known lexical terms for Chicago geographic markers (Navy Pier, Lake Michigan, Wrigley Field, the Eden's), which also familiarize White Earth for readers with a neat pairing of the Chicago referents with parallel and contrastive Anishinaabe markers of place: "open air pow-wows" paired with the pow-wow at Navy Pier, White Earth Lake with Lake Michigan, "Indian ball diamonds" with "Wriggly Field," and the home highway 113 with Chicago's Eden's.

There is one final rhetorical and prosodic tool that is used to great effect in the Blaeser, Noodin, and Schoolcraft poems. Along with the markers to ancestral lands and specific rhetorical pairings and repetition, we see a specificity of poetic expression that points us in distinctively Anishinaabe directions. Schoolcraft and Blaeser make powerful use of the emphatic and connective pause in the form of stanza breaks; all three manifest this in their strongly accented line endings. Whereas the emphatic pause is a poetic and literary tool that is part of all literary traditions and had been used throughout time in oral storytelling, there are aspects of Schoolcraft's, Noodin's, and Blaeser's use that indicate an Anishinaabe rhythmic.[7] The Schoolcraft and Blaeser poems include adjacent repeated phrases that end one stanza and begin the next: "Going to a pow-wow. // On the way to the Chicago pow-wow" (twice in the Blaeser poem) and "Ain dah nuk ke yaun // Ain dah nuk ke yaun" ("My homeland" which ends the third and begins the fourth and final stanza). Schoolcraft does this twice in her poem, but the first occurrence is less obvious, occurring in the break between the first two stanzas in which she writes, "Ain dah nuk ke yaun // Ne dau nis ainse e" ("My homeland // My little daughter"), with a relational repetition that emphasizes the extent to which her children are her last crucial link to tribe and homeland. Schoolcraft's pausal stanza breaks give space and silence for the speaker's sadness to sink in that much more deeply. Blaeser's repetition of "going to a pow-wow," of being "on the way to the Chicago pow-wow" is a light-hearted, excited, joyous assertion that converges in the final line of the poem, in which the phrasing of the indeterminate "*going to* a pow-wow" and the specific "*on the way* to the Chicago pow-wow" switch into "*going to* the Chicago pow-wow, / *on the way* back home" as the poem concludes with the strong affirmation that "going to the Chicago pow-wow" is indeed a journey not merely to Chicago nor to the pow-wow there but a journey of placefulness and a "way back home."

In these three journey poems, the authors clearly demonstrate the Anishinaabe rhythm of accented and elongated line endings that point forward in emphatic and connective ways as endings are also beginnings, leavings are startings, and goings away are returns. In Blaeser's English poem, other than the prosaic conversational shifts with "Collin talking / . . . [about] where you're heading" (/u /u and /u /u) with their ending trochees, virtually every other line ends with strongly accented syllabic beats. In this way, her English poem demonstrates an affiliative beat and rhythm with the Anishinaabe poems by Schoolcraft and Noodin. These are only three poems, but there are clear resonances in them that point to Anishinaabe poetic rhythms. In these and other poems by Schoolcraft, Noodin, and Blaeser are strategic uses of the accented and emphatic pause (for emotional and interpretive depth or for reader engagement), connective and affiliative rhythmics that move the lines of the poems forward in a lexicon and poetics of cyclic transmotion, conversive rhetorical strategies of familiarization that bring the world of the poem into the world of reader (through accessible diction, internal explication, and connective voice shifts in Noodin's "we," Blaeser's "you," and Schoolcraft's intimately expressed "I"), poetic patterns of repetition that reflect the oral and rhetorical patterns of traditional Anishinaabe storytelling and song, and the ever-present geographic centrality of Anishinaabe homelands with their "Indian ball diamonds," "open air pow-wows," "wrinkled birchbark," "shells in the sand," and Anishinaabe language.

One final journey poem by Gordon Henry Jr. demonstrates many of these patterns as well, even in the very different form of a block prose poem. "Traveling among Strangers," like the Schoolcraft, Noodin, and Blaeser poems is centered in the process of journeying and also structured in four distinct parts, each of which repeats the same refrain "This song is not from our language" (*Failure of Certain Charms* 128). Schoolcraft's poem is centered in past remembrance in the line "Ain dah nuk ki yaun" (Endanakiiyaan or My homeland), which is repeated four times. Noodin's poem is focused on movement forward as deeply informed by the past motions and resemblances of forefathers and foremothers (in four questions answered in the final four lines). Blaeser's poem is centered in the present progress forward "On the way / going to the Chicago pow-wow" (also repeated four times). Henry's poem follows the pattern of four poetic sections that are separated by his repeated refrain that, like the other poems, points forward through the remembered past and toward continuance.

Although the four poems discussed herein are radically different in their explicit subjects, structures, diction, and meter, each is nevertheless a decidedly Anishinaabe journey poem. In light of the patent differences between the poets and their divergent poetic styles, the parallels of the poems are that much more striking. Unlike the multistanza poems by the women poets, Henry's "Traveling among Strangers" is structured as a one-stanza block poem. As noted already, this one-stanza descriptor requires a caveat because the stanza is neatly divided by the repetition of one refrain that appears as the first, fifth, ninth, and twelfth lines—thereby dividing the poem almost equally into four quatrains (containing four, four, three, and five lines each). The repeated line in the Schoolcraft poem occurs internally in her poem in twice-stated refrains for added emphasis and impact. Blaeser begins and ends her poem and each stanza with the pow-wow refrains, giving added emphasis at her stanza breaks. Henry's poem gives the appearance of greater structural simplicity as a block poem, yet as is the case throughout his literary oeuvre, there are complexities that interweave his creative writing as ideas and language circle back on each other in deeply intricate structures. In his poem, like his sister Anishinaabe poets, he uses the poetic tools of repetition and division to structure the poem into stages of journey and travel. As Noodin explains, this is an inherent aspect of Anishinaabe worldview and understanding: "From an Anishinaabe perspective, indigenous literature is that trace of words, the circle of story, the lyric image of a nation connected by memory to space. . . . As our language teaches us, to live is to be in motion" ("Megwa" 1).

"Traveling among Strangers" relates the story of living and "traveling among strangers in sadness," away from home, away from tribe and language, away from family. Much like the other poems, it emphasizes the importance of language and story as vehicles of connection across worlds, times, and geographies. Schoolcraft's poem expresses her deepening sadness regarding her distance from her children, her tribe, and her tribal homelands and her children's sadness at their distance from mother and home. Schoolcraft poignantly and ironically turns to her tribal Anishinaabe language to speak the solitude and distancing of Euro-America. For Schoolcraft, it is language that on one hand speaks her sense of alienation and loneliness, while on the other drawing on Anishinaabe literary orality to effect the healing and restorative powers of language and story. Following in this traditional understanding of indigenous "literature and stories as involving both acts of connection and key acts of transformation" (Blaeser, "Wild Rice" 245), Noodin, Blaeser, and Henry use poetic language and craft to connect with their readers as their continuance and survivance songs face forward, even when that signifies geographic and tribal memory and physical distances from Anishinaabe community and homelands. In fact, Henry makes this point in an essay where he states, "Stories and songs know no distance; they tend to transcend distance and context" ("Eagleheart Narratives" 304). As he ends his poem, even the distances across physical and spirit worlds can be transcended through the creative force of poesis, thereby effecting emotional, psychological, and spiritual healing: "This song took away my sadness . . . I will sing this song. This song will take away the sadness of my dead father" (*Failure of Certain Charms* 128).

Henry's poem has the intricacy of a sestina, but it is far more complex in its open structuring of lines, phrases, and words that repeat and fold in back on each other in different ways, all within the fixity of the one block paragraph. In this way, words and prior referents take on new and different meanings in and of themselves and in conjunction with their prior and subsequent appearances. The poem begins with the common refrain and moves toward the title and thematic phrase: "*This song is not from our language.* [u/ u/ u//u] These sounds came out of the dark where I was *traveling among strangers* in sadness" (*Failure of Certain Charms* 128, emphases added). [u/ u/ /u/ u/ u/u/ u/ /u u/u]. The speaker of the poem affirms (1) that the poem is a song, (2) that the poem-song does not come from "our" language, (3) that the poem-song comes from "the dark," and (4) that the speaker is "traveling among strangers in sadness." Henry indigenizes and oralizes his poem at the outset in referencing it as a "song" and then by affirming the speaker's community through "our" language. Does "our" language signify Henry's tribal Anishinaabe language or English, or even academic language? Is the dark the past, the realm of the symbolic and dream state imaginary, the unknown, the dangerous? We know that the speaker is traveling "among strangers," that the speaker of the poem speaks out his community in the vocalization of the first-person plural "our," but the speaker is nevertheless surrounded within the alterity of strangers. Is it the speaker who is "in sadness," or the strangers, or both? As Noodin explains regarding the deep tribal connections and traces in contemporary Anishinaabe literature, regardless of its language of creation, "Today Anishinaabe authors move from one language to another by choice and necessity. The language of the original stories is now endangered, but translations and contemporary creations still reflect indigenous Anishinaabe patterns" (Noodin, *Bawaajimo* 19). In Henry's assertion that "This song is not from our language," he metrically affirms a traditional drumbeat of regular iambs with the metrical negation in the ending trochee that bespeaks the poem's cultural and linguistic hybridity.

The next and final lines of this first section of the poem reiterate the title phrase: "This song made a circle of light around me where I was traveling in sadness among strangers. These sounds made a circle of light in the darkness" (*Failure of Certain Charms* 128). The reference to sadness is now moved up in closer proximity to the speaker, but still with sufficient proximity to strangers to maintain the ambiguous referent. Here, as in the primacy of the song and language in the first line, the song and the sounds of the song are given reiterated emphasis and primacy, notwithstanding the thematic orientation around the literal journey or "travel among strangers." As this first section progresses and concludes, the prayer-song, the poem-song, the sounds "made a circle of light" that Henry reiterates in both sentences, crafting a circle poetic in the structure of the poem. Even though surrounded by strangers, the language of the song, the music of the song, less the English words and more the sounds, create the protective healing and illuminative circle. In a reconstructive inversion of Derridean hierarchy, Henry centers each section of his poem in *parole*, making it explicit that it is not *langue* that provides the needed grounds but *parole* and the fundamental interconnections among persons. Henry's turn toward *parole* and nonlinguistic sound is explained by Blaeser in her book-length study of Vizenor's work: "Another important means of communication . . . is nonlinguistic sound: vocables in song, the sound of drum and rattle, the sounds made in the voice of other beings, the sounds of spirit voices, and so on . . . [that] place his own writing in the oral tradition of the *midéwiwin* songs and alludes in a broader sense to the belief system inherent in that religious society"—vocables that are also present in Schoolcraft's poem (*Gerald Vizenor* 22, 23).[8] It is important to note that what Henry is doing in his poem is far more complex than pat distinctions between orality and textuality, for indeed the poem manifests both sides of the oral to written continuum in its rhythmic, syntactic, and lexical expression.

Noting the importance in recognizing the literary intricacies of craft on the part of indigenous writers, Craig Womack calls for "scholars of Native literature . . . to break down the oppositional thinking that separates orality and literacy wherein the oral constitutes authentic culture and the written contaminated culture" (15). In Henry's poem, in deconstructing the primacy of *langue* and affirming the fact that "This song is not from our/any language," in no way is Henry asserting that authenticity lies in the realm of orality. Whereas Womack critiques the hierarchized oppositionality that misrepresents story and orality as somehow fundamentally distinct from literature and textuality, Henry speaks the same concerns in the scope of one poem while affirming the living integration and coherence manifested in the poem and in poetry throughout the ages. Where language becomes a living song, the realms of orality, textuality, lexicality, and the paralinguistic and even nonlinguistic converge in relationships that are both internal and external to literature. Vizenor explains that this is inherent to the intersubjective relationality of Indigenous orality: "Words are rituals in the oral tradition, from the sound of creation . . . not cold pages or electronic beats that separate the tellers from the listeners" (*Landfill Meditations* 99). Accordingly, "Traveling among Strangers" performs convergent rituals of healing in the potencies of song and poetic story that literally bring together persons, real and imagined, living and remembered, and in the expansively relational intersections of poetry and its intricate webs, words and persons and communities are connected through "circles of light," much like the Platonic chain of inspiration that descends from muses through the interconnected links of poets and listeners and readers. As Dean Rader explains the crucial role played by such relationships, "The reliance on performative language, the connection between poetry and ceremony, and the necessity of speaker/audience interaction form a kind of interpretive web that, in my mind, helps us see the interrelation among language, culture, history, gender, land, and, perhaps most importantly, tribes" ("Epic Lyric" 141).

The pacing of the block format for Henry's poem moves the reader directly from section to section such that the stages and divisions become obscured while the interconnecting links of language and repetition create progressive cycles of movement, return, and continuance. In this way, the repeated phrase, "This song is not from our language," serves as both an ending and beginning as it simultaneously concludes each section in repetition while transitionally beginning the following section, as we can see in the framing of the second section of the poem:

> This song is not from our language. These sounds came from a singer sitting across from me in a circle of light. This song made light where I was traveling in darkness. These sounds took away the sadness I was traveling in. This song is not in any language. (*Failure of Certain Charms* 128)

The prior circle of light that encompassed the individual speaker is expanded as the song and its singer ("across from me" and also the poet) reverberate in the "circle of light." Here again, Henry uses ambiguous placement as the person "in a circle of light" points to the immediately preceding pronoun "me" and also to the "singer sitting . . . in a circle of light" that is "made" (poesis) as the singer's "song made light" and the "sounds took away the sadness," much as Schoolcraft turned to song and poetry for healing and connection. In Henry's poem, the singer and circle within his Anishinaabe orientation firmly root the poem in the realm of the sacred with the image of a circular sweat lodge or other sacred healing ceremony in which the healer/medicine person/singer brings the transforming power of conversive (transformative and intersubjectively relational) language and utterance to heal the speaker's sadness. The speaker then expands the "circle of light" outward and forward to encompass others as the speaker steps forward in the role of the singer to sing the song: "When I awake I will sing this song. My father is traveling in sadness among strangers in the dark. When I awake I will sing this song. This song will take away the sadness of my dead father" (*Failure of Certain Charms* 128).

    The repetition that concludes the poem is also significant in that the final four lines are essentially two lines that repeat. "When I awake" is repeated, followed by a variation of the affirmation regarding the father's sadness. The first mention affirms the father's sadness and the second mention affirms the healing removal of his sadness. In his essay "Word as Weapon," Rader notes that many poems by Native writers "function as tropes of agency and contingency, for in the final scene, they empower Natives and Native culture because each writer uniquely envisions alternative modes of being that do not define Indians in relation to Anglos but establish Natives as independent and interdependent communities" (165). Even beyond the poetic concept of the trope, poetry in the hands of writers such as Henry literarily and literally effect agency and empowerment through the creative force of relationally connective and intersubjective language—what Blaeser describes as the extent to which Native literatures elicit on the part of their listener-readers a "vital engagement in the questions of life," so that the literary work "becomes itself a spiritual force" ("Pagans Rewriting" 30).

    Schoolcraft, Noodin, and Blaeser sing forward the restorative relations through homeland, stories, forebears, and a Chicago pow-wow. As is true in the respective Anishinaabe hybridity of these poets, Henry sings a healing song forward whose specificity is not bounded by one "our" language but speaks the power of language, song, and sound for one's own healing and outward for the healing of others. In addition, his poem's consistent first-person voice and the shifts from the past-tense verbs (came, made, was traveling, took away) in the prior sections to the future tense (will sing, will take away) open up the poem to the articulations of survivance, forward in time, across worlds into the spirit world of the speaker's dead father and into the worlds of each reader. As contemporary poets Noodin, Blaeser, and Henry make patently clear with their modern visions, a Vizenorian "survivance" is possible even for Schoolcraft's words as they endure today, for as Vizenor asserts: "Native identities must be an actuation of stories, the commune of survivance and sovereignty" (*Fugitive Poses* 37).

    As Henry's poem articulates, the "circle of light" that emanates from sacred and connective song can also include those beyond this world—that even within a framework of physical absence (whether of one's children, of connections across time to distant grandfathers and grandmothers ["Can we see them"], one's distance from tribal homelands, or from a deceased father), the connective and restorative force of language can effect connection and thereby healing presence. Henry writes, "This song will take away the sadness of my dead father." In her scholarship, Blaeser emphasizes "the relational contexts of language" that permeate the integrity of personal and community well-being and that are part of the warp and woof of Anishinaabe oral tradition (*Gerald Vizenor* 27). As the four poems by Schoolcraft, Noodin, Blaeser, and Henry are brought into scholarly and poetic conversation, their respective personas along with the poets' voices speak out the centrality of home, homeland, and tribe. Explicit geographies of belonging in the Schoolcraft and Blaeser poems are more implicit in Noodin's and Henry's poems. White Earth and his Chippewa tribal community orient Henry's poem implicitly in their physical absence ("traveling among strangers") and spiritual presence ("a singer" making "a song" that in turn makes "a circle of light").

Returning. Remembering. Retelling. These steps inform much of the literature of sacred journey in American Indian traditions. The journeys vary greatly in length and circumstance, but the hearkening toward the sacred nearly always involves ritualized repetition of motion, memory, or voice. "Somehow through the enactment of connection, the immersion in the cyclical reality of experience and being, we outstrip our individual essence, are infused with a knowing power or arrive back on sacred ground" (Blaeser, "Sacred Journey Cycles" 84).

Blaeser's description of Native American sacred journey articulates the survivance journeys of her people as expressed in Anishinaabe literary and oral tradition. The diverse poems addressed herein demonstrate the realities of survival and resistance as they coalesce in the survivance of a tribal literary tradition that speaks its presence forward through the history of conquest, beyond the changes of language ("This song is not from our language") and in the continuance of Anishinaabe journeys throughout time and circumstance.

These poets all draw on Anishinaabe sonority in wielding the tools of repetition, silence and emphatic pauses, and Anishinaabe rhythmics. Future studies will need to explore this further, but all four poems demonstrate an interesting consonance in accented beats at the beginning and ending of lines, whether in the form of trochees ("Endan-"; "Waassa-"; "Ishe"; "Weaving"; "Driving"; "Taking"), amphimacers ("On the way"), or spondees ("This song"; "These sounds") in the former case or iambs, diambi, amphimacers, and spondees at the ends. In this way, the poets give strength to their poems' speakers and exemplify Anishinaabe survivance today and forward into the future. The distinctive rhythms made possible through different indigenous languages often include residual tribal, rhythmic patterns even when presented in the languages of conquest. In addition, there are rhythmic patterns evident in geographic regions manifesting the particular historical realities of place, what Tol Foster refers to as "the *interzones* where different constituencies collide and, as a result, renegotiate their communal cultural frames" (272). It would be interesting to look at the range of English-language poetry of the upper Midwest to see possible Anishinaabe rhythmic influence, as well as the convergent resonances of indigenous, Scandinavian, and French/Métis influence.

Although the scope of this essay is limited to poems by four different Anishinaabe poets, which is decidedly a small-scale study, there are sufficient parallels in these poems to merit specific hypotheses and points for future studies of Anishinaabe literature and oral tradition (e.g., meter and rhythm, repetition and parallelism, silence and intersubjective relationality, familiarization, geographies of belonging, and a semiotics of place). There is no question that the creative legacies of these writers are integrally informed by their tribal and geographic roots; this being said, even these poems demonstrate aspects of their writing that decidedly differentiate each from the others. For example, Schoolcraft's English poetry is fairly traditional for her time almost two centuries ago; it is also representative of both the American English-language lyric and her people's traditional Anishinaabe song and prayer forms. Noodin's poetry is deeply informed by her linguistic studies of the Anishinaabe language and song traditions, with her English versions explicitly guided by their Anishinaabe origins. Blaeser's eco-poetic story rhythms that pervade her poetry and prose are almost always firmly grounded in the images of living experience and known place and environment, whether actual, historical, or imagined. Henry's poetry moves in the realm of the philosophically abstract such that even historically grounded realities become transformed into linguistically rich and complex conceptualizations. Where readers are invited to touch Blaeser's poetic and photographic worlds, they are invited to conceptualize and contemplate Henry's.

Vizenor asserts that "Native American Indians are the stories of presence, the chroniclers in the histories of this continent" (*Fugitive Poses* 1), and Gabriele Schwab states that a text can become "a virtual life-form (in the Wittgensteinian sense of a 'language-game' as a life form), as a complex and dynamic pattern (of signifiers) that forms part of the self-shaping process of a living cultural system" (111). In the work of highly skilled and intentionally crafted creative writing, an aesthetic is reflected in the sounds and rhythm and silences of the literary work. This is patently true of these journey poems by Blaeser, Henry, Noodin, and Schoolcraft, in which distinctively articulated Anishinaabe realities are expressed in the specific ebbs and flows of poetic repetitions, emphatic silences, tribal and regional geographies of affiliation and belonging, and strong affirmations of the human longing for the presence of self, family, tribe, and community (narrowly and broadly defined). Noodin advocates for a depth of literary analysis that can "read Anishinaabe literature through the reality of the Anishinaabe language and storytelling culture" (*Bawaajimo* xx). Specifically in relation to Schoolcraft, Heid E. Erdrich points out that "The fact that Bame-wa-wa-ge-zhik-a-quay recast Ojibwe songs as poems, wrote about her Ojibwe lineage, and took care to give attribution (in the Ojibwe manner of saying who 'gave' the song or story) reveals a sensibility deeply within an Ojibwe literary tradition" (20). There are deep rhythms and resonances that echo the place and sounds of White Earth and broader ancestral homelands across time and across the histories of creation, change, conquest, and survivance, for as Henry explains, "Like a seemingly dislocated band moving beyond borders, driven from home and family, [these] stories and songs continue . . . , to live on, in ever-extending sites of struggle where the spirit of affiliation develops anew, to energize and empower people" ("Eagleheart Narratives" 304). And as we see in these four poems with the larger themes of children, community, ancestors, story, pan-tribal indigeneity, pow-wows, distance, strangers, and a father, there is also an identifiably Anishinaabe language and grammar of connection manifested in the "family resemblances" of Anishinaabe poesis and poetics.

Notes

1. Noodin's presentation in standardized Anishinaabe makes the poem understandable to Anishinaabe readers and listeners. The translation provides accessibility for non-Anishinaabe speakers. Noodin includes two lines that are not in the original poem, adding the final line "Endanakiiyan" at the end of the second and fourth stanzas. Although this provides consistency across the stanzas, it does change the meaningfulness and emphases of the original stanzas, so I keep Schoolcraft's original poem, along with Noodin's Anishinaabe edits and translation.

2. Noodin's reading is available at http://ojibwe.net/songs/womens-traditional/nindinendam-thinking/ and http://www.umich.edu/~ojibwe/audio/songs/Nindinendam.mp3.

3. Master's famous *Spoon River Anthology* includes a variety of poems that fondly reminisce about his early experiences, yet starkly critique his experiences of his later years as an older child and young man.

4. As I note elsewhere, "Just as the accomplished storyteller ensures permeable boundaries between the actual storytelling event and all those other events and times and places and persons potentially relevant to the story, Blaeser opens her own memories and stories up to her listener-readers, inviting us all gradually into her worlds and remembrances" (Brill de Ramírez, "Power and Presence" 98).

5. See http://www.umich.edu/~ojibwe/songs/.

6. See J. Noé Mitchell, "Anishnabe/Songs," http://www.reverbnation.com/anishnabe063 (accessed January 1, 2014).

7. See Blaeser's discussion of silence in the work of Gerald Vizenor (*Gerald Vizenor* 20–22).

8. I am thankful to Noodin for pointing out that "Jane's poem/song has vocables, too" (email correspondence).

References

Blaeser, Kimberly. *Absentee Indians and Other Poems*. East Lansing: Michigan State University Press, 2002.

———. *Gerald Vizenor: Writing in the Oral Tradition*. Norman: University of Oklahoma Press, 1996.

———. "Pagans Rewriting the Bible: Heterodoxy and the Representation of Spirituality in Native American Literature." *A Review of International English Literature* 25.1 (1994): 12–31.

———. "Sacred Journey Cycles: Pilgrimage as Re-Turning and Re-Telling in American Indigenous Literatures." *Religion and Literature*. 35.2/3 (Summer-Autumn, 2003): 83–104.

———. *Trailing You: Poems*. Greenfield Center, NY: The Greenfield Review Press, 1994.

———. "Wild Rice Rights: Gerald Vizenor and an Affiliation of Story." *Centering Anishinaabeg Studies: Understanding the World through Stories*, edited by Jill Doerfler, Niigaanwewidam James Sinclair, and Heidi Kiiwetinepinesiik Stark, 237–57. Lansing: Michigan State University Press, 2013.

Brill de Ramírez, Susan Berry. "The Power and Presence of Native Oral Storytelling Traditions in the Poetry of Marilou Awiakta, Kimberly Blaeser, and Marilyn

Dumont." In *Speak to Me Words: Essays on Contemporary American Indian Poetry*, edited by Dean Rader and Janice Gould, 82–102. Tucson: University of Arizona Press, 2003.

Erdrich, Heid E. " 'Name': Literary Ancestry as Presence." In *Centering Anishinaabeg Studies: Understanding the World through Stories*, edited by Jill Doerfler, Niigaanwewidam James Sinclair, and Heidi Kiiwetinepinesiik Stark, 13–34. Lansing: Michigan State University Press, 2013.

Foster, Tol. "Of One Blood: An Argument for Relations and Regionality in Native American Literary Studies." In *Reasoning Together: The Native Critics Collective*, edited by Craig S.Womack, Daniel Heath Justice, and Christopher B. Teuton, 263–302. Norman: University of Oklahoma Press, 2008.

Henry, Gordon. "The Eagleheart Narratives: Contexts, Process, Representation, and Ceremony in Making Texts." In *Stories through Theories / Theories through Stories: North American Indian Writing, Storytelling and Critique*, edited by Gordon Henry Jr., Nieves Pascual Soler, and Silvia Martínez-Falquina, 291–305. East Lansing: Michigan State University Press, 2009.

———. *The Failure of Certain Charms and Other Disparate Signs of Life*. Cambridge: Salt, 2007.

Mitchell, J. Noé. "Anishnabe/Songs." http://www.reverbnation.com/anishnabe063/. Accessed January 1, 2014.

Noodin (Noori), Margaret. *Bawaajimo: A Dialect of Dreams in Anishinaabe Language and Literature*. East Lansing: Michigan State University Press, 2014.

———. "Megwa Baabaamiiaayaayaang Dibaajomoyaang: Anishinaabe Literature as Memory in Motion." In *Oxford Handbook of Indigenous American Literature*, edited by Daniel Heath Justice and James Cox. New York: Oxford University Press, 2014.

———. "Waanimazinbiigananke / Writing Images in Circles." In "Ezhi-Waanimazinbiigananke Daphne Odjig: The Way Daphne Odjig Writes Circular Images," presented at the 41st Algonquian Conference / Le 41ème Congrès des Algonquinistes. November 1, 2009.

Parker, Robert Dale, ed. *The Sound the Stars Make Rushing through the Sky: The Writings of Jane Johnston Schoolcraft*. Philadelphia: University of Pennsylvania Press, 2007.

Rader, Dean. "The Epic Lyric: Genre and Contemporary American Indian Poetry." In *Speak to Me Words: Essays on Contemporary American Indian Poetry*, edited by Dean Rader and Janice Gould, 123–42. Tucson: University of Arizona Press, 2003.

———. "Word as Weapon: Visual Culture and Contemporary American Indian Poetry." *MELUS* 27, no. 3 (2002): 147–67.

Schwab, Gabriele. "Reader-Response and the Aesthetic Experience of Otherness." *Stanford Literature Review* 3 (1986): 107–36.

Sinclair, Niigonwedom James. "A Sovereignty of Transmotion: Imagination and the 'Real,' Gerald Vizenor, and Native Literary Nationalism." In *Stories through Theories / Theories through Stories: North American Indian Writing, Storytelling and Critique*, edited by Gordon Henry Jr., Nieves Pascual Soler, and Silvia Martínez-Falquina, 123–58. East Lansing: Michigan State University Press, 2009.

Vizenor, Gerald. *Fugitive Poses: Native American Indian Scenes of Absence and Presence*. Lincoln: University of Nebraska Press, 1998.

———. *Landfill Meditations: Crossblood Stories*. Hanover, NH: Wesleyan University Press/University Press of New England, 1994.

Womack, Craig S. *Red on Red: Native American Literary Separatism*. Minneapolis: University of Minnesota Press, 1999.

Chapter 5

Ambiguity and Empathy in the Poetry of Gordon Henry Jr.

STUART RIEKE

Leaving Smoke's
To Gogisgi and Claudia

Black
wings sun glanced

green, crows
circle and half circle
snowfields before scattering
over old barns falling
slowly paintless
against the sky

across the road.

Your car shivers
to start, windshield
trembling, Sky, Blue
barked breath floating
white through
fences behind his

back and the door
opening she waves from.

At the stop sign,

the prism hanging
between door curtains
still turns
sun colors
on the kitchen
floor.

On M-66

something or the wind
moves outside
and turns his head to
windowed dusk's sun
leaving behind barns
with glazed empty
snowfield
beyond the prism
still.

—Gordon Henry Jr., "Leaving Smoke's,"
Failure of Certain Charms

The poetry of Gordon Henry Jr. is deeply and refreshingly connective. It generates extreme empathy for a variety of human experiences, culturally related stances, feelings, and worldviews. Reading his poems allows this grace to connect wisdom, power, and needed compassion to the demonization, "otherness," broken families, wall talk, and cages for innocent children. Poetry is, of course, already an extremely empathetic practice and a way of imaginatively healing harsh views of otherness in human relations. When analyzed, Henry's poetry can offer even more ways to see deep, endemic connections between people that resonate in a resistant, encouraging way. These connections are written about in the subject matter of Henry's work *The Failure of Certain Charms*, and they can be found in the poetic techniques the poet applies.

One technique that Henry uses with inclusive effect is intentional ambiguity. His use of ambiguity, especially interesting in the poem "Leaving Smoke's" (12–13), represents a way of looking at the world that celebrates multiple perspectives. Ambiguity, by definition, takes a singularity, such as a single word or expression, and illustrates how this singularity can be seen or can express multiple experiences and multiple viewpoints with a single expressor. Whereas a narcissistic worldview might only include the will (or capacity) to grasp singularities based on a strict, monopersonal, tunnel-vision perspective, "Leaving Smoke's," and the ambiguity Henry uses to express its meanings, explore possibilities that open when multiple perspectives are valued in a single initiator and when empathy is applied to multiple participants in an experience. It defines experience as interpretable. It suggests that as humans, we can feel multiple things at once, that we aren't locked into a single, best, or "superior" response, and that considering the responses of others to simple life events makes those events richer.

"Leaving Smoke's" is a poem with themes of departure, arrival, nostalgia, transition, love, loneliness, place, season, timelessness, and warm friendship. As friends leave a place of safety and welcome, they begin to imagine the world beyond the reality of home. Yet because of the healthy empathy and love they feel for "Smoke's," they keep in their awareness a precious loved one, even as they leave this loved one behind. In this way, the poem can be looked at as a short piece about "staying" emotionally while "leaving" physically. It can be looked at as a way of expressing a bundle of emotions—those coming, mingling, perplexing, and twisting—taken on when exiting a beloved territory, a beloved stronghold of home. Leaving a place of love is never simple. There are many experiences within the "singular" action of exiting a place. Themes bloom from the poem because of its suggestions that a rich life means more than one "appropriate" response—and beyond "appropriate" to humane. We as readers know that Henry's poetry helps us be humane.

One theme in "Leaving Smoke's" that humanizes the reader is the emphasis on relatedness. This theme is discussed at length later in this essay, but briefly put, relatedness is skillfully central to the poem. Locations—"across the road" (l. 9), and "On M-66" (l. 25)—take prominence in the syntax of the poem because they occupy their own lines with line breaks before and after them. This emphasis on locations relates the reader to the world of the poem by insisting that the reader knows roughly where they are, but not exactly; the poem takes place exactly anywhere. In this way, with an emphasis on a kind of common element to the locations ("across the road" and "On M-66" aren't artificially sacred, aren't particularly poetic, or important, and are only understood to be important to the poem's speaker), the setting of the poem is seen more as a place of relational significance than as a place of specific meaning. The locations within the poem relate the reader to the setting since they could exist anywhere, and since the reader can fill in the exact location. The reader relies on relatedness to understand where the poem is taking place: somewhere vitally important to the poem's speaker. Because the reader doesn't see the setting as remarkably exotic, or specifically mystical—or even more than ambiguously placed—relatedness becomes a direct theme established by the location of the poem. This prominence of relatedness among the themes is humanizing to a reader.

Not only is "Leaving Smoke's" intentionally multifaceted thematically, it also offers multiple interpretations by way of symbols, motifs, and intentionally ambiguous punctuation. An analysis of these techniques helps bolster a deep message of Henry's work: that life usually offers, as in the definition of ambiguity, "two or more diverse attitudes or feelings" (Abrams and Harpham 9), more than one interpretation or understanding. Henry's poetry offers hope that we can choose a humane response to life's challenges, that we aren't locked into seeing things according to an outside authority, that we aren't dependent on an authority to design our life views, and that we can understand that life is not to be controlled but to be experienced to its fullest and in all its rich permutations.

"Something or the wind" (l. 26) stands out as a peculiar line of richness in the poem, and here, intentional ambiguity shows in a way that expresses diverse potential responses, responses that dodge authority and leave interpretive choice entirely to the reader. What is this "something?" Even the speaker cannot make it out. Maybe it is "the wind." Or perhaps an apparition or rougarou? The poem goes on without telling. Of course, a reader's response matters greatly depending on how they interpret the "something or the wind" line. One interpretation might call for a fearful rejection of this reality or imagined misperception. A reader might be disgusted or made sick by the possibility of its otherworldliness and imagine that the speaker is leaving so as to avoid this "something" once and for all. But this reading would limit the scope of the poem's intimated worldview, seeking to reject a possible supernatural element in everyday living. Perhaps a preferable reading is that there is a dream element to the poem, and this "something or the wind" is not entirely real but that our dreams, waking or sleeping, have deep effect and are worthy of examining in our poetry. This reading doesn't nullify the fearful reading of the rougarou but keeps it alive yet sequestered to the realm of the imagination. A third possible reading can be shown to further enrich the meanings of "Leaving Smoke's"—a reading that discounts neither of the two earlier possibilities. The openness of the final lines of "Leaving Smoke's" indicate that "something or the wind" is not the fulcrum of the poem and that the "something" is noted, certainly, but not what the poem is mostly about. "Something or the wind" could be frightening. It could be about the pervasiveness of dreams or the imagination. Or it could be just a passing observation of something that could be in our world—because we humans don't know all and shouldn't presume to—but that life continues and we must continue with feeling, experiencing, thinking about, and moving through life without stopping. In that way, the title of the poem is really the fulcrum, the pivotal phrase of the entire experience. It's a warm experience, despite the poem's imagery—and its peculiar line—from this reading's vantage point. We are always leaving a version of Smoke's, a warm place and a place of safety. We might get stuck on a line like "something or the wind," but the intentional ambiguity of the poem helps us keep going, keep thriving, and keep pressing on—even to perhaps return.

In the book *The Everlasting Sky* by Gerald Vizenor, there is a phrase used to describe unbroken Anishinaabe lifeways: "the sentient meaning of the past in the lives of the people today" (39). This special sentience might be one of the meanings floating among the themes and ambiguities of "Leaving Smoke's," and of *The Failure of Certain Charms*. One possible form of cultural reference is in the title "Smoke's," potentially a reference to a sweat lodge and the cultural practice of sweating, where smoke, steam, and heat are involved. The title also hints at the ongoing sentient meanings of nicknames and names given or granted to people by friends and family. Since Native peoples were historically hampered by Christianized name-giving and were assigned names, nicknaming can be viewed as a resistance practice. "Smoke's" is also ambiguous, if we remove the apostrophe and interpret a possible reference to pipe smoking, tobacco offerings. These all resonate with "sentient" lifeways. Like the prism refracting light symbolically in the poem, Henry uses an ambiguous word—the title, "Smoke's"—and "refracts" it. A prism is a prevalent symbol in the poem.

Henry opens the world of 'the poem with a sequence of grammatical ambiguities and ambiguities created by punctuation and line breaks that foreshadow later developments in the poem. These instances initiate an atmosphere of shifts, of shimmering, smoky meanings. Wordplay is key to the first lines, and here wordplay sets a light tone, even though images such as "crows," "snowfields," "old barns falling," "car shivers," and a "glazed empty snowfield" contrast their lonely wistfulness with the play of syntax. Play and longing mingle in Henry's poem.

Visual imagery of crows flying in repeating motions over snowy fields and a series of broken barns start a reader off almost seeing the crows functioning as smoky, transient characters themselves: "Black / wings sun glanced / green, crows / circle and half circle / snowfields before scattering / over old barns falling / slowly paintless against the sky / / across the road" (ll. 1–9). We see the image of black birds that are more than black; they are doubly colored black and green by to the transformative power of sunlight. In an instant, a glance, they change from black to "sun glanced green." These crows alter in iridescence, changing physical characteristics according to a mere look (glance) of the sun. Of course the looker is also the onlooker, the one who glances—the poem's speaker. But "glanced" can take on a third meaning: the way sun glances off of objects to shine differently, blindingly, or illuminatingly into an observer's perception. Sun is glancing off the wings of the crows. At least three perceptions are suggested by these nine lines. This ambiguity rolls themes that initiate a reader into the shifting, multiple meanings of "Leaving Smoke's" and provides an introductory metaphor for seeing in a nonsingular way: the doubling, iridescent effect of sun on black/green feathers.

Another sequence of visual/verbal ambiguities or choices of readings is created in these first nine lines by the author's omission of commas between "barns" and "falling" and between "sky" and "across." The line breaks between "falling" and "slowly" and between "sky" and "across" also create multiple perspectives. These omitted commas and particular line breaks offer different readings, one where the old barns are doing the falling and one where the crows are falling. Reading the crows as "falling slowly paintless against the sky" gives emphasis to the birds' naturalness and unbroken though shifting iridescence. It melds crow and barn, natural and human-made with "paintless," a possible descriptive term for the crows, if not the barns. The crows are "paintless" and natural, or of the Creator, and yet being paintless, they are without a splotch of human art: colorful, artful, yet distinctive because they have been painted only by the Creator. It seems that a patient reader of "Leaving Smoke's" who may delve into these ambiguities and multiple meanings must do so "patiently." This patience required of the reader contrasts with the imagery of glancing and adds to the poem's swirling atmosphere.

A last ambiguity, "against the sky / / across the road" (ll. 8, 9), are separated by a line break and a stanza break. This ambiguity hinges on "across the road." Here, a reader is invited to ask: are the "barns falling" across the road, the "crows circling" across the road, or, most interestingly, is "the sky" existing and being specifically placed across the road. With this last reading, personification and understatement are developed. Reading "the sky across the road" personifies sky by locating it (or a portion of it) in a limited space; this puts "sky" in a space, a human space, a partially humorous/absurd limit, an element of imaginative placing that the effect of humanizing causes. Vizenor quotes Anishinaabe writer Ted Mahto: "Some white teachers believe that *indians* just can't learn how to read well, but the people have the subskill of reading without knowing how to read through visual memories . . . through visual concepts—like daydreaming—which is an area of education that is almost totally ignored" (39). Daydreaming—a musing, pondering, creative, positive, freeing, and boundless action—is suggested by a creative rendering of a sky's behavior, locale, habitation, or zone. It is as if the speaker in the poem is sent into a daydream by the combination of these crows, barns, skies, all just across the street. "The sky across the street" makes a zone that mainly daydreamers can visit, an unnoticed zone "almost totally ignored," a "subskill of reading without knowing how to read," a creation that anyone inclined to and given to daydreams could see. Henry has omitted a comma and allowed a whole mode of thought—or seeing—to be suggested.

Fixico writes that meanings in "the traditional perspective" are seen as a "totality of one's universe" (3). He further writes that "The point of knowledge or an idea may not be apparent at the moment of its introduction, but, with patience, the message becomes clear. Sometimes this realization takes several minutes, days, or even years" (3). In the context of "Leaving Smoke's," the image of the prism takes on such a function. It intimates or symbolizes the kind of seeing that requires patience and a "message [that] becomes clear" and a realization that contains more than an initial observation can reveal. Therefore, with a prism, while light at "the moment of its introduction" appears to be singular—a simple, monocolored strand—later, "with patience," the light appears more complex and colorful, a rainbow initially hidden. Patience is the moral prism that breaks meanings open. This opportunity for patient seeing, seeing meaning refracted, as light through a prism, can be present in a reading of "Leaving Smoke's." As consideration of the poem continues and patience is exercised, a circular view of the poem is achieved, and meanings open up, rather than close off.

Vizenor writes:

> The tribal people in this nation have never forgotten that at the same time they were forbidden to speak their language and express their religion while living in poverty on colonial reservations, the federal government was subsidizing anthropologists and sociologists to study the people of the reservation and record what was being lost. (26)

This impulse to study the people misses vision and confuses the roles of the people and the non-Indian. "Being an *indian* is being related to the people," said Lee Cook, who was born on the Red Lake Reservation. 'It is the beautiful freedom to go back to the reservation—to the peace that is really mine" (Vizenor 26). As Cook is quoted in Vizenor's book, "being *indian* is being related"; relatedness is a way of looking at human consciousness as an interdependence between observer and observed, individual and community, family member and family, person and their environment or surroundings. "Being indian" is more of a continuing within a relationship. Fixico's and Vizenor's statements—the former about the relatedness of circular, patient thought and the latter about the integrity of being related rather than being studied and thus distanced or otherized—might be expressed in "Leaving Smoke's." The poet has created symbols, ambiguities, and themes that cause a reader to participate in circular or patient thought, thus relating reader and poet, creating empathy with a lifeway rather that informing a reader like sociologists might. Henry wants to show a different lifestyle and allow a reader to experience that lifestyle in a way that involves the reader to an empathetic level of relatedness. Therefore, Fixico and Vizenor, though seen sociologically are talking about difference, seen empathetically are talking about feeling sameness.

In these ways, it is interesting that Henry's poem begins in its title with an image of "Leaving" but ends with an image of remaining, staying, or being present and contented—of being still—and of never having left (in a circular sense). In a way, the poem ends to address where it begins with the speaker realizing the fact/relating to the fact that he or she is "still" and not leaving. Although the speaker has physically removed him- or herself from Smoke's, he or she finds that by way of noticing, contemplating, and musing on poetic levels he or she has placed themselves in Smoke's environment even more completely, though being "still" in Smoke's involves an imaginative reading. Instead of transcending a locale through physical removal—or succumbing to an illusion of physical removal—the speaker has related to Smoke's to the point that leaving becomes "still present"; the poem begins with a relocation but ends with a relatedness.

Kidwell and Velie write on the inexorable importance of place and traditional homeland to identity—therefore, "Leaving Smoke's" removal, "leaving," relocating is a bittersweet coming into awareness of the tension between the inability of removing and the exterior forced leaving that modern, patronizing, paternalistic, "civilizing" power regimes find necessary to extract physical resources from a human homeland. As readers, we are helped to understand the unresolved societal tension that "Leaving Smoke's" reveals. A concept addressed by Joy Harjo and Gloria Bird's collection of indigenous women's writings, *Reinventing the Enemy's Language*, shows "Leaving Smoke's" as a poem that reveals tension through an ironic adoption of "the enemy's language": it is written in the oppressor's tongue. But this oppressor's tongue can be used to reveal oppression as it, like modern life, still reflects elements of indigenousness that allow for the revelation of oppressive, hidden tension. Although place (as in ancestral homelands) has been separated, place still reveals consciousness, a consciousness sharp and righteous enough to see and reveal oppression's ways. Harjo and Bird write in the introduction of *Reinventing the Enemy's Language*:

> *Reinventing the Enemy's Language* was conceived during a lively discussion of native women meeting around a kitchen table. Many revolutions, ideas, songs, and stories have been born around the table of our talk made from grief, joy, sorrow, and happiness. . . . Some of this dialogue has been excerpted from letters, from notes drafted on yellow pads, typed carefully on a typewriter or a computer after reading manuscripts or cooking dinner. No matter, the kitchen table is everpresent in its place at the center of being. It has often been the desk after the dishes are cleared, the children put to bed. (19)

This dialogue and the discussion out of which the collection proceeds occurred during "a lively discussion," rather than a controlled think-tank environment, and came forward after "cooking dinner," rather than after a directed setting. In other words, although homeland and sacred space has been violated and continues to lie fragmented, pieces of a home, traditional, indigenous environment where such integrated practices as getting the "'children put to bed," "cooking dinner" and talking in a creative, revolutionary way occurs. In this perspective, Native peoples integrate action and thought, liveliness and ideas, of chaos and creation (and food), of randomness and form, of inclusivity and strategizing. This is a simple reality—the idea that things can be accomplished around collectivity, spontaneous action and experience—mentioned on the first page of *Reinventing the Enemy's Language*, and contrasts with "mainstream" North American education, in religious settings, in the accepted act of writing and composing, in performance of dance, and music and even in US democracy. We vote alone. We write alone. We pray alone. We study by ourselves. For indigenous people, whose lifeways were disrupted, perhaps cloistered ways have to be sifted through or acted around to maintain traditional modes of knowledge transmission and political or social action. School can stunt learning. This is what I believe is the importance of understanding Harjo and Bird's "table of our talk" as well as Henry's "Leaving Smoke's." Modern institutions, education systems, political arrangements, and religious organizations can obscure sight, vision, visionary action, and the ability to relate to the environment. Global histories can obscure local truth (Kidwell and Velie 42). We may be able to stay still while we leave, as is communicated by the end of "Leaving Smoke's," but there is pain and loss. The traveler down highway or road M-66 is in movement, as they are indeed traveling. But a part or the speaker is "still," unmoved, grounded, able to reason, able to see clearly without obscured sight, not disturbed. This stillness can be found in "the wind," "windowed dusk's sun," "barns." and the "snowfield" even after leaving a beloved place of 'stillness.'

Even "beyond the prism" several things are "still" there: the barns, the snowfields, the crows, the sun, the wind. "Beyond the prism" may be read to mean that beyond the refracting or multiplicative power of experience, time, nature, these circular and seasonal rhythms, objects or items are still there, still coming back, still resistant to change, still beautiful and amazing. Even beyond the prism of the poem, these ideas, spiritual presences, beings are still there. Beyond the card tricks and sleight-of-hand of ambiguity, spirit and simplicity are still there. These readings resonate morally and culturally with themes of resistance, return, survival, reorientation, and resurgence. Every color is distinct, has a sameness of source, is delightful in its own context and striking alongside its partners—and yet in this sameness, represents distinctness. Therefore, realizing this distinctness is to be run through the prism ourselves, to take a trial run at different sensibilities, to practice consciousness and sensitivity, to empathize and feel the working minds and hearts of other people and escape Eurocentrism, prejudice, narcissism and self-centeredness, even if for the brief duration of being tricked by an illusion of language with broad cultural and moral implications.

References

Abrams, Meyer Howard, and Geoffrey Galt Harpham. *A Glossary of Literary Terms*. Boston,: Wadsworth, 2012.
Fixico, Donald L., *The American Indian Mind in a Linear World*. New York: Routledge, 2003.
Harjo, Joy, and Gloria Bird. "Introduction." In *Reinventing the Enemy's Language*, edited by Joy Harjo and Gloria Bird, 19–31. New York: Norton, 1997.
Henry, Gordon, Jr. *The Failure of Certain Charms and Other Disparate Signs of Life*. Cambridge: Salt Publishing, 2007.
Kidwell, Clara Sue, and Alan Velie. *Native American Studies*. Edinburgh: Edinburgh University Press, 2005.
Vizenor, Gerald. *The Everlasting Sky*. Saint Paul,: Minnesota Historical Society Press, 2000.

Chapter 6

Justice *in absentia*

The Re-stor(y)ing of Native Legal Presence through Narratives of Survivance in Gerald Vizenor's "Genocide Tribunals"

SHARON HOLM

Preamble: "Dane White at Sand Creek"

> So much of the Native world is unnameable. Violence, silence, and the unnameable.
>
> —Gerald Vizenor interview (Isernhagen 123)

In his 1981 essay "Sand Creek Survivors," White Earth Anishinaabe writer, critic, and theorist Gerald Vizenor connects two seemingly disparate events: the 1864 massacre of Cheyenne and Arapaho at Sand Creek in eastern Colorado and the suicide of a thirteen-year-old Dakota boy, Dane Michael White, who hung himself in the early 1970s after forty-one days in jail without a juvenile hearing for his persistent truancy from a "white school." Vizenor was a reporter for the *Minneapolis Tribune* during the early 1970s, and the essay charts his struggle with journalistic expectations of "the facts" as demanded by his newspaper editor and what Vizenor, in his veiled persona as part-time journalist Clement Beaulieu, a "mixed-blood college teacher from the White Earth Reservation," sees as the real story of Dane's suicide (Vizenor, "Sand Creek" 34). For Beaulieu/Vizenor, Dane's death is as much about the genocidal massacres of Natives in the nineteenth century and the violent legacy of settler colonialism as contemporary limited socioeconomic opportunities, institutionalized racism, and the dissolution of extended familial relationships—all of which played parts in Dane's shortened life.

This intergenerational legacy of pain and loss is registered as ongoing, unresolved trauma structurally realized in the essay through the fragmented narrative irruptions of witness descriptions of Native corporeal trauma incurred during the genocide. Reports of bodily mutilation and murder at Sand Creek, the 1870 Marias (or Baker) Massacre of members of the Blackfeet Nation at Marias River, and the horrors of the 1890 Wounded Knee massacre starkly juxtapose themselves on the page against biographic sketches of White's difficult home life, juvenile detention, and eventual suicide:

> First Lieutenant James Cannon testifies at the hearing on the Sand Creek Massacre that the tribal bodies he saw after the attack were scalped and butchered by federal troops, "and in many instances their bodies were mutilated in the most horrible manner . . . I heard of one instance of a child a few months old being thrown in the feed box of a wagon, and after being carried some distance, left on the ground to perish. I also heard of numerous instances in which men had cut the private parts of females, and stretched them over the saddle bows, and wore them over their hats, while riding in the ranks."
>
> Dane Michael White buckled his wide belt around his thin neck and hanged himself from a shower rod in the Wilkin County Jail in Breckenridge, Minnesota. (Vizenor, "Sand Creek" 33)

In Cannon's witness testimony, Native people are presented as dehumanized spectacle: abject, anonymous, and literally in pieces, their butchered bodies fetishized as trophies. They provide a physically arresting contrast and a psychic correlative to Dane's body, which hangs whole and unmarked (except for bruises on his neck), seemingly a victim of his own hand "who turned his revolution inward to his own end" (Vizenor, "Sand Creek" 46). This narrative juxtaposition enables a temporal continuum where past and present trauma coexist and present intergenerationally through the body: these events may be "three generations apart in calendar time, but in dreams and visual tribal memories, these grievous events . . . are not separated in linear time" (Vizenor, "Sand Creek" 34). Playing on a continuous loop of memory and images—"the past can be found on tribal faces in the present"—Dane, like the murdered at Sand Creek, becomes "a victim of colonial domination, manipulation and cultural invalidation" (Vizenor, "Sand Creek" 34, 45). Beaulieu/Vizenor further extends the circumstances of Dane's suicide to resonate with the extralegal atrocities at Sand Creek when he notes that Dane was "trapped and *executed* in a white institution" only to finally suffer being "*mutilate[d]*" by the "funeral words" of the white apologists who presided over his burial service (Vizenor, "Sand Creek" 36, emphasis added).

The essay emphasizes added dis/connection between physical and psychic derealization through the violent, exclusionary discourse of dominant judicial and religious institutions: "in words he was abandoned at all the cruel crossroads in the white world" (Vizenor, "Sand Creek" 45). The culpability of law is attributed to racially motivated neglect, which occludes and abjects Native presence before the law and in the institutional parameters of its courts: "The white man smacks his law and order on the land . . . and then he goes hunting in the mountains while the tribes die in his institutions" (Vizenor, "Sand Creek" 43). The careless postponement of Dane's juvenile court hearings by the judge who was off hunting game in the mountains is combined with a misjudged assessment of Dane's "appearance of contentment" in jail. A mask of "indianness" that "he had been taught, as an Indian, to act in front of white persons in authority" has made him invisible to the system, contributing to his extreme vulnerability and decision to commit suicide (Vizenor, "Sand Creek" 43). This conveniently inert construction of indigeneity by those in charge—characterized by Dane's passive behavior as a "good Indian"— proves to be equally annihilating as the discourse of savagery defending Col. Chivington's action for his genocidal "appli[cation] of the scalpel to the ulcer" of the Indian problem at Sand Creek (Vizenor, "Sand Creek" 45–46). Both contribute to the effacement of Native presence involving denial of social identity, psychic health, legal subjectivity, and in the ultimate negation—death.

"Sand Creek Survivors" explores themes common throughout Vizenor's work in which the discourses of government institutions, social science, history, and law are exposed as "monotheistic" crippling "terminal creeds"—myopic beliefs producing one-dimensional, static simulations of what Vizenor calls the "*indian*"—a psychic and semiotic absence of Native presence—which, in turn, enables an internalized mind-set of "victimry" for Native peoples.[1] Although the social sciences—with anthropology often singled out—are the most damaging of Vizenor's terminal creeds, his work frequently considers the ramifications of occluded or absent Native presence before the law with the courtroom as the agonistic arena where a "monotheistic" interpretation of events and experience—a Vizenorean concept akin to Lyotard's idea of metanarrative—is most plainly in evidence. However, for Vizenor the court is also a space of possibilities where a "competition of facts . . . a verbal contest for a documented narrative" occurs; an arena where "multiple contradictions and procedures of evidence" offer opportunities for narrative and interpretative intervention (quoted in Isernhagen 124). Vizenor's response to the law and issues of justice—from his early journalistic treatment of "Thomas White Hawk" to the "trickster hermeneutics" of his fictional 1991 novel, *The Heirs of Columbus*, to his more recent role as principle drafter of the Constitution of the White Earth Nation (ratified in 2013)—has been to use imaginative narrative approaches drawn equally from Native cultural, legal, and political resources and a poststructural attention to language.[2] Such work offers counterstrategies and alternative interpretive vision(s) to the asymmetrical hierarchies of power enshrined in neoliberal settler-state legal regimes and is what David Carlson characterizes as Vizenor's "attempt to reimagine postindian literary practices in the realm of law" ("Trickster" 25). This is an ongoing focus in Vizenor's work and one that is intimately involved in the foregrounding of narratives of Native "survivance"—his often-cited, key theoretical/aesthetic concept developed from a Native cultural and political praxis of continuance, resistance, and survival—and the wider promotion of Native and specifically Anishinaabeg sovereignty in the legal arena.[3] Vizenor understands the necessity of working through such institutional entrenchment to challenge interpretive legal monotheism and "push back . . . colonial simulations to create a space for the recreation of the real" (Carlson, "Trickster" 24). However, in "Sand Creek Survivors," Dane never gets this chance—he never even makes it as far as the court. His personal circumstances and the weight of history—the "primal screams" of the spectral dead—turn his "revolutions of the heart" to defeat and victimry (Vizenor, "Sand Creek" 37, 36). The "white law" remains closed, and the indelible image of his hanging body is mute testimony to Dane's powerlessness and legal abjection.

Judith Butler speaks of the political necessity of making legible subjects that have, in the ground zero of state-sanctioned violence and through extralegal means, been "erased" through a process she calls "the derealization of the 'Other' " (33). Those who are "unreal" are not "subjects in any legal or normative sense"—that is, protected by international law or entitled to regular trials, lawyers, and due process—and their deaths remain "unthinkable and ungrievable" (33, xvi, xiv). For Butler, the recuperation of derealized Others—the re-presentation of lives absented through such extirpative violence and omitted from public discourse—is a deeply political act that not only speaks to who is "acceptably human" but, to extrapolate her ideas, fundamentally challenges and disrupts what and who constitute the normative embodiment of legal subjectivity. Butler sees the issue as "not a matter of a simple entry of the excluded into an established ontology, but an insurrection at the level of ontology, a critical opening up of the questions: What is real? Whose lives are real? How might reality be remade?" (33). Through its narrative form, "Sand Creek Survivors" strongly registers the inability of presenting a violent and traumatic past as legible or, to use Vizenor's imagery, "nameable" in official public space. This is also evident in the reflexive narrative of the essay's conception as Beaulieu/Vizenor struggles as a journalist to expose what he sees as the truth—*the real*—through competing discourses of Dane's experiences of isolation, the archives of graphic witnessing and military triumphalism, and his editor's demand for just "the facts" of Dane's death. However, Beaulieu/Vizenor does recuperate Dane's life through an act of Native remembrance that somewhat mitigates the damage of alienation from Native cultural contexts—a nascent form, I suggest, of Vizenor's concept of survivance, which he fleshes out in his later work. Through the affiliative power of the essay's narrative, Dane *is* made "grievable" in a Native context; he is "not now separated from our memories and the memories of the tribal 'caretakers of the land' " ("Sand Creek" 46). Kimberly Blaeser notes that we as readers of Dane's fate "share[d] responsibility for the transformative power of story by identifying its communal origins," realizing the potential of the "liberation of the narrative" through our active participation in Native memorialization through story: Dane "must not be forgotten . . . [h]e must soar in memories with millions of tribal people from the past" (Blaeser 82; Vizenor, "Sand Creek" 39). If Beaulieu/Vizenor's journalistic strategy is to recuperate Dane's death through story, the question remains as to why the essay exhibits a reluctance or resistance to transformatively recuperate the historically ventriloquized and unheard stories of the murdered at Sand Creek, the Marias massacre, and Wounded Knee in a similar way. "Sand Creek Survivors" arguably leaves its reader-participants as well as "the survivors"—the designated "pallbearers and ghost dancers" of Dane's story—as conflicted and unsettled witnesses neutered by the seeming lack of legal or political redress to its horrors (39). Perhaps it also reveals the difficulty of Vizenor's response (and responsibility) as a Native writer to encompass such a deeply traumatic history in a narrative form reflective of the reality of Native past and present experiences.

Yet the narrative offers possibilities in its irresolution: the faces of the Sand Creek dead and the faces of its survivors are turned toward all who share responsibility for this history and its legacy—we "all carry the wounds," as Vizenor says, "of collective trauma in our modern time" (*Genocide Tribunals*). They demand an ethical response encompassing legal and moral accountability. Anishinaabe legal scholar John Borrows, quoting the work of Judith Herman, observes: "to hold traumatic reality in consciousness requires a social context that affirms and protects the victim and that joins the victim in a common alliance. When a victim is already devalued (a woman, a child), she may find that the most traumatic events in her life take place outside the realm of a socially validated reality. Her experience becomes unspeakable" (172). Borrows offers an avenue for facilitating an affirming social context and a socially validated reality, which is through "the recognition and affirmation of Indigenous legal traditions" (173). I suggest that years later, Vizenor formulates an ethical and imaginative response to the survivors and the murdered of Sand Creek in his essay "Genocide Tribunals," one to which "Sand Creek Survivors" lends itself as a suggestive preamble.[4] Recognizing the importance for a public forum that attends to the moral and legal accountability of the genocide of Native nations and peoples by the US government in tandem with Native cultural, legal, and political contexts of recovery, "Genocide Tribunals," I argue, challenges existing legal paradigms and prejudice—those that contributed to Dane's invisibility before the law—to offer a critical and theoretical legal paradigm for contextualizing Native experiences of violent genocidal trauma and its intergenerational repercussions. Vizenor links this move to his wider remit of Native "visionary sovereignty" rooted in Anishinaabeg "consciousness and intellectualism," which informs a specific indigenous-led visibility before the law to insist on the "sovereign right of indigenous people to determine how, or how much they are seen by others" (Sinclair 129; Carlson, "Trickster" 24–25).[5]

"Genocide Tribunals" and (Im)Possible Justice

Vizenor's essay "Genocide Tribunals," published in *Native Liberty: Natural Reason and Cultural Survivance* (2009), is a work of political and legal "re-vision" in the continuing vein of a strong Native intellectual tradition of political essay writing. "Re-vision" is a term used by Janice Acoose to describe how the work of Vizenor and other Anishinaabe writers "signal[s] a political strategy for reconstituting Being Anishinaabe in written English" (39).[6] I use it to suggest that "Genocide Tribunals" is underwritten by Vizenor's continuing engagement with both traditional Anishinaabe values and cultural practices and what he names the *oshki anishinaabe*: the complex, diverse, divergent "one tribe" that is the cultural, social, and political experience of contemporary Anishinaabeg (Doerfler 193). Similar to the other essays in *Native Liberty* that utilize his key literary and political aesthetic of survivance as transformative praxis, "Genocide Tribunals" calls for the establishment of formal genocide tribunals in the United States to legally redress genocidal practices against Native peoples and their nations since colonial contact. Working as a public forum for retroactive justice and historical accountability, such tribunals would be initially realized as a "moot court" program at various US universities to "provide venues of judicial reason and equity that reveal continental ethnic cleansing, mass murder, torture, and religious persecution, past and present" ("Genocide" 139).[7] Their proposed judicial procedures "would justly expose, in the context of legal competition for evidence, the inciters, falsifiers, and deniers of genocide and state crimes against Native American Indians" ("Genocide" 139).

As contentious as the use of "genocide" continues to be in certain circles, for Vizenor, the term is justified to describe the murder, massacre, and forced removal of Native peoples during invasion and containment under a settler colonial state and it is requisite to pursue issues of moral and legal culpability that remain tellingly elusive from dominant contemporary and mythic narratives of American nation-building. Using the 2002 Rome Statute of the International Criminal Court (ICC) as a model for their structure and legal authority, the proposed tribunals, like the ICC, would allow hearsay and prosecutions *in absentia*, and—in line with Article 29 of the ICC—they would be able to waive the statute of limitations on war crimes and genocide and hear cases retrospectively.[8] This 'loosening of the legal seams' (in contrast to common law systems) would facilitate a unique evidential process enabling deceased victims, witnesses, and perpetrators of historical genocides to be summoned *in absentia* to have their stories and experiences presented before the court by proxy ("Genocide" 153). These narratives would be allowed as admissible evidence and would be composed of a bricolage of various official and unofficial written documents and oral sources, such as "archives, witness testimony, diverse narratives, remembrance, hearsay and indirect evidence, and by those imaginative storiers who have the right of consciousness and survivance" ("Genocide" 152–53). The allowance of hearsay and indirect evidence would enable a process of imaginative recall, invoking Native temporal and visual strategies of indirect witnessing and historical recollection—what Vizenor has referred to in earlier works as "new word cinemas from the oral tradition"—which he links specifically to Anishinaabe cultural, political, and linguistic praxis (*Summer* 14–15). This is a presence generated through a form of oral historical visualization or verbal (en)visioning by living Native peoples acting as legal conduits for the dead. A form, I suggest, of conjuring "testimonio," which George Yudice claims is an act "not of speak[ing] *for* or *represent[ing]* of a community but rather performs an act of identity-formation which is simultaneously personal and collective" (15). In the tribunals, Vizenor's introduction of imaginative recall and proxy testimony—what Carlson calls "imagic moments"—become a constitutive act of indigenous legal presence and, in its act of identity-formation, the concomitant instantiation of rights associated with Native (tribal/nation) sovereignty that "transform (albeit briefly and provisionally) the colonial order" (*Imagining Sovereignty* 173).

Alongside his proposal for a more procedurally and evidentially flexible criminal court model, Vizenor also employs an expanded temporal definition of genocide current in indigenous and settler colonial studies so that both court and law can accommodate the full experience of Native trauma incurred during colonial invasion and settlement:

> Genocides are events, even if they occur at very low speed and can only be perceived *ex post facto* in chronological acceleration. [T]his practice [is called] below the threshold of immediate visibility settler imperialism. This variety of imperialism will be defined as the rhizomatic expansion of settler colonies and

settler states, directed against "exterior" indigenous populations, achieved in the context of a democratic and egalitarian society of white, predominantly protestant Anglo-Saxon settlers, organized in family farm households. (Finzsch 219)

This would enable a forensic *ex post facto* legal examination of high-profile atrocities, such as the Mystic River massacre of the Pequot in 1637, the 1864 Sand Creek massacre, and the 1890 massacre at Wounded Knee, and "below the threshold" events, such as the desperate starvation precipitating the Dakota Conflict of 1862. It would include other criminal acts such as the removal and abuse of Native children perpetrated by Indian boarding schools, the destruction and theft of indigenous land, and the "forcible detention and placing in indentured labor" of Natives who fled the reservations, in the continuous systemic operation of settler colonialism and as genocidal in their effect and scope ("Genocide" 149). Finzsch's definition emphasizes the inherent hidden systems and cumulative processes of genocide over time rather than the singular intention of specific historic events that serve the deniers of genocide who regard such "conflicts" as the inevitable, if regrettable, consequences of European and American conquest and war now consigned to history (217). This is an important semantic and legal distinction. Because a major focus of the tribunals would be crimes against Native nations in Indian Territory and on the western plains during nineteenth-century expansion, this would also entail investigation into the "disturbing legal limbo" of extralegal exception, which made them particularly vulnerable in terms of the military, who were often charged with their protection but acted otherwise (Rifkin 89). For Vizenor, setting up tribunals as a moot court is not just a hypothetical juridical exercise but a pragmatic avenue for promoting serious dialogue challenging the continuing willed "eva[sion] of any national sense of guilt" about systemically imposed genocidal trauma and the tacit legal exemption from extralegal violence seen as the price of US settler colonialism (William Greider, quoted in Friedberg 357).

Envisaging the tribunals to be like the South African Truth and Reconciliation Commission but "much tougher," the use of the ICC model indicates Vizenor's support for a new way forward through transnational justice, where the application "of universal jurisdiction to crimes committed in other parts of the world . . . is an important new way to break the cycle of impunity for serious and massive human rights crimes" (*Genocide Tribunals*; Méndez 25).[9] This invocation of the ICC is deliberately provocative.

Vizenor is fully aware that the reason given for the initial US nonratification of the Rome Statute in 2002, and its continuing nonengagement with the ICC was the fear that it could result in the United States being "accused of war crimes for legitimate but controversial uses of force to protect world peace" (John Bolton, quoted in "Genocide," 142).[10] "The perpetrators of such serious crimes," Vizenor contends, "have seldom been punished, and the insidious deniers of genocide collude in the protection of the immunity of the perpetrators" ("Genocide" 140). The insistence on the rigors of the ICC as a legal model would refuse the flawed agenda of certain truth commissions that have granted amnesty for crimes against humanity to facilitate a narrative of reconciliation weighted to serve idea(l)s of "national redemption and transcendence" or those who have maintained their settler colonial status quo "by framing past wrongs in terms of historically delimited, specific injuries rather than acknowledging the systemic and on-going practices of colonialism" (Clarke 81; Wakeham 3).[11] Eradicating any questions of legal immunity for genocide, the tougher tribunals would seriously intervene in a US exceptionalism underpinned by the terminal creeds of colonialism—the ideologies of conquest and Manifest Destiny and the emergent racializing of "the Indian." This becomes a vital issue when settler-state sovereignty is predicated on a legal and economic system facilitating genocide as a route for the primitive accumulation of capital as Vizenor indicates: "Many of the very perpetrators of genocide appropriated the ancestral land and property of murdered, removed and exiled Native American Indians" ("Genocide" 157).

Bound by Law? Writing Rights

Given the prejudice that still viably underwrites what Eric Cheyfitz has described as "the imperial edifice of federal Indian law" (49), it is no surprise that Vizenor proposes an international juridical model for his tribunals (although, as he admits, it isn't a perfect solution). The instantiation and legitimation of US settler-state law has relied on various productions of Native legal subjectivities as less than human and Native political sovereignty as "diminished" under the precedents of key Supreme Court decisions. Historically, indigenous difference or "indigeneity" has been produced in response to various political, social, and economic forces as noble, primordial, demonic, and unpropertied. Native legal presence/absence has been produced within and by occidental law and in the wider social and institutional matrix through what Jodi Byrd calls a "paradigm of Indianness," emerging "not just in the scientific racisms and territorial mappings inaugurated through Enlightenment voyages for knowledge, but in the very constitutionality that produced the nation" (xxi). Held in tension in the various incarnations of Indian legal and political subjectivity "the indian," initially stereotyped as savage and later conveniently dying out in nineteenth-century discourse, came to delineate "the lines of the founding fracture and its putative resolution" (Fitzpatrick, *Modernism* 166) through which the new republic legitimated its nationhood and sovereignty claims. What are now identified as racial stereotypes—Natives as "fierce savages," "heathens," and "infidels" or Natives as child-like, incapable of managing their natural rights and so requiring "pupilage"—became then, as *obiter dictum*, translated and encoded in law in the nineteenth-century Supreme Court decisions by Chief Justice John Marshall known as the Marshall trilogy (*Johnson v. M'Intosh* 1823, *Cherokee Nation v. Georgia* 1831, and *Worcester v. Georgia* 1832).

As rationalizations for the diminishment of the inherent status of Native sovereignty from foreign polities to "dependent domestic nations," such "indianness" foundational to federal Indian law also "unmistakeably shaped national patterns of violence by establishing whom one could kill under propitious circumstances" (Drinnon 463). This relationship between Native sovereignty, law, and the instantiation of settler-state sovereignty in the United States follows too complex a political and legal trajectory to be rehearsed fully here, but it is one that is often charted by scholars of US and Native American history as a complex ideology of exclusion and inclusion based on the need to square the circle between various pressing political and legal concerns. Caught between the contested status of Native nations as foreign polities and as human beings with rights in natural law and the rights and interests of the individual states, it became necessary to sacrifice the higher principles of the American new republic "that supposedly inhered in the Revolutionary era's radical, natural-law-inspired vision of America as a land free of the oppression and feudal burdens of a Norman yoke" (Williams, *American Indian* 231). Accommodating the tensions inherent in this foundational compromise resulted in the ghettoization of Native political and legal standing and rights as "an aberration divorced from the principles at play in the rest of U.S. law" (Rifkin 97) and justified suspending the rule of law at key moments in the eighteenth and nineteenth centuries to consolidate ideas of an emerging US nationalism and open the way for westward expansion. As Mathew Fletcher and Peter

Vicaire remind us, during the nineteenth-century so-called Indian wars, the newly formed settler state exhibited "the worst violation of the rule of law . . . indefinite detention without charge, torture, and indiscriminate killing" (19).[12]

Not only did these legal and extralegal inclusive/exclusive moves open "the *space* for a legal geography predicated on the territorial coherence of the nation," as Mark Rikfin points out, "the state of exception produced through Indian policy create[d] a monopoly on the legitimate exercise of legitimacy" (97). That is, through this sleight of hand, law in tandem with dominant sovereign power produces its own legitimacy through which the settler-state constructs a seemingly "incontestable right to define what will count as a viable legal or political form(ul)ation"—which in turn has been described as effecting a "now you see it, now you don't" approach to Native sovereignty (Rifkin 91; D'Errico 10). Such a process of legal exception described as the "restless performance" of "state sovereignty tactically produced through the very mechanism of its self-justification" reveals itself as an anxious response from law when faced with its inability to make what it comprehends as indigenous political alterity intelligible to its own system (Rifkin 106; Butler 82).[13] Rifkin sees this as a "fundamentally circular and self-validating" co-dependent relationship between law and sovereign power, legitimated through "nothing more than the axiomatic negation of Native peoples' authority to determine or adjudicate for themselves the normative principles by which they will be governed" (91). The inevitable consequences of this state of exception for Native peoples were extreme: the suspension of law facilitated genocidal practices whose denial or negation effected (and continues to effect) the derealization of Native subjectivity before the law.

Given this legal fiction of legitimacy, historically settler-state common law has *appeared* to be adept at denying or occluding Native presence and *appeared* adept at regulating Native (collective, tribal, nation) experience and presence into normative recognizable legal entities and Natives themselves into individual (if delimited) legal subjects. I emphasize *appeared* to indicate that not only did Native polities, nations, and kinship systems have their own systems of Law (which I capitalize to distinguish from occidental law) that continued to operate in their societies, but their legal presence in occidental law was continuously exerting pressure on "official" settler-state legitimacy through various strategies—treaty negotiations, physical defense of sovereign homelands, and indigenous resistance via legal challenges in the courts to name the obvious (Rifkin 89; Fitzpatrick,

"Surpassing" 190–91).[14] However, continuing legal/political dominance in relations with Native peoples and their sovereign nations was accomplished either through the disciplinary rule of law (or its suspension), in tandem with a Foucauldian biopolitical power discursively producing the "civilized" or "assimilated" Indian in an effort to produce the Native subject in law through "inclusion and exclusion or extermination from the body politic" (Cheah, Fraser, and Grbich xvii).[15] In terms of Anishinaabeg, Amelia Katanski notes how such governmentality eventually produced the same aims as genocidal land clearance:

> Assimilationist discourse and the language of "scientific racialism" came together in the legal narrative of allotment laws to constitute a world in which Anishinaabeg identity was defined and determined by agents of the U.S. government, and "progress" toward "assimilation" was used as the justification for transferring land title from the tribe to the Anishinaabeg individual, and from there, far too often, to the logging companies or other U.S. economic interests. (66)

Pervasive and "inextricably linked" to everyday Native lives, this production of Native subjectivities before the law became "more than strictly legal" in that it "exceed[ed] the boundaries of legal institutions to become key discursive elements in social and political life in settler states" (Hamilton 2).

The terminal creeds associated with occidental law—what Robert A. Williams identifies as the "rights-destroying, jurispathic power" of endemic racism codified in the Doctrine of Discovery—are still resonant in the wider reaches of US federal Indian law and in any judicial decision that relies in particular on the nineteenth-century precedents of the Marshall trilogy underwriting federal Indian law today (*Like a Loaded Weapon* 22).[16] Such dualisms—savage/civilized, dependent/independent, progressive/backward, and inside/outside—form the "imperial binary" that Kevin Bruyneel observes has "vexed the politics of indigenous people in North America for centuries, because they legitimate the colonial rule of the liberal democratic state by imposing Western ways of knowing as the standards by which indigenous people's claims are understood and judged" (8). Although the historical severity of such legal and political occluding has been mitigated by advances on the ground by Native legal scholars, lawyers, and advocates, within the US judicial system a problematic politics of recognition involving "indigeneity" persists through concrete issues of blood quantum, land disenfranchisement, and "authentication" of spiritual/religious practices in repatriation disputes. Indigeneity in this incarnation—as a legal descriptor and political entity before the law—by necessity becomes "ultimately a cultural and political performance" (Birrell 18).

This isn't just confined to the US juridical system. As a result, there still exists a "representational crisis faced by Indigenous peoples worldwide whose legal and political campaigns hinge upon their ability to represent themselves at multiple levels and achieve a range of rhetorical effects" (Johnson 484).[17] This is particularly so when indigenous peoples are called on to legally represent themselves through narratives demonstrating their traditional or religious claims to remains and artifacts, fishing and hunting rights, land title, and so on. Such representations are adjudicated as "authentic" or "preexistent" under the aegis of indigenous rights formed under a liberal democracy, which admits the recognition of indigenous "difference" in law and then imposes qualifying degrees and static parameters for the legal viability and (visibility) of those rights (Johnson 484–85). The reality of occidental law, whether in the US domestic or international arena, is that it still produces a demand for indigeneity that is contextualized through nonindigenous legal paradigms of juridical procedure, so the ability to perform or narrate indigeneity before the law—to "master the assets and liabilities of alterity" in a form intelligible or visible to the court—is paramount (Johnson 485). The current "mastery" is motivated by competing interested parties—indigenous and nonindigenous alike—using differing historical methodologies and narrative technologies, which the hypothetical imaginary of Vizenor's tribunals will open up for debate, even if they can't entirely "clear the ground," so to speak.

For Vizenor, establishing the tribunals with international juridical space outside the US judicial system would signal the "commitment to adjudicate the serious rights of Native American Indians" ("Genocide" 138). These are rights that are "inalienable," preexisting, illimitable, and aligned with the 1948 Universal Declaration of Human Rights, which, Vizenor claims quoting from the declaration, are the "'foundation of freedom, justice and peace in the world'" ("Genocide" 155). This genesis of human rights, of course, is problematic for indigenous peoples because they are uncomfortably aligned with Enlightenment ideas of universality and monadic subjectivity antithetical to indigenous concepts of collective polity and identity. However, they seem at the time to have offered Vizenor a more tenable affirmation of Native legal subjectivity and rights under a constitutional democracy, taking into account that at the time of the essay's 2009 publication the United States had refused to adopt the (not unproblematic) UN Declaration of the Rights of Indigenous Peoples (2008).[18] Although Vizenor maintains a healthy cynicism and productive anger toward the universal rights "guaranteed" by the US Constitution, pointing out that for Native peoples "the reality of human rights provision is more literary irony than protection," he also cites them as a "profound source of endurance in native stories" and the "everlasting narratives of survivance," confirming that the affirmation of human rights is deeply connected to the act of survivance ("Genocide" 156). This reflects the guarded optimism in his prolific literary and critical engagement with the law and legal issues that stage the envisioning of (indigenous) rights in occidental law not as reactionary to what it perceives as the anxiety-inducing performance of indigenous alterity but as opening to possibilities beyond extant law. Writing about the responsiveness of law (and the "beyond" to which literature can push this responsiveness), Kathleen Birrell shares this view: "rights afforded the human being who is recognised as 'Indigenous,' while violently determinative in the moment of her recognition, are otherwise infinitely responsive and, therefore, may be radically 'intercultural'" (19). For Vizenor, this possibility of intercultural responsivity is a pivotal feature of his engagement with legal discourse. Demanding rights and allying them with Native (specifically Anishinaabe) concepts of Law and rights is arguably his way of chipping away at the existing system of law to widen the aperture for re-vision and visibility, enabling a more encompassing view of indigenous rights.

Narrative Rights: You *Can* Say What a Dead Man Says

> Charles Aubid declared by stories his *anishinaabe* human rights and sovereignty.
>
> —Vizenor, "Genocide Tribunals" (131)

In Vizenor's texts, legal prejudice is perceived as the favoring of constructions of indigeneity or "indianness" over Native "rights of perception" and emerge in his courtroom settings as competition over legal procedure and rules of evidence—that is, which and whose narratives are or are not allowed as evidence or, indeed, visible in the realm of an occidental legal real. For Vizenor, the judicial rules of evidence themselves are constructed by prejudice (and are therefore, he argues, *not* absolute): "The rules of evidence are selective by culture and tradition, and sanction federal cozenage over native presence and survivance" ("Genocide" 134). In his gesture to alleviate what is often seen in Native literature as an ontological impasse of incommensurate realities, Vizenor's tribunals remove the epistemic cultural and legal gatekeepers over "authentic" or "factual," so that a Native social and material reality can be constructed through the recall/revoicing of the dead—the narratives of genocidal victims and events—within the legal system he bases on the ICC. This move would have potentially far-reaching, destabilizing effects confirming Butler's assertion that producing grievable bodies demands an ontological challenge of the dominant real. It is true that "Genocide Tribunals," as a form of indigenous writing as resistance, through its hypothetically modified legal format presents a prime opportunity for a radical anticolonial critique. Opening up through its forensic legal examination the restless performance of settler-state sovereignty, the tribunals would expose its historical extralegal self-legitimacy, revealing "a fault-line in occidental political formation in the fissure between an ultimacy of ontological assertion either as sovereign or as law" (Fitzpatrick, "Surpassing Sovereignty" 16). However, the tribunals have another pressing aim—one that considers as important the promotion of indigenous-led processes of justice and healing in relation to the historical and intergenerational psychic trauma of genocide.

When asked whether he thought justice would emerge from the tribunals, Vizenor replied, "Justice, no, but a narrative will" (*Genocide Tribunals*). As "Genocide Tribunals" suggests, the act of Native narrative is not just a matter of accepting its ontological reality in law but of an active promotion of inherent Native/Anishinaabeg human rights and sovereignty that surpass the politics of legal recognition in occidental law. The essay begins with the true story of eighty-six-year-old Charles Aubid and his role as a witness in a trial that Vizenor covered for the *Minneapolis Tribune* in the late 1960s. Aubid's story, which Vizenor has recounted many times in various forms in his work, serves as a paradigm through which Vizenor advances his indigenous legal theorizing using a specific Anishinaabe framework of perception and presence.[19] Aubid testified in a court presided over by Judge Lord that a verbal agreement was made many years ago between a representative of the US government and another Anishinaabe man, Old John Squirrel, that Anishinaabeg would always retain the rights over their *manoomin* harvest. In another version of Aubid's story in *Fugitive Poses*, Vizenor elaborates that these rights were in jeopardy because federal agents had assumed the authority to regulate the harvest—"a bureaucratic action that decried a native sense of transmotion, survivance, and sovereignty" and one that blatantly denied the rights of harvest "inherent in most treaties" Anishinaabeg had made with the federal government concerning ceded territory (167, 168). On the witness stand, in Anishinaabemowin, "the language of his visual memories," Aubid related the agreement that occurred in the past between Squirrel and the government agents, concerning which any documentary evidence had been lost ("Genocide" 133). For Aubid, this loss of paper did not signal any loss of rights as "the *anishinaabe* always understood their rights in stories" ("Genocide" 132). Aubid's story in court in which he re-called Squirrel is an act of legal re-presentation as valid as any signed treaty document: "John Squirrel was there in memories, a storied presence of native survivance . . . [and] the court could have heard the testimony as a visual trace of a parol agreement, a function of discourse" ("Genocide" 132). Judge Lord pointed out that this was hearsay and inadmissible in court: "John Squirrel is dead . . . and you can't say what a dead man says." Aubid then turned and pointed to the legal books on the bench and observed that those books contained the stories of dead white men. "Why," he shouted, "should I believe what a white man says when you don't believe John Squirrel" ("Genocide" 133). This momentary yet fundamental epistemological impasse between the spoken and written word, between Anishinaabemowin and English was overcome through Aubid's persuasion—the judge conceded that he had a point and allowed for an equal competition of evidence eventually enabling a decision in favor of the Anishinaabeg. Aubid won this verbal contest for a Native-legitimated oral narrative to be admissible in court—not as hearsay but with the same legal weight as a written document.

Aubid is Vizenor's prototype for the proposed "imaginative storiers" of the tribunals who will orally summon the presence of the dead through stories—one who animates a "fourth presence" of Squirrel's absence and his legal subjectivity. This is Native jurisprudence that Vizenor grounds in a creative interpretation of linguistic praxis: the use of the obviative fourth person is a grammatical feature of the Algonquin family of languages, of which Anishinaabemowin is one, and its use here highlights how meaning and law can be altered in translation. Anishinaabemowin linguist Margaret Noodin explains, "What English accomplishes through the use of syntax, Anishinaabemowin accomplishes through obviation and more fine-tuned definition of pronouns including inclusive and exclusive plural second person and an additional third person, often referred to as the 'fourth person.'"[20] Vizenor inventively teases out the linguistic possibilities of Anishinaabemowin to "flesh out" what is already extant in the language. John Squirrel is called forth in a specifically Anishinaabe context of witness—visual memories and interpersonal relationships are clarified through language and social contexts—and this narrative truth has legal standing. In terms of the tribunals, the cumulative effects of these visual memories and oral reanimations as indirect witness statements would produce what Carlson describes as an indigenous-sustaining "*network of images achieving substantive ontological change*," facilitating "mutual recognition" in the existing judicial system benefitting both Anishinaabeg and nonindigenous alike (*Imagining Sovereignty* 174; emphasis in original).

Living Law, Speaking Justice

Aubid's claim that Anishinaabeg understand their rights in stories hearkens back to indigenous forms of Law emerging through the more traditional sources and processes noted by Borrows where "principles of acknowledgement, accomplishment, accountability, and approbation are embedded in the Annishinaabek creation epic" (79) as well as in other oral stories and other narrative materials and forms. Indigenous law as oral transmission remains an organic process—a "living law" that connects its legal instantiation to the affirmation of collective identity: "the spoken word ensures the law's vitality because it sustains connections to their communities' underlying cultural foundations. It also ensured that laws remain connected to a living community" (Borrows 56). Contemporary Native writing that participates in a similar process performs what Katanski sees as a form of Native "jurisgenesis"—"writing the living law"—where precepts of indigenous Law (both sacred and customary) are reexpressed and refiltered through contemporary social and legal parameters to create "new systems of law, to function as an agent of nation building" (64). Although "Genocide Tribunals" may not be making *new* systems of indigenous law, it promotes its own form of "jurisgenesis" by proposing a discursive legal space in which individual, tribally specific and Native trans/national narratives of survivance speak "truth in [their] own narrative form" (Katanski 64). The tribunals affirm a Native legal authority and sovereignty that emanates not only from "the basic ways in which tribal law [was and] is practiced" (Justin Richland and Sarah Deer, quoted in Katanski 56) but through a collective accountability inherent in survivance itself: "Original, communal responsibility, greater than the individual . . . animates the practice and consciousness of survivance" (Vizenor, "The Aesthetics" 18–19).

Through the witness testimonies produced by "Genocide Tribunals," long dead, occluded Native subjectivities are made legally visible and legally viable. Reiterated in this way, they become what Allen Feldman calls a "*politicized* anamnesis"—a "re-auditing of residual marginal, repressed, denied, and unreconciled historical fragments that can call the present into question, and to political accountability" (164–65, emphasis added). This Native-inflected jural legitimation of witnessing, I suggest, works similarly to the concept of antiphonic witnessing found in forms of "call and response" testimony of Xhosa and Zulu women during Truth and Reconciliation Commission testimony and in the lamentation in Greek women's culture discussed in Feldman's "Memory Theaters, Virtual Witnessing and the Trauma-Aesthetic." The antiphony of the many narratives of survivance that Vizenor's tribunals would produce would have similar political and healing possibilities acting as a performance site "through which anti-statist, kinship-based bereavement breaks into public culture and into the space of the nation-state as a critical political discourse" (Feldman 179). Recalling the dead in culturally contextualized narratives constructed by Native storiers performs a healing "ritual of social reincorporation" and "a rite of re-origination for the surviving kin-groups, from which the dead had been subtracted by violence" (Feldman 177). In its collective performativity, narratives of antiphonic witness that communicate the "shared emotional substance" of survivance render "testimony [as] collective speech" and present a counterstrategy to the individualization and atomization of the victims that is "part and parcel of the dehumanization process of state violence" (Feldman 177). Vizenor's genocide tribunals offer a Native "jural and historicizing structure" within which to realize the now grievable bodies of Native genocide (C. Nadia Serematakis, quoted in Feldman 177).

Presenting "Genocide Tribunals" as a legal "what if" engages its audience with the imaginative possibilities of survivance, asking them to envision survivance as both a narrative of healing and a narrative of justice. Embedded in the occidental legal paradigm and realized through an active narrative of survivance, the tribunals offer both a healing and inherently destabilizing and deconstructive impulse, which, through its autonomously constructed narrative matrix, surpasses the historical and contemporary productions of indigeneity or "indianness" as containable responses to social, economic, and political forces. If "survival is a response," as Vizenor posits, "survivance" in its wider resonance is "a standpoint, a worldview, and a presence" contextualized by the diversity of modern, global Native experience(s) and the temporal continuum of the traditional (quoted in Doerfler 192). This presence has roots in the Anishinaabe concept of *minobimaadiziwin*, what White Earth scholar Jill Doerfler describes as a "holistic view of life that includes the individual and the collective, physical and mental health, and moral and ethical well-being that has long guided Anishinaabe life" (190). Survivance and *minobimaadiziwin* are integral to Anishinaabe visions of sovereignty "that go beyond 'supreme political authority' to address ethics and health" (Doerfler 190).[21] There is a complementary parallel in traditional Anishinaabe legal praxis that also promotes the ethical and nourishing life described by Doerfler. Borrows has used the term *daebizitawaugaewin* [sic], when he speaks of health and ethics in Anishinaabe law. It is a word that suggests knowledge is relational and must take into account how rights and responsibilities are always intertwined in reciprocity and connected to duties or obligations to families, clan, and communities: "Whenever a potential right exists, a correlative obligation can usually be found, based on individual's relationship with the other orders of the world" (79). These rights are autonomous, organically modal, and not temporally or conceptually bound as in occidental law. They work as conduits across the connected, relational, and reciprocal concepts of the natural world, the human, and the other than human and challenge occidental law, which constricts them as "traditional" or "customary" rights or special "aboriginal" rights to protect settler-state sovereignty. These rights would become more visible through the indigenous legal lens of Vizenor's tribunals.

Conclusion: Hearing the "Callout" and the Response

It could be argued that "Genocide Tribunals" and Vizenor's engagement with the law in his work theoretically maps out a juridical complement to Bruyneel's concept of a "third space of sovereignty":

> Indigenous political actors work across American spatial and temporal boundaries, demanding rights and resources from the liberal democratic settler-state while also challenging

the imposition of colonial rule on their lives. This resistance engenders what I call a "third space of sovereignty" that resides neither simply inside nor outside the American political system but rather exists on these very boundaries, exposing both the practices and the contingencies of American colonial rule. This is a supplemental space, inassimilable to the institutions and discourse of the modern liberal democratic settler-state and nation. (xvii)

The open, transformative nature of narratives of survivance and the agonistic arena of the court continues to provide Vizenor with a supplemental space to mount creative challenges to occidental law. However, with the tribunals his aim is to critically unsettle the delimiting parameters of law to discursively create an admissible jural "third space" for Native "rights of perception." While "Genocide Tribunals" remains a theoretical premise, its intentions are deadly serious, and Vizenor presents it as integral to the consideration of justice in the work done on the ground in the domestic and international legal arenas by Native and indigenous peoples as suggested in the political example of sovereignty outlined by Bruyneel.

"Genocide Tribunals" is both a "callout" and response to recent critical calls for Native writers drawing on the "intellectual tradition of historically engaged political writing to introduce a theory of Native praxis" (Teuton 106). In its re-presentation of Native subjectivity (mis/un)recognized in law, the tribunals use the generative, creative, and political narrative process of survivance as a form of indigenous-led justice. These narratives, as produced through the tribunals, would construct specific contextualization around relational ties, clan, kinship, and nation in re-presencing and remembering the dead. They would also crucially link the generation of its narratives to a particular political goal underpinned by a surviving tradition within indigenous legal systems, which bases its legitimacy on the oral transmission of Law and mnemonic processes where a form of politicized anamnesis actively re-members and re-visions experience as collective. This process suggests an ethically responsible and relational healing narrative in light of the violent trauma of genocide—re-presenting formally "ungrievable" lives in public and legal arenas and rendering them visible and grievable through specific Native cultural, legal, and politically directed contexts. In Vizenor's jurisprudence, the law's encounter with an/other, which it perceives as alterity, is asked to be open to the "transgressive claims of the other" and to answer Native demands transformatively and ethically (Shildrick 40). In terms grounded specifically in Anishinaabe social, political, legal, and traditional reality, "Genocide Tribunals" insists occidental law hears this callout and responds by clearing the ground for indigenous due process and the possibility of justice through an immediate redress of America's genocidal past. Then will the healing truly begin.

This essay is dedicated to the memory of
Dane Michael White.

Notes

I thank Rebecca Tillett and Jacqueline Fear-Segal, who invited me to give an early version of this essay as a paper at the July 2009 NSRN conference "Indigenous Bodies: Reviewing, Relocating, Reclaiming" at UEA, Norwich, UK.

1. Many of these terms are further clarified and augmented in Vizenor's works *Fugitive Poses* and *Manifest Manners*.

2. "Trickster hermeneutics" is a phrase Vizenor uses in *Manifest Manners* to describe his Anishinaabe-led critical interpretive reading and writing praxis drawing on the power of transformation, translation, and imagination inherent in Anishinaabe trickster stories in tandem with poststructural inquiry and deconstructive impulses: "Trickster Hermeneutics is the interpretation of simulations in the literature of survivance, the ironies of descent and racialism, transmutation, third gender, and themes of transformation in oral tribal stories and written narratives" (15).

3. There are myriad mentions of "survivance" in Vizenor's work. This is just one of them: "The nature of survivance creates a sense of narrative resistance to absence, literary tragedy, nihility, and victimry. Native survivance is an active sense of presence over historical absence, the dominance of cultural simulations, and manifest manners. Native survivance is a continuance of stories" (*Native Liberty* 1).

4. "Genocide Tribunals" was also given as a lecture at the University of Minnesota and a keynote speech at the University of Geneva in 2006, and broadcast on public television in the same year.

5. Vizenor alludes to the concept of "visionary sovereignty" in *Fugitive Poses*, which is inextricably bound with his key idea of "transmotion"—the inherent indigenous right to move over the land both literally and via the imagination through oral, written, and visual cultural production. Most crucially, visionary sovereignty is a sense of reciprocity, survivance, and shared power with all forms—human and other than human—of the natural world and is opposed to a

settler-state territorial-based sovereignty. See the final chapter, "Native Transmotion," in *Fugitive Poses* (167–99) and "Mercenary Sovereignty" in *Native Liberty* (108–9).

   6. To clarify my use of Acoose's terminology, I cite the following from her dissertation: "I use the word *Anishinaabe* in both singular and plural references to acknowledge colloquial ways of speaking about ourselves. The word is also used to name the people who self-identify as Being Anishinaabe, relate themselves to specific clans and communities, and preserve the spiritual teachings of ancestors" (1). Acoose cites Vizenor as an honored Anishinaabe "re-vision-er" and in a textualized naming ceremony that forms her doctoral thesis as one of the "*Doodaem Ogimaawinini*, leading Anishinaabe visionaries who revive 'a small portion of the total fund of unwritten tradition' to show contemporary writers how to enhance the teachings of ancestors" (38).

   7. It is notable that in the 2006 broadcast of "Genocide Tribunals," Vizenor didn't envisage the tribunals as part of a moot court process. They were initially proposed as "deadly serious" legal forums in their own right. See, in particular, the discussion about this in the Q & A in the *Genocide Tribunals* broadcast.

   8. Vizenor points out that Article 24 of the ICC states "no person shall be criminally responsible under this Statute for conduct prior to the entry into force of the Statute," seemingly contradicting the statue of limitations waived by Article 29. See the debate in "Genocide Tribunals" (140–41).

   9. Although Vizenor is specifically referring to the TRC of South Africa, instantiated in 1995, his 2006 talk "Genocide Tribunals" was prescient. In a similar model closer to home, the Truth and Reconciliation Commission of Canada (2008–2015) provided a platform where First Nations, Métis, and Inuit survivors could bear witness to the violence of removal, the horrific physical and sexual abuse, and life-long trauma they incurred through the genocidal policies of Canada's residential schools.

   10. At the time of this essay's publication, the United States continues to refuse ratification of the Rome Statute and its relations with the ICC have become increasingly hostile under the current Trump administration.

   11. Pauline Wakeham cites Jeff Corntassel and Cindy Holder's concept of a "politics of distraction," which "shift[s] the discourse away from a restitution of indigenous homelands and resources and ground[s] it instead in a political/legal rights-based process that plays into the affirmative repair policies of states and ultimately rewards colonial injustices" (3). Wakeham makes the argument that current gestures of Canadian and New Zealand atonement and reconciliation do not perform an "unsettle[ing] of settler privilege" and therefore fail to "destabilize the power asymmetries underpinning white authority" (3).

   12. I have called attention to Indian wars as "so-called" to highlight their questionable legal status—as Sidney Harring points out: "Congress, with the sole

power to declare war under the Constitution, never declared a war against an Indian tribe" (16).

13. Butler describes the legitimating process of sovereign exception succinctly: "It is not, literally speaking, that a sovereign power suspends the rule of law, but that the rule of law, in the act of being suspended, produces sovereignty *in its action and as its effect*. This inverse relation to law produces the 'unaccountability' of this operation of sovereign power, as well as its legitimacy" (66). Rifkin and Butler draw heavily on the works of Giorgio Agamben (*Homo Sacer: Sovereign Power and Bare Life* and *State of Exception*), for different, if related purposes. Agamben's work has become particularly important (if somewhat problematic) in theorizing settler-state sovereignty in relation to nineteenth-century extralegal abuses of Native peoples, such as forced removal and internment. See Byrd (185–220). See also Santiago.

14. Rifkin sees this pressure registered as "gaps" in nineteenth-century discourse. There are of course many "nameable" cases of Native resistance and engagement with law, which could be produced alongside this reading.

15. Wendy Brown argues in *Regulating Aversion* that Foucault's concept of governmentality doesn't "chronologically supercede[s] or fully replace[s] sovereignty and rule" (82). "For Brown, both 'governmentality' and 'sovereignty' characterize modes of conceptualizing power rather than historically concrete phenomena that might be said to succeed each other in time" (Butler 60).

16. There is an enormous body of criticism and legal theory written on the Marshall trilogy. For a recent overview of Marshall's influence, see Fletcher, "The Iron Cold of the Marshall Trilogy." See also Cheyfitz.

17. For a comprehensive discussion on the production of indigeneity under state systems of a neoliberal multiculturalism such as Australia, see Povinelli. See Birrell for an extended discussion of performative indigeneity before the law.

18. In December 2010, President Barack Obama pledged US support for the declaration: "The United States supports the Declaration, which—while not legally binding or a statement of current international law—has both moral and political force" ("Announcement of U.S. Support" 1).

19. See *Fugitive Poses* (167–69) and the chapter "Bone Courts" in *The Heirs of Columbus* (63–90).

20. Personal correspondence with Margaret Noodin, August 7, 2020. I am grateful for her help in furthering my understanding of how Vizenor and Borrows interpret certain terms and linguistic characteristics of Anishinaabemowin.

21. However, Carlson sees a specific indigenous political currency between the relationship of Anishinaabeg contemporary holistic and ethical beliefs and law in his discussion of the 2013 ratification of the Constitution of the White Earth Nation, which "seeks to . . . integrate aspects of Western law (certain forms of rights consciousness, for example) into the realm of *mino-bimaadiziwin*, to redefine Anishinaabeg legal and political identity, dialectically, in a way that speaks to the realities and contingencies of the present moment" ("Trickster Hermeneutics" 36).

References

Acoose, Janice M. "Minjimendaamowinon Anishinaabe: Reading and Righting *All Our Relations* in Written English." PhD diss., University of Saskatchewan, 2011.
Agamben, Giorgio. *Homo Sacer: Sovereign Power and Bare Life*, translated by Daniel Heller Roazen. Stanford, CA: Stanford University Press, 1998.
———. *State of Exception*, translated by Kevin Attell. Chicago: University of Chicago Press, 2005.
"Announcement of U.S. Support for the United Nations Declaration on the Rights of Indigenous Peoples." April 23, 2015. http://www.state.gov/documents/organization/184099.pdf.
Birrell, Kathleen. *Indigeneity: Before and Beyond the Law*. Abingdon, UK: Routledge, 2016.
Blaeser, Kimberly M. *Gerald Vizenor: Writing in the Oral Tradition*. Norman: University of Oklahoma Press, 1996.
Borrows, John. *Canada's Indigenous Constitution*. Toronto: University of Toronto Press, 2010.
Brown, Wendy. *Regulating Aversion: Tolerance in the Age of Identity and Empire*. Princeton, NJ: Princeton University Press, 2006.
Bruyneel, Kevin. *The Third Space of Sovereignty: The Postcolonial Politics of U.S.-Indigenous Relations*. Minneapolis: University of Minnesota Press, 2007.
Butler, Judith. *Precarious Life: The Powers of Mourning and Violence*. London: Verso, 2004.
Byrd, Jodi A. *The Transit of Empire: Indigenous Critiques of Colonialism*. Minneapolis: University of Minnesota Press, 2011.
Carlson, David J. *Imagining Sovereignty: Self-Determination in American Indian Law and Literature*. Norman: University of Oklahoma Press, 2016.
———. "Trickster Hermeneutics and the PostIndian Reader: Gerald Vizenor's Constitutional Praxis." *Studies in American Indian Literatures* 23, no. 4 (2011): 13–47.
Cheah, Pheng, David Fraser, and Judith Grbich."Introduction: The Body of Law." In *Thinking through the Body of the Law*, edited by Pheng Cheah, David Fraser, and Judith Grbich, xi–xix. New York: New York University Press, 1996.
Cheyfitz, Eric. "The (Post)Colonial Construction of Indian Country: U.S. American Indian Literatures and Federal Indian Law." In *The Columbia Guide to American Indian Literatures of the United States since 1945*, edited by Eric Cheyfitz, 3–124. New York: Columbia University Press, 2006.
Clarke, Jennifer. "Australia: The White House with Lovely Dot Paintings Whose Inhabitants Have 'Moved On' from History." In *Indigenous Peoples and the Law*, edited by Benjamin J. Richardson, Shin Imai, and Kent McNeil, 81–109. Portland, OR: Hart, 2009.

D'Errico, Peter. "Native Americans in America: A Theoretical and Historical Overview." *Wicazo Sa Review* 14, no. 1 (1999): 7–28.

Doerfler, Jill. "Postindian Survivance: Gerald Vizenor and Kimberly Blaeser." In *Gerald Vizenor: Texts and Contexts*, edited by Deborah L. Madsen and A. Robert Lee, 186–207. Albuquerque: University of New Mexico Press, 2010.

Drinnon, Richard. *Facing West: The National Metaphysics of Indian-Hating and Empire Building*. 1980; Norman: University of Oklahoma Press, 1997.

Feldman, Allen. "Memory Theaters, Virtual Witnessing, and the Trauma-Aesthetic." *Biography* 27, no. 1 (2004): 163–202.

Finzsch, Norbert. "'[. . .] Extirpate or Remove That Vermin': Genocide, Biological Warfare, and Settler Imperialism in the Eighteenth and Early Nineteenth Century." *Journal of Genocide Research* 10, no. 2 (2008): 215–32.

Fitzpatrick, Peter. *Modernism and the Grounds of Law*. Cambridge: Cambridge University Press, 2001.

———. "Surpassing Sovereignty." In *Sovereignty: Frontiers of Possibility*, edited by Julie Evans, Ann Genovese, Alexander Reilly, and Patrick Wolfe, 181–93. Honolulu: University of Hawai'i Press, 2012.

Fletcher, Matthew L. M. "The Iron Cold of the Marshall Trilogy." *North Dakota Law Review* 82, no. 627 (2006): 627–96.

Fletcher, Matthew L. M., and Peter S. Vicaire. "Indian Wars: Old and New." *Michigan State University College of Law Indigenous Law and Policy Center Working Paper Series* (May 4, 2011): 3–25.

Friedberg, Lillian. "Dare to Compare: Americanizing the Holocaust." *American Indian Quarterly* 24, no. 3 (2000): 353–80.

Hamilton, Jennifer A. *Indigeneity in the Courtroom: Law, Culture and the Production of Difference in North American Courts*. New York: Routledge, 2009.

Harring, Sidney L. *Crow Dog's Case: American Indian Sovereignty, Tribal Law, and United States Law in the Nineteenth Century*. Cambridge: Cambridge University Press, 1994.

Isernhagen, Hartwig. *Momaday, Vizenor, Armstrong: Conversations on American Indian Writing*. Norman: University of Oklahoma Press, 1999.

Johnson, Greg. "Narrative Remains: Articulating Indian Identities in the Repatriation Context." *Comparative Studies in Society and History* 47, no. 3 (2005): 480–506.

Katanski, Amelia V. "Writing the Living Law: American Indian Literature as Legal Narrative." *American Indian Law Review* 33, no. 1 (2008/2009): 53–76.

Méndez, Juan E. "National Reconciliation, Transnational Justice, and the International Criminal Court." *Ethics and International Affairs* 15, no. 1 (2001): 25–44.

Povinelli, Elizabeth A. *The Cunning of Recognition: Indigenous Alterities and the Making of Australian Multiculturalism*. Durham, NC: Duke University Press, 2002.

Rifkin, Mark. "Indigenizing Agamben: Rethinking Sovereignty in Light of the 'Peculiar' Status of Native Peoples." *Cultural Critique* 73 (2009): 88–124.

Santiago, Charles R. Venator. "From the Insular Cases to Camp X-Ray: Agamben's State of Exception and United States Territorial Law." *Studies in Law, Politics, and Society* 39 (2006): 15–55.

Shildrick, Margrit. "Transgressing the Law with Foucault and Derrida: Some Reflections on Anomalous Embodiment." *Critical Quarterly* 47, no. 3 (2005): 30–46.

Sinclair, Niigonwedom James. "A Sovereignty of Transmotion: Imagination and the 'Real,' Gerald Vizenor, and Native Literary Nationalism." In *Stories through Theories/Theories through Stories: North American Indian Writing, Storytelling and Critique*, edited by Gordon D. Henry, Nieves Pascual Soler, and Silvia Martinez-Falquina, 123–158. East Lansing: Michigan State University Press, 2009.

Teuton, Sean. "The Callout: Writing American Indian Politics." In *Reasoning Together: The Native Critics Collective*, edited by Craig S. Womack, Daniel Heath Justice, and Christopher B. Teuton, 105–25. Norman: University of Oklahoma Press, 2008.

Vizenor, Gerald. "The Aesthetics of Survivance: Literary Theory and Practice." In *Survivance: Narratives of Native Presence*, edited by Gerald Vizenor, 1–23. Lincoln: University of Nebraska Press, 2008.

———. *Fugitive Poses: Native American Indian Scenes of Absence and Presence*. Lincoln: University of Nebraska Press, 1998.

———. "Genocide Tribunals." In Gerald Vizenor, *Native Liberty: Natural Reason and Cultural Survivance*, 131–57. Lincoln: University of Nebraska Press, 2009.

———. *Genocide Tribunals: Native Human Rights and Survivance*. Institute for Advanced Study, University of Minnesota. Broadcast talk given on October 10, 2006. http://ias.umn.edu/2010/03/06/vizenor-gerald/.

———. *The Heirs of Columbus*. Hanover, NH: Wesleyan University Press, 1991.

———. *Manifest Manners: Narratives on Postindian Survivance*. 1994; Lincoln: University of Nebraska Press, 1999.

———. *Native Liberty: Natural Reason and Cultural Survivance*. Lincoln: University of Nebraska Press, 2009.

———. "Sand Creek Survivors." In Gerald Vizenor, *Earthdivers: Tribal Narratives on Mixed Descent*, 33–46. Minneapolis: University of Minnesota Press, 1981.

———. *Summer in the Spring: Ojibwe Lyric Poems and Tribal Stories*. Minneapolis: Nodin Press, 1981.

———. "Thomas White Hawk." In Gerald Vizenor, *Crossbloods: Bone Courts, Bingo, and Other Reports*, 100–151. 1976; Minneapolis: University of Minnesota Press, 1990. Print.

Wakeham, Pauline. "Reconcilling 'Terror': Managing Indigenous Resistance in the Age of Apology." *American Indian Quarterly* 36, no. 1 (2012): 1–33.

Williams, Robert A., Jr. *The American Indian in Western Legal Thought: The Discourses of Conquest*. Oxford: Oxford University Press, 1990.

———. *Like a Loaded Weapon: The Rehnquist Court, Indian Rights and the Legal History of Racism in America*. Minneapolis: University of Minnesota Press, 2005.

Yudice, George. "Testimonio and Postmodernism." *Latin American Perspectives: Voices of the Voiceless in Testimonial Literature* Part 1, 18, no. 3 (1991): 15–31.

III
Jiibayaaboozo

Chapter 7

The Exceptional Power of the Dead in Heid E. Erdrich's *National Monuments*

DEBORAH L. MADSEN

> Mostly I want people to think about the line: When is a body sacred and sovereign, and when is it scientifically significant and what happened in between? Is it more about *whose* bodies remain sacred? How does relationship to the body define our larger culture, our scientific belief system?
>
> —Heid E. Erdrich interview (Goetzman)

> We shall find a new place. We shall be happy and the old place will always be ours, for the bones of our uncles, our aunts, our grandmothers, and our grandfathers have blended with the earth there and the strangers cannot erase that.
>
> —Ignatia Broker

Even before opening Heid Erdrich's volume of poetry, *National Monuments*, the cover image raises questions of nationalism, indigeneity, memory, and history. As David Stirrup remarks of the painting, Andrea Carlson's "Vaster Empire," "ironically undermines the strategies and assumptions of imperial/colonial histories and re-presents its subject matter as an Anishinaabe storied landscape" (303).[1] This is precisely the work performed by the poems in Erdrich's book as they challenge the exceptionalist history of the United States, re-placing the US national narrative into the discursive environment of Anishinaabe storying. American exceptionalism—the idea that the United States was created by God's will to be a model to the world—works largely through the territorial narrative of Manifest Destiny, which claims a divine mission to occupy the entire North American continent. Of course, this narrative must disavow the violence with which the settler nation occupies the land on which are constructed the social, political, and cultural institutions of the United States.[2] Whether the bloodshed of the American Revolution, the brutality of "King Philip's" (Metacomet's) War of the 1670s, the violence of the so-called Indian wars that coincided with the relentless westward expansion of the nation throughout the nineteenth century, or the ongoing conflict between indigenous nations and the settler nation that is the United States, this history of devastation is disavowed by the rhetoric of American exceptionalism. Beneath this narrativized history lies a trail of dead human bodies, lifeless bones, that refuse the disavowal of their stories. The history of settler violence in the United States is signified by the human remains—indigenous and settler—that are the primary product of this violent process of colonial nation-building. What sets apart the corpses of settlers and Natives who died in the same conflict? Most fundamentally, the answer lies in the disposal of the corporeal remains that endure to tell the story of their deaths. While the heroic remains of US soldiers are feted and memorialized, the remains of indigenous people are shipped to hospitals, museums, and research collections—institutions in the structure of the federal government. Indigenous human remains become wards of the state, hostages to the claim of Manifest Destiny.[3]

The rendering invisible of indigenous presence on the North American continent has taken place epistemologically by appropriating bones as the object of empirical science and physically by removing the material traces of indigenous occupation from the landscape and placing human remains and funerary objects in museum vaults and laboratory files. In these ways, Gerald Vizenor argues, an absence is created by colonial "manifest manners," an absence that makes available a space to be filled with invented images of "the Indian."[4] A similar point is made by Suzanne Crawford, who suggests "that the creation of the fictitious 'Authentic Indian' of non-Native American lore effectively cuts contemporary Native Americans off from their heritage, enabling the appropriation of Native identity by non-Natives. The ultimate goal of this appropriation is to secure a sense of place, what Yi-Fu Tuan has called 'geopiety' " (212).[5] Geopiety is defined by Thomas Parkhill, quoted by Crawford, as "the sense of country as one's native home, the sense that one had sprung out of its soil and was nurtured by it; the belief that one's ancestors since time immemorial were born in it" (225). The image of the fictitious Indian consigned to prehistory by the inexorable forces of modernity serves the interests of settler-colonial "geopiety" by sustaining the fiction of the land as an uninhabited wilderness that was awaiting civilization by the United States. The appropriated markers of indigenous occupation or "relics" are divorced from their lived tribal contexts and, in the environment of museum or laboratory, recontextualized within the alien settler-colonial narrative of nation-state formation. Thus, Native human remains play a key role in the ideological operations of American exceptionalism and the conflicts over tribal versus settler nationalisms, which are fundamentally conflicts over stories. As Crawford explains, the European empiricist approach to indigenous human remains poses questions that "are constructed from a history of colonial discourse, which seeks to understand the Other so as to better colonize them: understanding the origins of the Natives, how they fit within the Euroamerican conception of human history, and how to integrate, assimilate, or do away with them most effectively" (229). Out of this interpretive control and domination emerges "power over history, power over identity, and hence power over those peoples whose heritage has been stolen" (Crawford 229–30). Thus, when Lee Schweninger quotes Greg Sarris's claim that "a culture under glass is a culture robbed of its story" (173), he is half right. The culture on display has been more than physically appropriated; the story has been stolen and strategically replaced with another.

In her study of the American Indian Repatriation Movement and NAGPRA (the 1990 Native American Graves Protection and Repatriation Act), Kathleen Fine-Dare implicitly connects the historical revisionism of settler colonization with the nation-forming ideology of American exceptionalism through the concept of Manifest Destiny, the definition of which she nuances as follows:

> Perhaps the most powerful sense of the term is a millennial one that signals a new world order . . . where insiders, or natives, are transformed into outsiders, or enemies, by newcomers who see themselves as the true Americans God destined them to be.

> When this religious and cultural impulse is combined with the activities of empire building, much light can be shed on the reasons why millions of American Indian and Native Hawaiian human remains and cultural objects were obtained by museums and private collections. It takes not only territorial expansion, population growth, and ethnic cleansing to ensure the success of continental expansionism, but also some kind of "mass communication" to convince the public that the possession of territories, resources, bodies, and property of natives-turned-enemies is justified. (13–14)

In the section of her chapter "Museums and Objects of Empire," titled "Native Americans and the American Project," Fine-Dare begins by noting the role played by indigenous peoples in the founding narratives of the United States. First they were the agents of the "trials" sent by a providential God to test the faith of settler Puritans, then they were the subjects of "American ideals of progress, civilization, and Christian *lebensraum* (literally, 'living room' expansionism, as it would come to be called in Germany), known in North America as Manifest Destiny" (19). She explains that the "quasi-religious status of museum holdings took on a large significance in the United States and Canada, which had no heritage on the North American continent other than what they could appropriate from American Indians or invent based on European traditions" (19). She underscores the role of the "museum process" by quoting Curtis M. Hinsley's 1989 essay, "Zunis and Brahmins: Cultural Ambivalence in the Gilded Age," in which he gives an account of the resolution of long-standing ambivalence about the status of indigenous Americans in the territorial space of the settler nation: "The resolution was achieved by announcing and then demonstrating the end of Indian history. The museum process constructed a meaning of Indian demise within the teleology of manifest destiny . . . and it did so by encasing, in time and space, the American Indian. Dehistoricization was the essence of the process" (21). Erdrich references this process of dehistoricization in the poem "Girl of Lightning," which directly addresses the corpse of an Andean girl, one of three children taken from a ritual grave site, the one corpse not selected for public display because of the damage inflicted by a lightning strike: "blackened flesh looks less asleep / flashes back the fact you're dead" (ll. 43–44). The damaged corpse—"Singed cheek and blasted chest" (l. 42)—is too real, too much historicized, too grounded in the natural world to function effectively as the indigenous mannequin of the "authentic Indian."

I suggest that Heid Erdrich, in her poetic engagement with material objects—landscape monuments, the monuments of popular culture, living bodies, and above all human remains (in poems like "eBay Bones," "My Beloved Is Mine," and the Kennewick Man sequence)—deconstructs the settler narrative of American exceptionalism by recontextualizing these artifacts, human remains in particular, by taking them out of the context of US national formation and reinstating them as monuments to indigenous sovereignty. The extraordinary power of the poems collected in *National Monuments* arises from the performativity of Erdrich's poetic language, which enacts interpretation through an Anishinaabe epistemology. In her use of images, the complex weaving of thematic and imagistic threads, and the grounding of her poetic ontology in the concept of *bimaadiziwin*, the traditional understanding of being in the world that is profoundly disrupted when proper respect for the dead is not practiced. Throughout the volume, the settler claim to a national identity arising from occupation of the land is subverted. The exceptionalist myth of US national origin is exposed as a creation myth through repeated contrasts with tribal myths of origin and powerful images of the people as arising from the land itself. For example, the bearer of the corpse addressed in "eBay Bones" is spoken of as "Woman of volcanic earth so rich she probably / eased into the loam like her shawl" (54, ll. 5–6); in "The Theft Outright," the settler claim to possess and belong to the land is subverted by Native images of "loamy risers," "formed of clay" (ll. 5, 6), which articulate indigenous identity and being as the "flesh of earth" (l. 28). The physical and discursive disruption of this relationship with land—by the rhetoric of American exceptionalism and the appropriative acts it motivates and legitimates—inhibits people's ability to "live a good life" (*bimaadiziwin*) and die a good death.

American Exceptionalism, or the Settler-Colonial Creation Myth

"The Theft Outright" is Erdrich's most explicit engagement with the fictive narrative of US origins as she rewrites the poem delivered by Robert Frost at John F. Kennedy's inauguration ceremony in 1961. Dean Rader describes Frost's "The Gift Outright" as "a swan song for the chauvinism and ethnocentrism of Manifest Destiny. Suffice it to say that when in the first line the speaker says, 'The land was ours before we were the land's,' he was not channeling Chief Seattle, Wovoka, or any person of color. Frost, frosty as they come, embodied whiteness" (n.p.). As Rader suggests, Erdrich reworks Frost's images and phrasings to expose his rhetoric of Manifest Destiny and restore the indigenous presence that is so absent from his poem.

Frost's "The Gift Outright" is a sixteen-line sonnet written in free verse. There are no stanza breaks, and punctuation creates the thematic structure; thus, the logical flow of the poem is punctuated by three end-stopped sentences, the last of which is broken by a single-line parenthesis. The first section begins with the claim "The land was ours before we were the land's" (348, l. 1), which is evidenced by the subsequent account of the colonial origins of the United States. The poetic voice, speaking for an indeterminate collective "we," ponders the contradiction between physical possession of the land and cultural alienation from it in favor of a continued allegiance or belonging to the metropolitan center of England. The poem's terms of reference are thereby established as the Old World/New World dichotomy, which is foundational to the narrative of American exceptionalism, while bracketing the indigenous dispossession that was a precondition for territorial possession and colonial occupation. Frost plays on the notions of "possessing" and "being possessed by" to evoke the dynamic between severing cultural ties to Europe and establishing a new form of national belonging in America. These seven lines are followed by two quatrains, the second of which consists of five lines due to the parenthesis in the position of the second line.

The first quatrain diagnoses the settler-colonial malaise as a form of "weakness" that arises from withholding a complete lived relation to the land and identifies "surrender" as the remedial source of "salvation." The surrender of the metropolitan ties that forestall the establishment of an authentic settler identity becomes, in the final quatrain, the "gift" bestowed by settler-colonists on the land. The poem's account of this process of gifting is disrupted by the insertion of a dramatic parenthesis in the second line of what becomes a five-line quatrain: "Such as we were we gave ourselves outright / . . . / to the land . . ." The subject and verb of the sentence—"we gave ourselves" find their object only after the line-long parenthetical pause. The parenthesis gestures to the nature of the gift that has been given: "(The deed of gift was many deeds of war)." In the context of the earlier lines, "She was our land more than a hundred years / Before we were her people" (ll. 2–3), the war to which Frost refers here is the American Revolution, only after which did the US nation-state exist as a national territory to which settler communities could belong. As commentators have noted, "deed" is a multivalent term here, signifying a conscious action and legal proof of ownership or possession. However, the repressed indigenous presence of the exceptionalist myth returns in the paradoxical semantic field created by the twin phrases "deed of gift" and "deeds of war."[6] A gift is an act that expects no return, as Jacques Derrida reminds us, and contradicts the notion of a deed that formalizes the exchange of ownership.[7] More problematically, this sense of possession evoked by the word "deeds" in the context of war cannot help but evoke the history of colonial violence with which indigenous peoples were dispossessed of their lands. These territorial implications assume prominence in the concluding lines, when the poet's vision turns westward, to the "still unstoried, artless, unenhanced" lands that await the settler-nation's future "becoming." These implications are made explicit in Erdrich's revision of the poem's title from "The Gift Outright" to "The Theft Outright."

If the two poems are placed side by side, the quality that becomes apparent first is the contrast between Frost's single block of text and Erdrich's "deconstructed" structure of tercets, couplets, and single lines; second is the dominant verbal register the poems share. Erdrich reuses Frost's phraseology—the repetition and variations on possession and dispossession, the claims that "we were the land's" and "she was our land," the terms "gift" and "deed"—but inverts the meanings of his exceptionalist vocabulary. This inversion, which is more accurately a reversion or return in the sense of restoring original meaning, is performed dramatically by the chiasmus that structures the couplet (ll. 11-12) enacting the first thematic transition. This move from Erdrich's meditation on the nature of indigenous belonging to the land to evoking tribal narratives of origin is punctuated by the following lines:

Un-possessing of what we still are possessed by,
possessed by what we now no more possess. (ll. 11-12)

Frost's diagnosis of settler "weakness" as the in-between condition of living physically in colonial space while living culturally in the metropolitan center—possessing land that has not become home while living possessed by the claims of an England that has been left behind—is interpreted here as the condition of indigenous peoples who have never claimed to "own" the land and yet have been shaped or possessed in every way by that land, who are possessed by land of which they have been dispossessed. Erdrich's repetition of "possessed by" at the end of the first line and the beginning of the second draws a conceptual line across the poem; the convergence of the meaning of the phrases "Un-possessing" and "no more possess" draws a less obvious line in the opposite direction—a line that is emphatically conceptual, underscoring the conceptual reversal of Frost's poem that is performed by her poem. The conceptual cross drawn in these lines could be thought of as an act of "crossing out," putting under erasure, an exceptional narrative that remains and yet is superseded or written over by the restitution of a Native narrative.

The poetic voice of both poems uses an indefinite third-person mode of address ("we") but, as Robert Dale Parker notes, "Frost's poem begins 'The land was ours before we were the land's' and then goes on to proclaim how 'we' became the land's. . . . Erdrich responds to Frost and to the dominant ways of thinking that Frost's poem so suggestively represents. Her 'we,' it turns out, is not Frost's 'we'" (77). Not just in her reinterpretation of the object of the pronoun but in her careful choice of grammatical forms, Erdrich performs the conceptual transfer of sovereignty over the land from a settler discourse to an indigenous ontology. The use of articles in the early lines, for example, enacts the colonial struggle over the meaning of "possession":

> Or the land was ours before you were a land.
> Or this land was our land, it was not your land. (31, ll. 2–3)

In the first of these lines, the definite article to name "the land" is in tension with the indefinite article that makes a distinction between the encompassing indigenous understanding of the land and the nation-specific epistemology of settlers who would become "a land." These demonstrative articles enact the subtext of colonial epistemological violence that is the work of rhetorical discourses like Frost's. In the second of these lines, Erdrich's use of determiners similarly deconstructs the rhetoric of settler possession. The adjectival element of the phrases "this land," "our land," and "your land" shifts from the simple determiner "this" to the possessive determiners "our" and "yours." If we turn to the assertions in the corresponding (third) line of Frost's poem, we find that he does not use a possessive determiner but the claim that "She was ours" takes the form of a possessive pronoun—a form of naming that encodes in itself the assumption of the fact of colonial possession. On the level of linguistic minutiae, Erdrich's poem exposes the ideologically charged nature of Frost's poetic minutiae.

Larger structural features of Frost's poem are subjected to Erdrich's relentlessly deconstructive gaze: that dramatic and contradictory parenthesis, for example. "The Theft Outright" also uses parenthesis—indeed, it is possible to read the end dashes in lines 6 and 15 as opening and closing a lengthy parenthesis—but where Frost uses the closed form of brackets, Erdrich chooses to complement brackets with the more open form of parenthetical dashes—and we can note that the dash that ends line 28 is never closed. The long parenthesis between lines 6 and 15 interrupts the poet's reflections on myths of origin. The people who "we were" are specified by the images "loamy roamers rising," "formed of clay, spit into with breath reeking soul" (ll. 5–6)—images that evoke the emergence stories of tribal nations like the Diné, stories of the first ancestor emerging out of the land into the world on the land. Indeed, the reference to contemporary "Dineh in documentaries" closes the parenthesis by linking ancestors to modern Native peoples. Where Frost interrupts his narrative of Manifest Destiny to mention the bloody gift of war that bound the settler nation to the land, Erdrich interrupts the theme of tribal origin with images of bloody birth. The blood of birth is introduced by the image "red rocks" (l. 8) with which is juxtaposed, in the following image, "blood clots bearing boys" (l. 8). The origination of the individual in maternal blood finds a parallel in the origin of community in emergence from the maternal land. The juxtaposition of "we originate / originally" (ll. 9–10) takes us from the birth of a person at the end of one line immediately to the origin of all the people. This relationship between the individual and community is underscored by the repetition of the phrase "we were people" (ll. 4, 13) in the repeated line "We were the land before we were people"—referencing the origin of each human within the loam, clay, and mud of the land—which is subtly transformed by the introduction of the indefinite article in the repetition in line 26: "We were the land before we were a people." "A people" distinguishes communities and tribal nations as collectivities and links them to the concepts of individual humans and humanity. This "people" is specified with reference to the Anishinaabe creation story of the earthdiver who made the land by collecting grains of sand and dirt, a myth that complements the Diné stories of emergence recalled in the alliterative phrases "emerging, fully forming from flesh of earth" (l. 28). To the land, in these lines, is attributed agency; rather than being created by the earthdivers, "her darling mudpuppies" (l. 27), the land has created these agents of her own creation in a cyclical process of mutual creativity.

The groundedness (in all meanings of that term) of indigenous people and their communities in the land fatally subverts the claim to settler possession encoded in the language of Frost's poem. This is underscored by two interposed single lines that take the form of rhetorical questions: "What's America but the legend of Rock 'n' Roll?" (l. 7) and "What's America but the legend of Stop 'n' Go?" (l. 19). Dramatically, the questions are left hanging, unanswered; yet they are answered by the implicit contrast between the indigenous ontological bond with land and place, on the one hand, and the absence of "grounding" that is a condition for settler mobility on the other hand. Erdrich's speaker is perhaps taking up Frost's allusion to westward expansion in the images of rock and roll, and Stop 'n' Go which, with their emphasis on active verbs, emphasize an activity of unceasing movement. For Frost, the continual move westward was toward "the land vaguely realizing westward, / But still unstoried, artless, unenhanced" (ll. 14–15): a land passively awaiting its creation with the arrival of settlers. As I noted already, Erdrich's land is active, agential, and symbiotic in its relation to human creation.[8] The land creates humans collectively and individually, and part of this creation is the stories that are about creation and *are* this process of creation. "The Theft Outright" is punctuated with the repeated phrase "so the stories go" (ll. 5, 14, 27). The word "go" in these repetitions is in ironic tension with "Stop 'n' Go" because it signifies the continuance of grounded indigenous storytelling. The stories "go" from the land to the people and return to the land, an emphatically storied land as the penultimate line stresses—"still storied, art-filled, fully enhanced" (l. 30)—in direct, phrase-by-phrase contradiction of Frost's description of a land that appears "unstoried" to those who cannot understand the language of the stories because they do not stop to understand. They stop . . . but then they go. In a poem that rarely uses rhyme, Erdrich echoes "go" with "know" (l. 18) and "Go": a storied "going" or the continuance of the stories connects human experience with knowledge and belonging to the land through the half-rhyme with "home" (l. 18). But the rhythmic identity between the phrase "they don't know" (l. 18) and "Stop 'n' Go" (l. 19) creates a semantic connection between these settler "legends" and their lack of ontological knowledge of the land.

Stories go beyond myths and legends. The "deeds" the poems reference are the actions recorded in stories and the written legal texts that have the power to act, to change reality. Whereas Frost plays on the double meanings of "deed" as act and legitimation to describe the settler claim to land through the gift of warfare and blood, Erdrich, also writing parenthetically, stresses the acts or deeds of theft that are identical with the performative power of language, texts, and stories: "the deed of the theft was many deeds and leases and claim stakes / and tenure disputes and moved plat markers stolen still today . . ." (ll. 24–25). As Dean Rader notes, Erdrich "plays with Frost's line and its sentiment, inverting the poem's claim to land by invoking the transgressive history of land reclamation, removal, and theft" (n.p.). Settler claims to the land are inverted by the poem's allusions to land theft, but there is a further irony in that this performative power of language is used in the poem—and throughout *National Monuments*—to enact a counter colonial epistemology.

Bimaadiziwin and Exceptional Violence

The intertextual relations between Erdrich's and Frost's poems enact the discursive struggle for possession of the land, in its fullest sense, that marks Native–settler relations. For an indigenous person like Erdrich, this struggle for the national narrative is a matter of survival. As Anishinaabe scholar Lawrence Gross explains in his essay "Cultural Sovereignty and Native American Hermeneutics in the Interpretation of the Sacred Stories of the Anishinaabe" and other writings (Gross, *Anishinaabe Ways* and "Bimaadiziwin"), culture and religion cannot be separated in the context of Native nations. He notes that "in regard to the Anishinaabe . . . we do not have a religion, we have a way of life. Unless a people's religion can be maintained, it is not likely the rest of the culture can survive intact" ("Cultural Sovereignty" 127). Indeed, viewed in terms of *bimaadiziwin*, religion and culture as distinct concepts become meaningless. One of the authorities on Anishinaabe ontology cited by Gross is Michael McNally. In his study of Anishinaabe singing, hymns, and grief, McNally describes how

> *Bimaadiziwin* could be translated as "the Circle of Life," for it is derived from a verb that describes a kind of motion that sweeps by or continues along. The term in its fullness encompasses notions of well-being, balance, profound interdependence, and right relations . . . *bimaadiziwin* is more than just "nature";

it is the ultimate goal of life. The Circle of Life is not just a matter of "what is," but a matter of "what ought to be." (24)

Ojibwes understood that *bimaadiziwin* embodied the force of sacred powers that animated it. As a consequence, to live well in light of *bimaadiziwin* was to maintain auspicious and proper ethical and ritual relations with the sacred powers that animate *bimaadiziwin*. In this state of affairs, there was no clear distinction between the natural and the supernatural, between the material and the spiritual, or between the sacred and the ordinary. (25)

Erdrich's poem "Ghost Keeper" recounts the year-long mourning practices of a "Ghost Keeper"—"the father of the fallen child" (ll. 6, 23)—the proper behaviors for dealing with the dead, the prohibitions and ritual requirements to satisfy the needs of the recently dead and usher them onto the spirit road to the ancestors, the giving of gifts at the end of the mourning period. The "shadow sibling" (l. 17), the "one who lingers" (l. 2) must not be disturbed and must not be given cause to envy "the living children" (l. 16). The keeper of the still present spirit must "be as a ghost himself" (l. 12). The poem concludes with an affirmation of life that is individual, familial, and above all communal: "the Ghost Keeper lifts each child / gallops them about like a pony gone wild" (ll. 29–30, 24). We might recall Arnold Krupat's observation that in many Native American tribal communities, "while death and loss were inevitably felt personally, they were intensely felt socially: someone who had contributed to the People's well-being was now gone. Native American elegiac expression traditionally, orally, and substantially in writing as well offered mourners consolation so that they might overcome their grief and renew their will to sustain communal life" (3). Erdrich's poem describes respecting *bimaadiziwin*, underscoring the communal nature of grief, mourning, and recovery. But respect for the living and the dead portrayed in this poem is disrupted when relations among the human, the natural, and the spirit worlds are severed.

The eponymous poem that opens *National Monuments* explores this disruption in relation to clan totems or doodems, the visible symbols of the complex ontological connectivity among individuals, the land, and the people. The poem opens with the poet's delighted appreciation of a traditional Anishinaabe grave-house, a "low house of rough bark" (ll. 1, 3), which shifts as the grave underneath is discovered and the grave-house is seen to have been "stained deck-red / shingled with asphalt" (ll. 5–6). A park official, the poet speculates, has attempted to preserve this ritual object by reconfiguring it as an artifact divorced from its purpose "to moss / and rot and fall" (ll. 8–9). The decomposition of the grave-house is situated as part of a cycle of mutual support between the human and the land, a cycle of interconnectedness symbolized by the clan markings that map individual identity to community and the Earth:

> Bear tracks tell complex genealogy,
> map land and tongue and history
> to crane's stick legs and turtle's shell. (ll. 16–18)

Doodems function as "national markers" (l. 19), marking the status of the body as a sign of tribal national belonging and survivance. In the essay "*Name'*: Literary Ancestry as Presence," Heid Erdrich defines the Anishinaabe term *Name'* as "a verb transitive animate [that] means 'to find/leave signs of somebody's presence'" (14). She explains further,

> I choose to be guided by a metaphor that involves a play between the notion of landmark literary works and the pictographic marks/signs/presence that Anishinaabe people left/leave/find on rock and elsewhere. This metaphor arises from an Anishinaabe-centered epistemology that relates writing with landmark, and marking with ongoing presence in place. . . . What helps us know a place? Landmarks. What helps us know a people? The marks/signs they leave, that we find. These marks and landmarks help us follow their path across a landscape of time. . . . When we find what another leaves, we are connected across time. (14)

The doodems marking the Anishinaabe grave-house function as *Name'* in this sense; the clan marker is a sign of indigenous presence inscribed in the landscape as a landmark of the individual's and community's ongoing presence. "Doodem signs" (l. 19) performatively integrate the individual into the history of clan and tribal nation and into the land itself. The positioning of the image "tongue" between "land" and "history" suggests that the tribal tradition of storying—telling the histories of the people and the stories of the land—creates and sustains a complex indigenous genealogy. This genealogy is a record or story to be told, a text, and it is an action or activity of inheritance: genealogy tells and acts, like the "map" produced by the bear's tracks that is at once a noun and a verb or active process of mapping. A bear tracks, and it leaves tracks; Erdrich's poem likewise performs the work of passing on the stories at the same time it tells the stories that are this inheritance and continues the cycle of *bimaadiziwin*.

Bimaadiziwin is disrupted most profoundly by the appropriative actions of the settler-state that render traditional ritual practices impossible. The theft of artifacts and human remains under the activity of "collecting"—whether for scientific or commercial purposes—inflicts great violence on indigenous ontology, in the basic interest of promoting and legitimating the settler claim to land. In his account of the early republican settler narrativizing of the ancient mound-builders of Ohio, Curtis M. Hinsley Jr. notes that no one is "more desirous of creating the founding and legitimating myths that secure title to the land" (38) than the founders of settler colonies. He argues that these myths are validated largely by the physical and discursive appropriation of indigenous material objects and human remains. Quoting Henry Rowe Schoolcraft's assertion that "America is the tomb of the red man" (43), Hinsley observes that "the particular force of the prehistoric narrative lay in granting primal, deep meaning to place(s), in a timescape prior to the speeches, signings, and other nation-building acts of more recent national memory." Key to this narrative is the "attribution of deep, grounded history" (43) based on the claim to ground, to Earth and land. By removing indigenous human remains from the ground, by vacating this primal relationship to the Earth, and inscribing these bodies along with funerary and other ritual objects into a new "prehistoric" narrative, the settler nation cleared the discursive ground for its own myth of origin staged on "virgin land" and asserted power over the capacity of Native peoples to practice *bimaadiziwin*.

The poem "eBay Bones" offers a complex interweaving of strands of thought that converge on the concept of *bimaadiziwin*, playing partly on the double meaning of "web" (l. 10) as both the modern internet and also the "web of life" of Anishinaabe cosmology. In the following line, the homophones site/sight generate multiple meanings: "sites" signify websites as well as sacred places and sacred "sights" in the sense that the dead can be seen as sacred spirit beings after casting off the material body through death. This play on "sight" is continued at the end of the stanza, in the image of an empty eye socket exposed to light. Opposed forms of seeing and understanding—conflicting indigenous and settler epistemologies—converge at the same time as they are kept distinct by the play on tribal-cosmological versus exceptionalist-settler visions of the significance of the human remains exposed in the "flash" (l. 16) of an archeologist's torch. How the remains of the dead are to be properly respected and valued is the center of the discursive conflict enacted in the poem. The repetition of the word "fine," for example,

> the grave may be a fine and secret place,
> but kept a fine secret only for some. (ll. 12–13)

establishes the grave as a location that marks a definite end but also carries a financial connotation. As an adjective, "fine" derives from the Latin word for "finished"—pure, keen, perfected, delicate, and skillful—but as a noun, the word signifies a fee or penalty paid to be exempt from punishment. In the poem, the grave marks the perfected end of life only for those who are left undisturbed in repose. For the "Others [who] are History" (l. 14) it has a commercial value. For those who are subjected to the universalist claims of human patrimony and the nationalist claims of settler history, the grave is the site of appropriation, where punitive erasure is avoided only at the cost of exposure and public display. Erdrich's careful capitalization of "History" underscores the universalist claim to the significance of indigenous human remains; the capitalization of "Others" signifies not innocent difference but the active process of "othering" that produces the "Indian-as-enemy" cited by Kathleen Fine-Dare (14). The profundity of this settler-colonial need to "other" through appropriation is emphasized by the assonance of the poem's line endings—"sleep," "deeply," and "needs"—where depth is attributed to the ancestor's need for undisturbed repose in death but also applies to "science's creepy needs" (l. 9). Here, "creepy" links with the multiple meanings of "web" in the following line to sustain tension between the web or cycle of life and the settler-scientific epistemology that threatens it.

Complementing the rhetorical value of indigenous remains, the poem focuses relentlessly on the theme of financial value and the commodification of human bodies, culminating in a powerful final stanza. The careful management of verb tenses throughout the poem contributes significantly to the power of the conclusion. The poem begins in the conditional past ("would," "probably"), then moves into the conditional future tense (the repeated word "should"), the conditional present ("may"), and then shifts to imperatives ("must," "will"): "Someone will pay for this / Someone did" (ll. 17–18). "Pay" works doubly here: in the sense of remuneration and idiomatically as vengeance. The following lines are notable for the absence of verbs. However, in the lines "Her ivory grin worth / less than human curiosity" (ll. 19–20) the line break attributes to the term "worth" an ambiguous doubleness as both the individual word "worth" and the first syllable of the construction "worthless." The lines suggest that in one perspective, this ancestor's remains are only valuable as a curiosity; in another perspective the skull is worthless in comparison to the value of human knowledge and the global patrimony represented by "the rest of all humanity" (l. 21). Here, the double meaning of the word "rest" is made explicit; working as a verb in the penultimate line ("all humanity at rest," (l. 22) "rest" signifies resting in peaceful death. However, in the preceding line (21) "rest" works as noun and verb to signify repose and remainder or remnant. Thus, the lines signify doubly: either these indigenous human remains are worth less than all other humans—"the rest of all humanity"—or their sacrifice is worth the repose accorded to those who are "at rest" because their remains have been respectfully disposed. The double meanings in these lines work not just through the careful positioning of the end-stopped words but also through the poetic technique of chiasmus. The reversal of the terms "rest" and "all humanity" in the lines:

> less than the rest of all humanity,
> all humanity at rest. (ll. 21–22)

highlights the two meanings attributed to "rest" throughout the poem and forces the stresses in the final line to fall on the final two words "us all." This emphasis on "us" highlights the she/me, me/they, they/her oppositions in the first stanza but, more important, questions the identity of the poetic speaker and her identification with a collective "us" that cannot be the universal category of "humanity" critiqued as a product of settler-colonial thinking but a more inclusive humanity defined by Anishinaabe ways of seeing, knowing, and being in the world: *bimaadiziwin*.

Voicing the Dead

Throughout *National Monuments*, the issue of poetic voice dominates: who speaks for whom? How does speech inscribe monuments of all kinds into powerful cultural narratives of nation, tribe, community, and humanity itself? The very title of the poem "My Beloved Is Mine" raises the question of possessive claims made through language. The poem is spoken by the "husband" of an ancient indigenous "fossil," named Toumai by scientists, who question her status as a human (*National Monuments* 55). The form of the poem permits access only to the speaker's hermeneutic perspective. The second-person style of address does not give voice to the dead but adopts the position of speaking for the dead. Even as Toumai is spoken of, her presence is only implicit in what the speaker does and does not say. We are told, "She loved me—that I know" (l. 15), but whether and how he loved her is not said. What he sees in her is the expression of nothing but "love and urgency" (l. 6), an urgency that is later identified as her urgent sexual desire for him. The "tender moments" (l. 23) shared with her are juxtaposed with the bald statement "we / bred" (ll. 23–24), bringing into play the human/animal binary that marks his discourse.

Toumai has no voice; the voice of the poem, while profoundly lyrical, expresses a form of exceptionalism that goes beyond that of the nation-state to a species or human exceptionalism. The speaker uses the verbal register of savagery in relation to Toumai and a corresponding vocabulary of "the human" with respect to himself. This is suggested by the placement of the word "man" (l. 21) in the context of an uncontrollable eroticism attributed to Toumai: she is "helpless" in her "wild heat" (l. 20); the speaker describes his response as almost involuntary: "I could not help but be a man" (l. 22) by providing her with erotic "relief." She is described by him almost exclusively in corporeal terms: her hands, her lips, her height, "her tufts of fur" (l. 32). He addresses her in species terms: "*H. sapiens* I whispered, *H. floresiensis*" (l. 16) using the vocabulary of the scientists he later reproves for carbon-dating her remains. Their children he describes using an animalistic vocabulary: they are "mooncalves"—the abusive term applied to Caliban's monstrous deformity in Shakespeare's play—"young" and "whelps" (another term applied to Caliban) rather than children; they resemble lemurs and are the result of breeding ("we bred and brought forth young," l. 24). In *The Tempest*, Caliban regrets the failure of his attempted rape of Miranda because his desire to "people the island" is thereby frustrated. This allusion creates a sinister subtext in the subsequent lines: "we fed among the lilies, / while I peopled the island" (ll. 26–27). The speaker's shift from the plural pronoun to describe sharing food to the first-person singular to describe the nature of their sexual relations suggests that his putative elevation of himself in Toumai's estimation to that of a god ("her Zeus—her Jove," l. 3) exposes a will to domination and control that is also evidenced by his relentless inscription of her into canonical narratives of the Western European tradition. The speaker presents himself as the father of the race, locating their relationship at an evolutionarily historic bifurcation: they did not share ancestors, he explains, nor were their descendants separate. In his narrative, Toumai becomes Eve, but only to his Adam. There is a tone of arrogance, of species-based human superiority, in the speaker's words that lends ambiguity to his final eulogistic description of her: "She elevated me, made me my best, made me a man." Apart from the focus on what Toumai has given him, implicit is the suggestion that the contrast with her savagery is what made him "a man." Also implied is the suggestion that the children she bore, in the speaker's estimation, "made me my best" (l. 42). By producing "humans" she produced something of the utmost value—in the material human bodies of the children and in the status as "father of a race," which the speaker appropriates for himself.

Partly in reference to her allusions to Shakespeare, in her essay "National Monuments" (2008), Erdrich explains that the collection began "as a response to monuments of literature that use indigenous figures as metaphor." But her interests soon extended to the human body. Her view that "the body itself is the place of monument and has been treated as such by science as well as religion across cultures" ("National Monuments" 249) is contradicted by the violation of the body when transformed into a text for scientific or scholarly study: "The rules in place to protect our bodies when we die simply do not apply to anyone who has been dead long enough. That seeming contradiction troubles me and made me want to express my dis-ease learning that an ancestor's bones had been crushed for testing" (249). The political implications of Erdrich's questioning are made clear in her interview with Dylan Thomas for the *Southwest Journal*: "When Erdrich said her poems addressed bodies, she meant bodies both living and dead. In a series of what she called 'persona poems,' Erdrich gives voice to child mummies, Marie Antoinette and the 9,200-year-old Kennewick Man, all of whom have had their resting places disturbed. 'I want people to rethink their political view of the body,' she said. 'When is it ours? When is it no longer ours?'"[9]

The three poems that make up the "Kennewick Man" sequence are voiced directly by him, and each offers a distinct take on the incongruity of appropriating his ancient remains into the contemporary United States. "Kennewick Man Tells All" gives voice to Kennewick Man, but his direct speech is doubly embedded in modern discourses. In the epigram, the words of forensic anthropologist James Chatters are quoted from the *New*

Yorker (*National Monuments* 59); the poem then opens with the programmatic introduction of the press conference; only then does Kennewick Man speak. The visual irony of the poem lies in the fact that despite the promise that Kennewick Man will "tell all," the poem is dominated by other voices: four lines are devoted to Chatters, three to the anonymous host of the press interview, and only two to Kennewick Man himself. The poem plays on the fact that the more words given to a speaker, the more time that must be given to reading or listening to that speaker. An ironic tension is created between Chatters's claim that Kennewick Man has a story to tell and it would be wrong to repatriate his remains "without waiting to hear the story he has tell," and the interview, which is limited to "a brief statement" and questions "as time permits." This irony is heightened by Kennewick Man's reminder of the time he has at his disposal: "I am 9,200 years old." The incommensurability of worldviews captured in these ironies is underscored by the fact that Kennewick Man offers very little in the way of a "story" such as Chatters expects. The poem seemingly refuses to attribute to Kennewick Man a story beyond the known facts of his contemporary existence. The poem does not speculate; Kennewick Man is not ventriloquized by the poet. He speaks not of who he was in life but of what he has become in death.

Although Kennewick Man seems not to have a story and seems to speak only of facts, what he does utter in his two lines are seventeen syllables arranged in three sentences that present vivid images: age, bone, isolation. He offers no explicit commentary on these images, although the third sentence clearly provides a context for their interpretation. What I am suggesting is that Kennewick Man speaks in the form of a haiku or Anishinaabe dream song. The form—even more than the content—of his speech tells his story, which can be read in two ways, both of which lead to the same point. The Asian associations of the haiku evoke the theory of Native American origins as a migration narrative in which ancestors are said to have traveled across the Bering Strait land bridge from Asia to the Americas. As Erdrich points out in "The Theft Outright," that bridge "was a two-way toll" (l. 21, 31): the tradition of haiku could just as likely have traveled to Asia from communities like Kennewick Man's. Similarly, Kennewick Man's use of the tribal dream song form, when he is finally allowed the opportunity for self-expression, underscores the long, continuous cultural and physical presence of Native peoples on and in the land. Within the haiku/dream song, the three dominant images—particularly the perfect rhyme of "bones" and "alone"—tell a story of the consequences of appropriation for human remains: Kennewick Man is "alone" because after "9,200 years" his bones have yet to be repatriated to his community and properly restored to the cycle of life and death. In a museum vault, he is alienated from the land, the source of his being.

In the next poem in the sequence, "Kennewick Man Swims Laps," the eponymous speaker critiques the study of ancient human remains for evidence of Caucasian ancestry, which can be used to deny Native presence by supporting a narrative of "European indigeneity." The controversy over the ancestral claims to Kennewick Man's remains is well known, and I will not rehearse it here except to note that the US Army Corps of Engineers, acting under the provisions of NAGPRA, was ready to repatriate his remains to a coalition of tribes headed by the Colville when a group of scientists that included James Chatters and then the Asutru Folk Assembly (AFA) sued for the right to examine the bones to determine Kennewick Man's race. Suzanne Crawford has explained the AFA's focus on the putative Caucasian lineage of Kennewick Man to support their belief that "ancient Caucasians were in fact the first settlers of America, predating the ancestors of contemporary Native American tribes" (212). These efforts, Crawford points out, along with those of non-Native scientists, support a settler narrative of territorial occupation of indigenous homelands. Quoting Randall McGuire, she notes that Europeans appropriate Native heritages "for nationalistic and scientific purposes. Archeologists lifted dead Indians from their graves, in part, to help create a national heritage, and the myth of the vanishing Americans. By routing the red savages, the new, civilized white American race inherited the mantle, the heritage, of the old civilization and the legitimate claims to the land" (224). Kennewick Man references this conflict between "Tribes and pre-Christian Folk groups" (l. 19) over his "water-logged bones" (l. 20) but devotes an entire stanza to the Morris dancers whose putative Druidic origins place them among the pre-Christian groups that would appropriate him to their origin stories, to their heritage, and to their claims to prior "indigeneity." In Kennewick Man's words, it is only in the imagistic coincidence of the location of his corpse by a riverside and what he calls the "subversive" (l. 22) performance of the Morris dancers "along chilly urban river banks" (l. 23) that creates identity. As his meditation continues, he rejects not only the suggestion that they are his "kind" but that he can have any form of belonging: "There is no mine" (l. 27), he concludes.

The poem is punctuated with his repeated claims to being outside the temporal frame of organized religion: "older than prayer" (l. 8), "older than religion" (l. 14), "older than any name for God" (l. 28), so the identity marker "pre-Christian Folk" is meaningless. The first-person mode of address lends Kennewick Man a perspective that is both lived and immanent, historical and transcendent. In the poem he speaks for himself and all the appropriated dead whose bones comprise the "12,000 Native Americans . . . kept in drawers and cabinets under the swimming pool of the Hearst Gymnasium, next door to the museum" (*National Monuments* 60) at the University of California, Berkeley, as the poem's epigram reports. Their "watery voices" (l. 4) are reported in italicized direct speech (ll. 6, 7) to characterize Kennewick Man as both a listener and a speaker; yet he speaks directly in the present moment, occupying a discursive position that is both ancient and contemporary.

The confessional poem that completes the sequence, "Kennewick Man Attempts Cyber-Date," brings into comic relief these historical perspectives as he contemplates the prospect of online dating. Here the challenge of self-representation in the constraints of a bureaucratic form—"My age / My race / My God" (ll. 8–10)—highlights the lack of identity that is the consequence of appropriation. Divorced from a lived context, Kennewick Man cannot "fill all required fields" (l. 6). Yet he knows what he is not. He is not an "Authentic Indian" along the lines of the model that fills the absence of actual indigenous presence in the settler-colonial narrative. Juxtaposing a pop-cultural lexicon with his anthropological designation, he refuses stereotypes—"Not looking for 'Barbie and Kennewick Man'" (l. 4)—rather, he desires a living embodied presence. "But to smell a woman's neck again!" (l. 5) he exclaims. In this way, his words refute the identification made in the epigrammatic quotation from Chatters, the anthropologist who saw in the forensic facial reconstruction of Kennewick Man's skull the image of Captain Jean-Luc Picard of *Star Trek*.

Erdrich's Kennewick Man poems underscore the point made by Suzanne Crawford in relation to the controversy, that it is in "reading the various texts that have been inscribed on this body that *latent power relations* are made manifest" (213, emphasis added). Erdrich's manipulation of temporal perspective, the use of direct and indirect speech, her historical and contemporary allusions, and the formal construction of the poems work together to expose the relations of power inscribed in the narratives constructed around the remains of Kennewick Man and, by extension, all appropriated indigenous human remains. Crawford goes on to cite Larry Zimmerman's explanation of the distinct attitudes of Native and non-Native peoples toward the past:

> To Native Americans, the idea that discovery is the only way to know the past is absurd. For the Indian interested in traditional practice and belief, the past lives in the present. Indians know the past because it is spiritually and ritually part of their daily existence and is relevant only as it exists in the present.... When archeologists say that the Native American past is gone, extinct, or lost unless archeology can find it, they send a strong message that Native Americans themselves are extinct. (Crawford 214)

Conclusion

Diana Fuss has coined the term "corpse poem" to define a genre of predominantly Anglo-American poetry that gives voice to the cadaver, to "make dying 'Dying' once again. Speaking in the voices of the dead provides a way for poetry to make present a certain kind of absence" (25). Although Fuss offers a compelling account of non-Native literary expression in this mode, what is at stake for indigenous writers like Erdrich is not to reconstitute the material conditions of death. For the appropriated corpses of Kennewick Man, Toumai, the "Girl of Lightning," or the anonymous woman whose consciousness once lived in a skull auctioned on eBay, all that is left is materiality. Erdrich's poetic reanimation of these human remains serves only the wider purpose that Fuss attributes to twentieth-century corpse poetry: as "a critique of politics, history, or even literature itself" (3). By engaging the monuments of literature and the exceptionalist assumptions they disseminate through their literary rhetoric, by reanimating the stolen Native dead, Erdrich performs the radically subversive act of refuting the assertion that indigenous presence is a thing of the prehistoric past. She exposes the workings of exceptionalist rhetoric as a settler myth of origin that is grounded in the theft of Native bodies and material objects and in the attempted theft of indigenous stories. By locating her critique in the Anishinaabe ontology of *bimaadiziwin*, in Anishinaabe ways of seeing, knowing, and being in the world, she tells and shows the continuance of sovereign tribal cultures.

In this sense, Erdrich's "talking dead" exercise a form of "necropower": the corpse speaks to its own political significance and capacity to force epistemological change, by virtue of its status as a material corpse, as bones.[10] In the very different context of postcommunist practices of exhumation and reburial, Katherine Verdery addresses this issue of the political power of the dead. She notes that the management and display of the dead play a significant role in the marking of political change, whether a move to national or ethnic independence or, in the cases she discusses, the beginning of the postsocialist era. Diana Fuss, writing of Verdery's work, highlights "the two principal properties that make cadavers especially potent political symbols: their capacity to instill awe and respect and their capacity to instill fear and terror" (13). Applying Verdery's insights to political corpse poems, Fuss observes that these poems

> fall into two general categories: poems that deflate and poems that redeem. The first group humbles those corpses that have been culturally canonized, while the second group elevates those corpses that have been culturally debased. Both kinds of corpse poems aim to correct a social injustice—the politically opportunistic overvaluation of the dead on the one hand, and the no less calculated undervaluation of the dead on the other. (13)

Erdrich neither casts down nor raises up the Native dead. Rather, her indigenous corpse poetics works to recognize the fundamental humanity of the dead—and in that recognition lies the political power of these human remains. Repatriating by poetic proxy the appropriated remains of Native people to the proper discursive space of *bimaadiziwin*, Erdrich achieves the reconstitution of "culture + religion" without which tribal sovereignty cannot exist.

Rather than the literary genre of the corpse poem, a more productive description of Erdrich's achievement in *National Monuments* would be the concept of "situated knowledges" that Crawford, drawing on Donna Haraway's work, applies to the case of Kennewick Man. Generalizing from this case she proposes that

> situated knowledge grants the object of study her or his own subjectivity, the voice to speak, to provide situated vision not available to the scholar. . . . This means granting both living and deceased indigenous peoples both agency and subjectivity. It means treating Kennewick Man not merely as a bundle of bone to be radiocarbon dated and DNA to be deconstructed. It means facing the remains with the respect granted to a living human being, and it means granting Native peoples

the semiotic sovereignty to speak for themselves, as subjects and not objects; to provide their own equally valued notion of history, time, space, and ancestry. (232–33)

How does Erdrich achieve the affective power of situated knowledge of the dead? Through the powerful performativity of her poetry. Through those humorous moments, as in "Nefertiti's Close Up" (*National Monuments* 72–73), when Nefertiti compares the exposure of her body under a museum's unforgiving lighting to the dramatic moment of revelation on a TV reality show: the "make-over reveal" (l. 20); through the careful choice of poetic form (like the dream song/haiku); through the skillful use of poetic technique (like chiasmus); through the masterful placement of every word in precisely the right place in the line to create rhythms and rhymes that like the Girl of Lighting's shawl "weave threads" (l. 16), "weave cover" (l. 18), "pull stitches so that wound closes" (l. 20)—the "soul wound," the exceptional ontological wound inflicted by settler-colonialism, sutured and restored by the narrative threads of *bimaadiziwin*.[11]

Notes

1. See David Stirrup's detailed analysis of Carlson's painting in his essay, "*Aadizookewininiwag* and the Visual Arts," 303–6.

2. Throughout this essay, I draw on Patrick Wolfe's concept of settler colonialism as a process that is both eliminative and constructive: signs of indigenous occupation must be erased from the land so that a new settler nation can be constructed on that land. Mishuana Goeman uses Wolfe's concept to discuss *National Monuments* in a paper presented to the 2012 American Studies Association meeting; her abstract can be accessed at: http://citation.allacademic.com/meta/p569962_index.html.

3. On the history of the idea of Manifest Destiny, see Madsen, "The West and Manifest Destiny."

4. Gerald Vizenor develops the concept of the invented "Indian" most extensively in *Manifest Manners* (1994).

5. Crawford's essay, "(Re)Constructing Bodies: Semiotic Sovereignty and the Debate Over Kennewick Man" is cited by Heid Erdrich at the beginning of the "Author's Note" with which *National Monuments* concludes (93).

6. On the ambiguities of Frost's use of the terms "deed" and "deeds," see the summary provided by Jeffrey Gray in "The Dream of Possession."

7. See Derrida, *Given Time*.

8. Robert Dale Parker notes this quality of the land in a different context: "for Erdrich the land is not the passive object of Euroamerican manipulation, not feminine in that colonialist sense. Instead, . . . it has agency, and it has its agency not in Frost's past or future ('was' or 'would') but instead in the ongoing present ('is,' 'wills')" (78).

9. In fact, in "Girl of Lightning," the poet addresses the child mummy in the second person and in "Prisoner No. 280" describes the experience of Marie Antoinette in the third person.

10. On the concept of necropower, see the work of Achille Mbembe.

11. Eduardo Duran, Bonnie Duran, Maria Yellow Horse Brave Heart, and Susan Yellow Horse-Davis discuss the concept of the "soul wound" in the context of trauma in "Healing the American Indian Soul Wound" (1998).

References

Broker, Ignatia. *Night Flying Woman: An Ojibway Narrative*. Minneapolis: Minnesota Historical Society Press, 1983.

Crawford, Suzanne J. "(Re)Constructing Bodies: Semiotic Sovereignty and the Debate over Kennewick Man." In *Repatriation Reader: Who Owns American Indian Remains?*, edited by Devon A. Mihesuah, 211–36. Lincoln: University of Nebraska Press, 2000.

Derrida, Jacques. *Given Time: I. Counterfeit Money*, translated by Peggy Kamuf. Chicago: University of Chicago Press, 1992.

Duran, Eduardo, Bonnie Duran, Maria Yellow Horse Brave Heart, and Susan Yellow Horse-Davis. "Healing the American Indian Soul Wound." In *International Handbook of Multigenerational Legacies of Trauma*, edited by Yael Danieli, 341–54. Boston: Springer, 1998.

Erdrich, Heid E. "'Name': Literary Ancestry as Presence." In *Centering Anishinaabeg Studies: Understanding the World through Stories*, edited by Jill Doerfler, Niigaanwewidam James Sinclair, and Heidi Kiiwetinepinesiik Stark, 13–34. East Lansing: Michigan State University Press, 2013.

———. *National Monuments*. East Lansing: Michigan State University Press, 2008.

———. "National Monuments." *Museum Anthropology* 33, no. 2 (2008): 249–51.

Fine-Dare, Kathleen S. *Grave Injustice: The American Indian Repatriation Movement and NAGPRA*. Lincoln: University of Nebraska Press, 2002.

Frost, Robert. "The Gift Outright." In *The Poetry of Robert Frost: The Collected Poems, Complete and Unabridged*, edited by Edward Connery Latham, 348. New York: Holt, Rinehart & Winston, 1969.

Fuss, Diana. "Corpse Poem." *Critical Inquiry* 30 (Autumn 2003): 1–30.

Goeman, Mishuana. "Affective (Re)Mapping in Heid Erdrich's Poetic Disinterment of National Monumentalism." Paper presented at the 2012 American Studies Association Annual Meeting, San Juan, Puerto Rico, 2014.

Goetzman, Amy. "Poet Heid Erdrich Speaks Up for Sanctity of Human Artifacts in 'National Monuments.'" *MinnPost*, March 10, 2009. http://www.minnpost.com/arts-arena/2009/03/poet-heid-erdrich-speaks-sanctity-human-artifacts-national-monuments.

Gray, Jeffrey. "The Dream of Possession: Frost's Paradoxical Gift." In *The American Dream*, edited by Harold Bloom, 57–66. New York: Chelsea House, 2009.

Gross, Lawrence. *Anishinaabe Ways of Knowing and Being*. Burlington, VT: Ashgate, 2014.

———. "Bimaadiziwin, or the 'Good Life,' as a Unifying Concept of Anishinaabe Religion." *American Indian Culture and Research Journal* 26, no. 1 (2002): 15–32.

———. "Cultural Sovereignty and Native American Hermeneutics in the Interpretation of the Sacred Stories of the Anishinaabe." *Wicazo Sa Review* 18, no. 2 (2003): 127–34.

Hinsley, Curtis M., Jr. "Digging for Identity: Reflections on the Cultural Background of Collecting." In *Repatriation Reader: Who Owns American Indian Remains?*, edited by Devon A. Mihesuah, 37–55. Lincoln: University of Nebraska Press, 2000.

Krupat, Arnold. *That the People Might Live: Loss and Renewal in Native American Elegy*. Ithaca, NY: Cornell University Press, 2012.

Madsen, Deborah. "The West and Manifest Destiny." In *A Concise Companion to American Studies*, edited by John Carlos Rowe, 369–86. Malden, MA: Blackwell, 2010.

McNally, Michael D. *Ojibwe Singers: Hymns, Grief, and a Native Culture in Motion*. Oxford: Oxford University Press, 2000.

Parker, Robert Dale. "Another Indian Looking Back: A Review Essay on Recent American Indian Poetry." *Studies in American Indian Literatures* 22, no. 2 (2010): 75–85.

Rader, Dean. "The Theft Outright, A Poem by Heid Erdrich." *Weekly Rader*, December 19, 2008. http://weeklyrader.blogspot.ch/2008/12/theft-outright-poem-by-heid-erdrich.html.

Schweninger, Lee. "'Lost and Lonesome': Literary Reflections on Museums and the Roles of Relics." *American Indian Quarterly* 33, no. 2 (2009): 169–99.

Stirrup, David. "*Aadizookewininiwag* and the Visual Arts: Story as Process and Principle in Twenty-First Century Anishinaabeg Painting." In *Centering Anishinaabeg Studies: Understanding the World through Stories*, edited by Jill Doerfler, Niigaanwewidam James Sinclair, and Heidi Kiiwetinepinesiik Stark, 297–316. East Lansing: Michigan State University Press, 2013.

Thomas, Dylan. Interview with Heid Erdrich, "Sacred Sites: Heid Erdrich's New Poetry Book, 'National Monuments,' Explores the Landscapes of Spiritual Places." *Southwest Journal*, March 9, 2009. http://www.southwestjournal.com/node/13372.

Verdery, Katherine. *The Political Lives of Dead Bodies: Reburial and Postsocialist Change.* New York: Columbia University Press, 1999.

Vizenor, Gerald. *Manifest Manners: Narratives on Postindian Survivance.* Lincoln: University of Nebraska Press, 1994.

Wolfe, Patrick. "Settler Colonialism and the Elimination of the Native." *Journal of Genocide Research* 8, no. 4 (2006): 387–409.

Chapter 8

Anishinaabe Being and the Fallen God of Sun-Worshiping Victorians

CARTER MELAND

Gerald Vizenor created me as a thinker about Native writing.¹ The love affair he has with Naanabozho, the Anishinaabe trickster, dove down deep inside me and reached some kind of ground that helped me understand who I should be as a writer about Native writing.² That fascination touched the deep ground of me, grabbed a handful of it, and brought it to the surface.

    Vizenor's unapologetically complex critical and literary conception of Naanabozho as an ever-shifting, never fully knowable but always known spirit who lives in stories as a means to teach Anishinaabe people how to live as Anishinaabe people excited my imagination and stirred my blood.³ I needed to understand this Anishinaabe being to understand my critical interests. Vizenor's work introduced Naanabozho to me, and in the years since I have read articles and books and paid attention to stories about Naanabozho and tricksters from other tribal national literary traditions. As I moved through these works, I was at first enlightened, finding myself coming to richer understandings of the Anishinaabe trickster's creative-destructive, subversive-transgressive life. In the scholarly literature about this being, I found myself coming up against a critical limit. That is, I began to see that all these works referred to the same narrow band of citations to help determine what this being means; they treated Naanabozho and other tricksters as if they were questions with answers, rather than as beings with lives—and that those answers could be found in the interpretations of scholars like (primarily) Paul Radin and Carl Jung.

I saw a kind of detachment developing out of this critical limit. When I read critical works about tricksters in Native writing, I found most critics using Radin and Jung to elaborate a theoretical framework from which the tricksters in the literary works take meaning. In such works, "trickster" becomes an ointment applied topically (superficially?) to highlight a selected feature of a piece of Native literature.

While Radin's and Jung's works on tricksters may be thoughtful and speak of many significant philosophical and psychological ideas, there is little reflection on what tricksters mean to Native peoples. In the works that depend on them—in the works that dwell at this critical limit—we lose sight of Naanabozho's life as we find apparent answers that explain the meaning of his actions. We lose this Anishinaabe being; he is foreclosed on when rendered as a property in such a cultural matrix. Vizenor taught me how to worry about this foreclosure when he talked about "all the bad things anthropologists have said about the trickster," but he also encouraged me to see past the critical limit when he said, "the thing I want to emphasize about him in my experience and in my writing is that he is a liberator" (quoted in Blaeser 146–47). Anishinaabe being exceeds capture at critical limits, yet to understand Naanabozho's potential for liberation, we need to examine the attempts to capture him and understand their implications. What I undertake here is a discussion of a specific incident of literary historical capture: the creation of the trickster in modern discourse as a universal cultural object rather than an agent in the literary traditions of specific nations. I focus on the anthropological construct of the trickster and argue that understanding a particular case of literary abduction is necessary to appreciate what Anishinaabe writers (like Vizenor) are seeking to liberate themselves—and us, their readers and commentators—from. In the following pages, I look at Daniel Brinton's analysis of Michabo and Manibozho as this being is named in the differing Anishinaabe traditions that Brinton draws on. I examine Brinton's analysis to discuss the means by which tricksters are abducted from specific cultural meanings to the status of a universal archetype. This archetyping decultures the tribal trickster compelling his recuperation by Native writers as a liberation of indigenous meanings from "all the bad things . . . said about" him (quoted in Blaeser 146–47).[4]

To begin this discussion, I want to step outside Anishinaabe literature for a moment and tell a little story—perhaps it may serve as a parable—about another trickster, Coyote. Only it doesn't start with Coyote going along, as such stories often do. It starts with Lewis and Clark and their expedition of discovery.

Meriwether Lewis and William Clark were going along that summer in 1804, collecting data about the little known (to Americans) territory and recording the observations that would aid in the later American settlement of these Native lands. While making their way up the Missouri River along what is now the border of Iowa and Nebraska, they sighted something so mundane that it was only briefly mentioned in Clark's journal on August 12. He describes a bluff along the river, and here I am quoting his words just as they were written, which is "Covered with timber, a fiew red Ceeder is on this bluff, the wind coms round to the S.E. a *Prarie Wolf* come near the bank and Barked at us this evening, we made an attempt but could not git him, the animale Barkes like a large *ferce* Dog" (quoted in Thwaites 108).[5] A prairie wolf, *Canis latrans* (Latin for "barking dog"), is, as you have probably anticipated, Coyote,[6] and of course Lewis and Clark can only fail in their attempt to "git him" because their obligation to gather observations deafens them to Coyote's voice. They can only hear that he "Barkes like a large *ferce* Dog"; they cannot hear what Coyote is saying.

The impulse to "git" Coyote, as Clark puts it, to kill him, skin him, and maybe inventory the contents of his gut, all in an effort to understand him, is the same impulse that motivates Brinton in his analysis of Michabo and Manibozho. He wants to understand this being not by listening to him, but through careful analysis, and in doing so his work denies this being its beingness. Brinton finds himself trying to resolve what he sees as the conundrum at the core of Michabo's character. Why, Brinton wonders, are the stories of this "highest divinity" (163) burdened with tales of his "ludicrous failures" (162)?[7] In an attempt to "git him," Brinton remakes this Anishinaabe being in his own analytic image.

Brinton recorded his analysis of Michabo and Manibozho in *The Myths of the New World*. What puzzles Brinton is why this highest Anishinaabe divinity is spoken of as the Great Hare. "It is passing strange," he writes, "that such an insignificant creature as a rabbit should have received this apotheosis" (164). What, he wonders, leads a people to denigrate their own cultural hero and reduce him to a vain trickster who, in the process (regress?), morphs from a revered figure into a giant rabbit? Brinton continues, "No explanation of it in the least satisfactory has ever been offered" (164). He proposes to set this matter right through a linguistic analysis of what the nineteenth-century philologist Max Müller referred to as the "diseased language" of mythology (quoted in Stocking 60).

Brinton's analysis of Native story is informed by ideas of linguistic monogenesis sifted (in part) through a school of thought known as "solar mythology" or solarism. Solar mythology came out of the tradition of mid-nineteenth-century comparative philology promoted by thinkers like Müller and exercised by Brinton. Comparative mythology sought to develop a genealogy of the world's languages through linguistic analysis that would eventually get down to the one "true" language from which all others descended. Once the monogenetic basis of language was established, it would demonstrate, in Müller's words, that all of humanity were "children of the same father—whatever their country, their colour, their language, and their faith" (quoted in Stocking 59). As one of the primary advocates of this school of thought, Müller pushed its methods of analysis into what was then the "newly baptized field of folklore" (Dorson 25). The comparative philologists imagined a pure world hidden in the roots of language, and Müller applied these methods to linguistic explorations of mythology.

As George Stocking discusses in *Victorian Anthropology*, one of the great philological problems of the era was to find the "single community and race [that] existed at the base of the Indo-European linguistic tree." Müller was instrumental, through his practice of comparative mythology, in "propagating the notion of the 'Aryans' as the primitive ancestors of modern European civilized populations" (Stocking 59). He proposed to "reconstruct the life of the [in his words] 'primitive and undivided family of the Aryan nations'" through a method that came to be referred to as "linguistic paleontology" (Stocking 59).

Müller argued that the "Aryans,"[8] the nomadic horsemen of the ancient Near East, were the "primitive ancestors" who populated Europe and India, and their language was the base of the Indo-European languages. He further asserted that Aryan myth stood at the root of all religious feeling. Aryan myth was built around the "wonderment," in Müller's words, of the Aryan forefathers with the reenactment of the "whole solar drama . . . every day, every month, every year, in heaven and earth" (quoted in Stocking 60). For Müller, the "solar drama"—the daily (or annual) birth-death-rebirth of the sun—inspired the idea of the divine and underlay all religious traditions.

Linguistic paleontology examined the root form of words in Indo-European languages in an attempt to reveal the original Aryan meaning of a word. If the words in question had the same root form, Müller assumed it was, as Stocking explains, "part of the primitive Aryan heritage; any [word] for which there were two or more different roots must be a later innovation" (60). Müller argued that "whenever any word, that was at first used metaphorically, is used without a clear conception of the steps that led from its original metaphorical meaning, there is a danger of mythology; whenever those steps are forgotten and artificial steps put in their places, we have mythology, or if I may say so, we have diseased language" (quoted in Stocking 60). For Müller, mythology was a diseased language where what started as a metaphor in the Aryan original comes to be mistaken as a literal description as the "clear conception of the steps that led from its original to its metaphorical meaning" are lost (quoted in Stocking 60). Language was not corrupt, but forgetting the genealogy of a word could profane it. Mythology grew out of this disease of forgetting and, Stocking explains, "Müller argued all of Aryan mythology was built . . . on the observation of those natural phenomena that [in Müller's words] 'bear the character of law, order, and wisdom impressed in them'" (60). As discussed already, the natural phenomena of primary importance for Müller was the "solar drama" that excited the "wonderment" of the Aryan forefathers and inspired their creation of the (metaphoric) myths of the gods and heroes of the Indo-European tradition.

Müller's method of linguistic paleontology allowed him to interpret "Aryan mythology" by "making equations in the roots of names (Greek Zeus = Sanskrit Dyaus, from the verb *dyu*, to shine) and following out the solar pattern in each myth" (Stocking 60). This method could be applied to the myths concerning heroes as varied as Baldr, Sigurd, and Achilles. These characters share one of the solar patterns identified by Müller: that of the hero who dies in his youth. Müller wrote that this mythic theme was "first suggested [to the Aryans] by the Sun, dying in all his youthful vigor, either at the end of the day, conquered by the powers of darkness, or at the end of the sunny season, stung by the thorn of winter" (quoted in Stocking 60).

Müller's articulation of this theory in an essay titled "Comparative Mythology" "swept all the materials of British folklore," Stocking reports, "'into its orbit' [as a later commentator put it] for almost two decades" (60–61). What Müller provided was a method of linguistic analysis driven to support a theory that commentators now refer to as solarism.[9]

Solarism sought to demonstrate that humanity was an undivided family with a common religious understanding that had been buried under layers of diseased language. The ideals and methods of solarism drew British folklore studies "into its orbit" in the mid-nineteenth century, but others felt its pull as well, including American scholars like Daniel Brinton. In solarism, it was the scholar's job to take truth back from mythology, and Brinton used this method to unpack the truth hidden in the gut of the Great Hare of the Anishinaabeg.

Having established the monogenetic "solar orbit" as the context for Brinton's analysis of Michabo, we can now turn to his discussion of his ideas about this Anishinaabe being in *The Myths of the New World*. Brinton announces that in his book, "the inquiry will be put whether the aboriginal languages of America employ the same tropes to express such ideas as deity, spirit, and soul as our own and kindred tongues" (5). Although perhaps obvious, the phrase "our own and kindred tongues" refers to the languages of the Indo-European family, and it is Brinton's professed goal to seek comparisons between the linguistic stocks of Native America and those of the Indo-European family as a means of demonstrating that the monogenetic assumptions of human cultural origins are correct. Brinton writes, "If the answer [to this inquiry] prove affirmative . . . [there] arises evidence of the unity of our species far weightier than any mere anatomy can furnish, evidence from the living soul, not from the dead body" (5).

The living soul that is human language is more important than the physical evidence of the human body in the monogenetic premises that underlay solarist interpretations. Echoing Müller's ideas about mythology as a disease of language, Brinton writes, "Penetrated with the truth of these views . . . the race will be studied as a unit, its religion as the development of ideas common to all its members, and its myths as the garb thrown around these ideas by imaginations more or less fertile, but seeking everywhere to embody the same notions" (38–39). Taking this monogenetic premise justifies Brinton's investigation of Native peoples not as distinct nations and cultures but as "the race" (as stated in the quote). Establishing the monogenetic foundation of his analysis, Brinton advances other ideas crucial to his interpretive method. He writes, "As the dawn brings the light and with light is associated in every human mind the ideas of knowledge, safety, protection, majesty, divinity as it dispels the spectres of night, as it . . . brings forth the sun and the day, it occupied the primitive mind to an extent that can hardly be magnified beyond the truth" (91–92). Here he establishes the centrality of the "solar drama" to the "primitive mind" (which could here mean both the "American race" of Brinton's work and the "Aryan family" of Müller's work). Brinton underscores this assertion when he notes that coming from the east, "according to the almost unanimous opinion of the Indian tribes, [are] those hero gods who taught them arts and religion, thither they returned, and from thence they would again appear to resume their ancient sway" (91).

Although these premises seek unifying parallels between American and Indo-European languages, Brinton locates a problem in tribal languages that complicates the ability of tribal people to truly perceive the solar truth. The polysynthetic construction of a Native language like Anishinaabemowin, he explains, "seeks to unite in the most intimate manner all relations and modifications with the leading idea," in effect seeking "to express the whole in one word." He asserts, "Thus in many American tongues there is, in fact, no word for father, mother, brother but only for my, your, his father, etc. This offers marvelous facilities for defining the perceptions of the senses with utmost accuracy," Brinton admits, "but regarding everything in the concrete, it is unfriendly to the nobler labors of the mind, to abstraction and generalization" (7). Native languages are thus enormously capable of describing the world with an unmatched specificity that unfortunately also articulates the inability of Native people to truly understand their relation to the greater truth of the solar drama. Because their languages are rooted in concrete description, Brinton asserts that tribal languages are hard put to generate the "nobler" aspects of human thought. He regards Native peoples as being challenged because of their languages in their ability to generate abstract philosophical insights, and in this they lose, he writes, "the best part of their religion" (296).

Nowhere is this deficit more apparent than in the conception that the Anishinaabe have of their "supreme god," whether he is spoken of as Manibozho or Michabo (the two names from different Anishinaabe dialects that Brinton discusses). Brinton writes that throughout their range, the Anishinaabe "were never tired of gathering around the winter fire and repeating the story of Manibozho or Michabo, the Great Hare. [They all] spoke of 'this chimerical beast,' as one of the old missionaries calls it, as their common ancestor" (161–62). In the stories concerning Michabo, Brinton writes, "he seems half a wizzard [sic], half a simpleton. He is full of pranks and wiles . . . in short, [he is] little more than a malicious buffoon delighting in practical jokes, and abusing his superhuman powers for selfish and ignoble ends" (162). Though describing Michabo, the "common ancestor" of the people, in these less than flattering terms, Brinton means no disrespect because his analysis will reveal that these tales of Michabo's "ludicrous failures' are nothing but "a low, modern, and corrupt version of the character of Michabo" (162).

To see past this "low" and "corrupt" conceptualization, Brinton argues that to understand "What he [Michabo or Manibozho] really was we must seek [out] . . . the part assigned to him in the solemn mysteries of religion" (162). In the "solemn mysteries" of Anishinaabe tradition, Manibozho is spoken of as the founder of the *midewiwin* (the Anishinaabe medicine society) and of pictography, as well as the creator of the "habitable" world (162).

As noted earlier, what Brinton finds most puzzling is why this powerful culture hero is referred to as the "Great Hare." Pursuing this puzzle leads Brinton "to the suspicion that there may lurk here one of those confusions of words which have so often led to confusion of ideas in mythology" (164). With the Great Hare we are dealing with a conception of solar mythology (that is, the source of all "true" religious feeling), Brinton asserts, only it has been hopelessly confused (or diseased) by the Anishinaabe in their language, and the solar drama has changed into an oversized rabbit.

The source of this confusion can be rooted out, Brinton demonstrates, by exercising a bit of linguistic paleontology on the words *Michabo* and *Manibozho*. In Brinton's reading, Michabo is formed from the Algonquian words for "great" (*michi*) and "hare" (*wabos*) and Manibozho is formed from the words for "spirit" (*manitos*) and "hare" (*wabos*). "But looking more narrowly at the second member of the word," he writes, "it is clearly capable of another and very different interpretation . . . which discloses at once the origin and the secret of the whole story of Michabo, in the light of which it appears no longer the incoherent fable of savages, but a *true* myth" (164--65; emphasis added). (A true myth is the opposite of a false mythology.) The disclosure of "the secret of the whole story of Michabo" is found in "attentively examining" the root *wab* found in the word *wabos* (rabbit). Brinton writes that *wab* "gives rise to words of very diverse meaning . . . [and] that, in fact there are two distinct roots having this sound. One is the initial syllable of the word translated hare or rabbit, but the other means *white*, and from it is derived the words for the east, the dawn, the light, the day, and the morning" (165). Having asserted that *wab* is the root syllable for light, Brinton can complete the disclosure of the "whole story of Michabo" and its expression of the solar drama. Of *wab* he writes, "Beyond a doubt this is the compound in the names Michabo and Manibozho which therefore mean the Great Light, the Spirit of Light, of the Dawn, or the East, and in the literal sense of the word, the Great White One, as indeed he has sometimes been called" (165–66).[10] Once it is understood that *wab* refers to the east, to light, to *white*, Brinton holds that "all the ancient and authentic myths concerning him are plain and full of meaning" (166). In the "ancient" myths of Anishinaabe peoples, "Michabo is the spirit of light who dispels darkness," he "is the grandson of the moon, his father is the West Wind, and his mother, a maiden, dies in giving him birth at the moment of conception" (Brinton 166). Brinton glosses this summary of Michabo's family story in this way: "For the moon is the goddess of night, the Dawn is her daughter, who brings forth the morning and perishes herself in the act, and the West, the spirit of darkness as the East is of light, precedes and as it were begats the latter as the evening does the morning" (166). In light of these relations, it is little wonder that "in the oldest accounts of the missionaries," Michabo "was alleged to reside in the east, and in the holy formulae of the meda [*midewiwin*] craft [which Michabo founded] . . . the east is summoned in his name . . . and there . . . he has his house and sends the luminaries forth on their daily journies [*sic*]" (164).

That the Anishinaabe trickster made his home in the east and his name carries the root of the word *light* coupled with his birth out of the dying dawn suggests to Brinton the justness of his understanding of Manibozho. He notes, "As daylight brings vision, and to see is to know, it was no fable that gave him as the author of their arts, their wisdom, and their institutions" (168). The fabular "Great Hare" is a mask encrusted with generations of diseased language that the cunning linguist penetrates with his superior knowledge of the tongue, opening the word to its full and neglected wonder. The story of Michabo or Manibozho is, Brinton asserts, "a world-wide truth, veiled under a thin garb of fancy" (169). For Brinton, the story of the Great Hare is the story of "that beneficent Father who everywhere has cared for His children. Michabo, giver of life and light, creator and preserver, is no apotheosis of a prudent chieftain, still less the fabrication of an idle fancy or designing priestcraft, but in origin, deeds, and name the not unworthy personification of the purest conceptions they possessed concerning the Father of All" (169).

Across the Atlantic, Müller read Brinton's *Myths of the New World*. According to Dorson, Müller "happily . . . underscored Brinton's contention that Indian myths conformed to the world-view of early man everywhere, and in the etymology of 'wab' [Müller] saw the Algonkin counterpart of the Sanscrit word root *div* or *dyu* that produced [the Vedic] Dyaus and Zeus" (49). Although Dorson notes that Brinton declared "he was no slavish solar mythologist" (49), given the attention he puts on the light in Michabo's gut, Brinton still shared with Müller a vision of humanity's unity. In his analysis of *wab*, he arrives at a link that ties the "American race" of his analysis back to the Aryans that Müller posited as the source of the Indo-European language family. More important, Brinton's analysis restores Anishinaabe peoples and their "fabled" gods to the family of those who recognize the "Father of All," but have merely been led astray by their misunderstanding of their language. Brinton writes, "The Algonkins, who knew no other meaning for Michabo than the Great Hare, had lost, by a false etymology, the best part of their religion" (296). Unveiling the true etymology, Brinton is able to find a purer conception of the Father of All shrouded in the "thin garb of fancy" that is Anishinaabe mythology. Naanabozho stories are symbols of Anishinaabe confusion, rather than sources of ongoing cultural vitality.

In Brinton's discussion of the Anishinaabe trickster culture hero, we get the picture of a god fallen out of light and into a "low" and "corrupt" darkness through the degeneration of language. With this conceptualization of Michabo and Manibozho, we also get an implicit explanation of why Anishinaabe people will speak of the wonderful things this god provides while simultaneously addressing the "ludicrous failures" of this "selfish and ignoble" creature, who seems nothing more than a "malicious buffoon" (Brinton 162). In Brinton's analytic framework, the stories of Manibozho's "pranks and wiles" and their often "ludicrous failures" can be regarded as symptoms of Müller's disease of language. Just as *wab* will come to express "rabbit" rather than "light" over the course of generations, so will the stories concerning the "Father of All" come to be diseased. Stories expressing "true" religious feeling will come to be confused with "ludicrous" tales of Manibozho's misadventures, and Anishinaabe sacred history will become a conglomeration of religious truths and "idle fancies" as the Father of All becomes a low trickster as well as the source of all beneficence. In this analysis of Michabo's deterioration from the Great God of Light to the Great Hare, Brinton finds in the stories of the culture hero expressions of true religious understanding that have become diseased with trickster tales and so contain a trace of true but incorrect human spiritual knowledge. The anthropologist's task is to revitalize the truth hiding under the layers of false etymologies; their task is to save the Father of All from the Anishinaabeg.

Brinton's analysis recharges Michabo as the God of Light, smoothing out the complexities and ambiguities of this Anishinaabe being's character while excising complicating factors as a disease of language. By removing complications, Anishinaabe articulations of cosmological understanding can be demonstrated (by the en*wab*ened scholar) to contain a grain of the truth, even as they are recognized as degenerate. Brinton erases the multiplicitous nature of Michabo and Manibozho as he reveals the light that is the truth at the core of this Anishinaabe's being.

My argument is not with the linguistic analysis Brinton undertakes. For all I know, his analysis of the root forms of *wab* in Anishinaabemowin are right on target. I do not argue that "light," "enlightenment," and an emphatic relationship to the east as the source of light are not important in Anishinaabe spiritual practice. Instead, my argument is with the notion that there is some universal means one can use to measure whether a people have a clear conception of "true religious feeling." Such universalist impulses denigrate indigenous teachings, obliterating them with bombastic blasts of light. As stated earlier, for the solarists, it was the scholar's job to take truth back from the diseased language of mythology. But Vizenor in his—yes, I'll say it—trickster fashion asks us, through his example, to invert this equation and take mythology back from the disease of universal truth-making. He asks us to take Anishinaabe meaning back from reductionist truths that eclipse Anishinaabe being—as muddled, enlightened, contradictory, ludicrous, and complex as it may be—in favor of the "true religious feelings" of a universalized humanity. A universalized conception of humanity—a focus on those truths that unite people across cultural lines—denies the claims of indigenous peoples to their unique cultural, political, and spiritual ways of life, especially when those truths are used to assess others (the Anishinaabeg!) as having a degenerate, fabular, or diseased form of religious feeling.

Why look at an obscure, nearly forgotten scholar from the nineteenth century then? Why look at an abduction that took place over a century and a half ago and seemingly never had an effect on succeeding generations?[11] We need to look at such events not for what they are or were but for the paradigms they propound. Brinton does not originate a universalist mode of thinking that abducts Anishinaabe meanings from Anishinaabe lifescapes, but in our attention to his ideas and ideals, we can read other universalist assumptions that were used to dispossess Anishinaabe and other indigenous peoples of their lands, languages, and literary traditions. In our attention is the liberation of Anishinaabe being from universalist paradigms that excise indigenous ideals as "diseased."

In his focus on the universal, Brinton fails to ask what Naanabozho means to Anishinaabe people. Instead, he declares what Manibozho means to all people, to the world culture of "true religious feeling," and to a solar dream of human unity. He ignores this Anishinaabe being's sovereignty and assumes—nay, asserts—that this being arose thousands of miles away, at the remove of countless generations, in a land as different from the woodland homes of Anishinaabe peoples as Naanabozho is from, say, Jehovah. The theory Brinton uses to unveil the truth within Naanabozho's gut leads to (in Vizenor's words) "bad things" being said about this powerful figure.[12]

Voiding indigenous claims to aboriginal lands is one of the methods that European and Euro-American peoples exercised in their colonization of Native homelands. Brinton's revelation of the light in Manibozho's gut and stripping that light of its Anishinaabe meanings symbolically removes Anishinaabe peoples from their indigenous homelands, lifting them out of the North American woodland and transporting them by this trace of light to the plains of the Near East from which the Aryans were said to people Europe. Excising the diseased elements, the enlightened scholar masters the indigenous, Anishinaabe meanings of Naanabozho, erasing the ambiguities in the stories as a means of revealing the light that is the truth in the trickster's gut.

If Manibozho is Zeus is Dyaus, the Anishinaabe are related to the Aryans, and if the Anishinaabe are descendants of the Aryans, just as the Angles and Saxons are, then the European colonization of indigenous lands and lives is moot. Colonization is not just or unjust, it is merely the rejoining of the many families of the Near Eastern plains. Although in later life he entered the debates on tribal American origins and ultimately settled on Europe as the source of the aboriginal migrations into North America,[13] Brinton makes no claims about the relation of his work and what I perceive as its ameliorative effect on the Euro-American colonization of Native America. I take note of this idea because I find it interesting that in terms of the United States's "Indian Problem," the 1870s—the era immediately after Brinton's *Myths of the New World* was published—are dedicated to two of the most wide-reaching and devastating programs to assimilate Native people to the universal standards of "civilized" people. I am speaking of the Allotment Act and the federal boarding school program. Brinton's monogenetic analysis connecting Anishinaabe people back to a true, if dim, perception of the proper religion of humanity might be seen to allay any contemporary American feelings of guilt that these devastating policies may have evoked. Brinton's analysis might be seen to allay guilt because what he reveals is that indigenous people like the Anishinaabe lost the clear sight of the truth—of enlightenment—and thus need to be returned to the right path. His analysis can be seen as assimilating Manibozho and Michabo to the real truth; in their assimilation to (ultimately) the Aryan strain, Michabo and Manibozho disappear—just as Native languages will in boarding schools and communal title to land will under the Allotment Act (to say nothing of the vast tracts of indigenous homeland that are also lost).

Native writers and scholars and their allies have the task of liberating indigenous ideas and truths from the straitjackets, such as the one crafted by Brinton, that suppress (in this case) Anishinaabe meanings. Although this book was written in 1868 and might not seem immediately relevant to the study of contemporary Native writing, its universalizing and deculturing impulses continue to surface. In the 1950s, anthropologist Paul Radin, like Brinton, smoothed out what he perceives to be the ambiguities in the Ho-Chunk trickster cycle, theorizing that the myth enacts an archetypal narrative of psychological development, and so the stories as he received them are in the wrong order.[14] By the end of his influential book, the Ho-Chunk narrators of Wakdjunkaga's teachings disappear as Radin's insight into the text's universal meaning is asserted. Carl Jung weaves a discussion of the trickster out of Radin's work, asserting that it is an expression of the collective unconscious that is really not so distant in expression from the ideal of the primitive Aryan unity we find in solarism. Contemporary New Age writers and teachers spin off from Jung and encourage us to embrace the Trickster within (by now capitalized, as it is universalized) and never mention the indigenous peoples whose intellectual property they are appropriating.[15]

When we return to the question of what we need liberation from, it should be clear that we need liberation from universal theories that erase Manibozho to find the "Trickster." In the process of that erasure, Anishinaabe people are rendered invisible as well. Anishinaabe writers like Vizenor who use Naanabozho in their works undo this erasure, replacing the universal Trickster with indigenous—and, I should add, sovereign—tricksters that exist in specific relationships to specific homelands and the specific peoples who call that land home. By being in the stories, tricksters help their people realize who they are and how they should live; they are indigenous to particular places and particular voices. Tricksters in Anishinaabe writings like Vizenor's are rejoinders to universalist theories that would reduce Manibozho to a pile of ash in a flash of light rather than see him as the powerful ground of Anishinaabe being. Even if the solarists and their successors are blind to this reality, Naanabozho is as much earth as light.

We might find a similarly powerful rejoinder in the parable I shared earlier. Like Brinton and Radin and Jung, Lewis and Clark fail to "git" Coyote when they see him along the river. They shoot at him and compare his voice to that of "a large *ferce* Dog," but they neglect to listen to what he might have to say about their attempt to understand him to death.

Notes

1. Of course, Vizenor did not create my critical obsessions with humor, the subversion of dominant paradigms, and subversive humor alone. He wasn't even the first to inspire me. The Marx brothers and S. J. Perelman taught me the joys of subversive wit—of the power of saying no to the inane and the absurd with language loaded with irony, puns, double entendre, and non sequitur, as did Monty Python. Leslie Silko turned me on to Native writing—giving voice to my alienation from the witchery of the American nuclear nation of the 1980s (when I read *Ceremony* for the first time). Silko, a writer rarely celebrated for her humor, hid a simple ironic joke at the heart of her many-layered novel that continues to delight me: Tayo—the Indian—is a cowboy, but one who avoids riding off into any sunsets (think the opening and closing words of the novel: "Sunrise"). Of course, it took Thomas King to introduce me to Vizenor, but only after he had introduced me to Momaday, Bullchild, McNickle, and Erdrich, among others (not the least of whom was himself). It may be overstating things to say that Vizenor created me as a thinker about Native writing, but his work has provided much direction for me.

2. Naanabozho creates the world in Anishinaabe sacred histories. The previous world has been flooded (as a result of Naanabozho's actions), and as he floats on a log or stands atop a white pine, he sends his animal brothers down into the flood, promising that if they bring up some earth from the world below, he will make a new world for them all to live on. The humble muskrat succeeds, and from the few grains of earth clutched in his paws and his mouth, Naanabozho makes this world. See Benton-Banai (29–34) and Vizenor (8–9) for versions of this story that, although differing in detail, share similar overall arcs.

3. Naanabozho has differing names in differing parts of the Anishinaabe world. Wenebojo, Nanapush, Nanabush, Menabojo, Manibozho, and Michabo are just a few of the variants.

4. The recuperation I discuss is limited to the word wars of the printed page. I assume that Naanabozho needs no such recuperation in the voices of Anishinaabe people.

5. I preserved Clark's original spelling, sentence structure (or lack thereof to our ears), and peculiar emphases on "Prarie Wolf" and "ferce" in the quote.

6. See Dobie 8 and 32–34 for more on the coyote's various names.

7. Though my bibliography contains three books by Brinton, the only one I refer to in the body of this essay is *The Myths of the New World*. All parenthetical citations to Brinton in the body of the essay refer to pages in that book and no others.

8. Müller used the term "Aryan" to refer to, in Stocking's phrase, "a community of language and race" (59). His solar mythology seemed to propose a kind of universalist notion that humanity were all one, with no "race" being greater or lesser than another, yet Stocking finds that in many passages Müller waxes rhapsodic in a manner that is "resonant of Aryanist racial ideology" (59).

9. See Dorson for an extensive discussion of the rise and fall of solarism.

10. With the assertion that Michabo and Manibozho are best translated as the "Great White One," you may be tempted to hear echoes of the conventional translation of the Aztec culture hero Quetzalcoatl. You are correct, in Brinton's point of view, to hear this echo. In later work, he explores this theme of the Great White One and its relation to Quetzalcoatl. See Brinton, *American Hero-Myths*.

11. Lee Baker explores Brinton's importance as a scholar during his lifetime and his lack of impact after his death in "Daniel G. Brinton's Success on the Road to Obscurity, 1890–1899."

12. As I finished typing this paragraph, the song that popped up on the shuffle mode of my iTunes was "I Don't Buy Your Shit No More" by those pioneers of avant-gardist "krautrock," Faust. *Miigwech* to the "Great God of Light" for his excellent DJ work!

13. In his 1891 volume, *The American Race*, Brinton tackled at length the question of how tribal people arrived in the Americas. He dismisses the Bering Strait theory, arguing that the Aleutian islands "were peopled from America, and not from Asia," adding that in fact all movements "have been *from* America into Asia, the Eskimos pushing their settlements along the Asian coast" (20, emphasis in original). Brinton asserts, that during an inter-glacial period of the late Pleistocene a huge geologic event resulted in the uplift of the earth's crust in the north Atlantic that had the effect of connecting Western Europe and North America. He argues that this land bridge provided humanity with its opening to the Western hemisphere. He writes that "the conclusion seems forced upon us that the ancestors of the American race could have come from no other quarter than Europe" (32). In light of my discussion of Brinton's participation in the debates surrounding monogenesis, it should be no surprise that we end up back in Europe when we look for the origin of Native peoples, because that is where their gods, like Michabo, ultimately come from.

14. See Radin. On pages 132–46 he offers an extensive discussion of how to reorder the stories his informant shared with him to make this arc of

psychological development more clear. It almost as if he thinks the order of the stories is diseased in that Müller sense of the word.

15. See Chinen and Mazis for representative New Age-ist engagements with the "Trickster," which is invariably referred to as "Native American" (a universalist category in such works that eliminates the need to understand the differences between Anishinaabe and Ho-Chunk peoples, for instance).

References

Baker, Lee D. "Daniel G. Brinton's Success on the Road to Obscurity, 1890-1899." *Cultural Anthropology* 15, no. 3 (2000): 394-423.

Benton-Banai, Edward. *The Mishomis Book: The Voice of the Ojibway.* Hayward, WI: Indian Country Communications, 1988.

Blaeser, Kimberly M. *Gerald Vizenor: Writing in the Oral Tradition.* Norman: University of Oklahoma Press, 1996.

Brinton, Daniel. *American Hero-Myths: A Study in the Native Religions of the Western Continent.* 1882. New York: Johnson, 1970.

———. *The American Race: A Linguistic Classification and Ethnographic Description of the Native Tribes of North and South America.* New York: N.D.C. Hodges, 1891.

———. *The Myths of the New World.* 1868. Baltimore: Clearfield, 1992.

Chinen, Allan B. *Beyond the Hero: Classic Stories of Men in Search of Soul.* New York: Putnam's, 1993.

Dobie, J. Frank. *The Voice of the Coyote.* Lincoln: University of Nebraska Press, 1961.

Dorson, Richard M. "The Eclipse of Solar Mythology." In *Myth: A Symposium*, edited by Thomas A. Sebeok, 25-63. 1955. Bloomington: Indiana University Press, 1965.

Jung, Carl. "On the Psychology of the Trickster Figure." In Paul Radin, *The Trickster: A Study in American Indian Mythology*, 193-211. New York: Schocken Books, 1956.

Mazis, Glen A. *The Trickster, the Magician, and Grieving Man: Reconnecting Men with Earth.* Santa Fe: Bear, 1993.

Radin, Paul. *The Trickster: A Study in American Indian Mythology.* 1956. New York: Schocken Books, 1972.

Stocking, George W. *Victorian Anthropology.* New York: Free Press, 1987.

Thwaites, Reuben Gold, ed. *Original Journals of the Lewis and Clark Expedition, 1804-1806.* Vol. 1, 1904. New York: Antiquarian Press, 1959.

Vizenor, Gerald. *The People Named the Chippewa: Narrative Histories.* Minneapolis: University of Minnesota Press, 1984.

IV
Nanabozho

Chapter 9

Beyond the Borders of Blood
An Anishinaabe Tribalography of Identity

JILL DOERFLER

Tribalography
quantum leap
revolution and evolution
weaving and writing
new worlds and old
keyboard drumming
indelible marks on the page
take shape
come together
like a sweetgrass basket
blade words
twirl together
circle around
form something whole
transform life

The Overture

This is a tribalography—not completely fiction or history but a story that draws on the past, present, and future; documents and imagination; the spaces between reality and rumors of memory (Howe 42). Choctaw scholar LeAnne Howe created the term "tribalography" to explain her observation that "Native stories, no matter what form they take (novel, poem, drama, memoir, film, history), seem to pull all the elements together of the storyteller's tribe, meaning the people, the land, and multiple characters and all their manifestations and revelations, and connect these in past, present, and future milieus (present and future milieus mean non-Indians)" (Howe 42). In this essay I use tribalography as a methodology and connect multiple elements in a textual weaving that constructs an Anishinaabe tribalography. As an Anishinaabe tribalography,[1] this work follows in the tradition set forth by Gerald Vizenor and Gordon Henry Jr., who, as Kimberly Blaeser asserts, "shift and reshift their stories' perspectives, turn the tables of historical events, unmask the stereotypes and racial poses, challenge the status of history's heroes and emerge somewhere between the probable and the possible, in some border area of narrative" (Blaeser 39). Likewise, I hope this tribalography will "incite the reader to an imaginative reevaluation of both the accounts and processes of history" (Blaeser 43). Maybe this essay will rise up among the Anishinaabeg and bring us new understandings of ourselves, our families, and our nation.

This tribalography is also a Native survivance story.[2] Vizenor asserts: "Native survivance stories are renunciations of dominance, tragedy, and victimry. Survivance means the right of succession or reversion of an estate, and in that sense, the estate of native survivancy" (*Manifest Manners* vii). This survivance story explores the varied ways the Anishinaabeg of White Earth defined their identity in the early twentieth century. I explore their creative and persistent resistance to the US government's attempt to racialize their identity. They refused the terminal dominance of race and insisted on succession. In addition, my goal is to immerse the reader in a story that extends beyond history and focuses on the people. Vizenor has asserted: "In the past the tales of the *anishinabe* were not an objective collection of facts. The *oshki anishinabe* writer tells stories now was in the past—stories about people, not facts" (Vizenor, *Everlasting Sky* 69). Indeed, this story is about people, not facts.

I have organized this essay two primary parts.[3] In part 1 I go beyond the "facts" to enliven the (hi)story,[4] to offer an alternative way of remembering the past. In this section, I have created several characters and collapsed events, but I draw heavily on historical interviews. I use many direct quotes and highlight all direct quotes with the use of italics. This section also includes historical photographs that provide an additional element of framework for the construction of the tribalography. In part 2, I offer a typical academic presentation of the "facts," including details about federal and state legislation as well as a scholarly analysis of the interviews. The two parts of this story create a weaving by pulling together a wide variety of sources, including primary documents, secondary sources, photographs, and the works of other storytellers.

Part 1

Niibidoon: "Weave Something"

In late July 1913 the sun shone brightly, heating the air to 84 degrees.[5] Ivy Giizhig gathered with the other Anishinaabe women in the cool air of the basement of St. Columba's to make sweetgrass baskets and listen to the words of Father Vincent.[6] The women welcomed the coolness of the stone basement and the company of others.

Ivy smoothed her long, dark blue skirt after taking a seat next to her best friend, Suzette Spruce. As usual, the priest was very intent on talking about the burning fires of hell that awaited nonbelievers. Few of the women were actually concerned with the afterlife the priest discussed, but they nodded their heads in silence, knowing full well the economic value his approval brought. Last Christmas each family had received a wool blanket, three pounds of coffee, and a small bag of sweets for the children as payment for their devotion to Christ.

After what seemed like forever to Ivy, Father Vincent finally left the women for other obligations. The room came to life as the women began to talk with each other while they worked. Suzette dampened the sweetgrass to make it pliable. She watched the water easily transform the sweetgrass from brittle and dry to supple and sinuous.

Ivy took the latest edition of the *Tomahawk* out of her purse and pointed out the article on land policies to Suzette. It stated that scores of people at White Earth had "sold" their allotted lands but that many of these so-called sales involved coercion and outright lies (Meyer, *White Earth* 153–60). Of course, Ivy knew that this was not really news to

St. Columba Episcopal Church and congregation, White Earth. Photographer: Robert G. Beaulieu, Photograph Collection ca. 1905, Location no. E97.7W r37, Negative no. 6443-A, Minnesota Historical Society. http://collections.mnhs.org/cms/display.php?irn=10576534.

Pembina band Indian girl, White Earth Reservation. Inspiration for Ivy Giizhig. Photograph Collection ca. 1897, Location no. E97.1 p33, Negative no. 91192, Minnesota Historical Society. http://collections.mnhs.org/cms/display.php?irn=10688824.

Press room of the 'Tomahawk weekly newspaper at White Earth.'" Photographer: Robert G. Beaulieu. Photograph Collection ca. 1910, Location no. HC1.11 r6, Negative no. 6487-A, Minnesota Historical Society. http://collections.mnhs.org/cms/display.php?irn=10813663.

Suzette. Suzette had sold her allotment over a year ago because she had four younger brothers and her family had been struggling to keep food on the table. Every day for weeks, an aggressive man wearing a brown suit had come by asking if she was ready to sell. Finally, out of sheer desperation, she signed the paper. The meager amount of money she received had only been enough to pay her family's debt at the Fairbanks Store and purchase enough flour for three months. She deeply regretted her decision, but it was sell or starve.

Ivy's brother had been told that the paper he signed was to rent his land, only to find out later that it was actually a bill of sale. He was trying to challenge the "sale," but Simon Michelet, the Indian agent, had warned him not to hope for much. Ivy's allotment had just been seized by the state because she had never paid the taxes on it.

"How can the state tax lands that are not theirs?," Ivy asked bitterly as she twisted the moistened sweetgrass together and began to create the bottom of a basket.

"It seems like they just do whatever they want," Suzette sighed as her lips turned into a frown.

Ivy stopped to examine her work. The basket was taking shape; the spiral coil that formed the bottom was complete. The uneven colors of green, yellow, and tawny contrasted just enough to complement each other. "My brother George just found out that he might be able to overturn his land sale if he can prove he is full-blood. Rumor has it that the United States government has made a law that says that people who are full-bloods are not allowed to sell their land, but he hasn't figured out exactly what they mean by full-blood yet. I told him this has nothing to do with blood! He was lied to about the paper he signed. This business about blood is just plain nonsense," Ivy said.

"Hmmm," said Suzette. "The ideas that those Americans come up with are so strange—I have never heard anything about that." she said, shaking her head with annoyance.

"I think they made up this idea of mixed-blood and full-blood just to try and get more land from us. My cousin Mikinaak said that there is no such thing as a mixed-blood." Ivy admired the shades of green and yellow of each blade as she added new ones to the basket. She had quickly woven nearly half a basket during their short conversation and she held it out in front of herself to see how it was taking shape. The once disparate blades of sweetgrass had transformed into a round basket. The red thread she used to stitch the coils of sweetgrass to each other formed veins around the basket, holding it together.

"Well, I hope he is right," said Suzette. Little did she know that there was already a plan in place to protect the swindlers and buyers.

Aabaabiigin: "Unravel Someone (as in Something String-like)"

Attorney Ransom Powell was appointed by the United States to investigate the genealogy of the Anishinaabe families and determine which were "mixed-bloods."[7] It was a crisp fall day when he arrived with his assistants. The pines held their unchanging form, but only a few golden leaves clung tightly to the branches of the tall birch trees. Rumors swirled like dry leaves around the reservation; Ivy heard that they would set everything straight and the illegally taken allotments would be returned, but she wasn't convinced.

Meanwhile, the investigators were already asking questions at the agency. Michelet had set up a room in the back for them to work in.

R. J. Powell, a lawyer, possibly at White Earth and three Indian women. Photograph Collection ca. 1910, Location no. E97.1 r206, Negative no. 91623, Minnesota Historical Society. http://collections.mnhs.org/cms/display.php?irn=106 89927.

He had a table for Powell and his associates to sit behind while the person they were interviewing sat in a wooden chair a few feet in front of them. A small picture window let in enough light. Suzette and Ivy joined the crowd gathered in the back of the room, curious to watch the proceedings.

Powell had already explained to several Anishinaabe witnesses that "full-blood" meant someone with no white blood, no white ancestors.

Amik was on the stand.

"Amik, will you please state your age and place of residence?" Powell asked.

"I was born just about the time of the 1867 treaty. My grandfather signed that treaty. You can go and look up his name. I am a Mississippi Indian. I have lived most of my life right here around the White Earth Village."

White Earth Chippewa Indians. Inspiration for Amik. Photograph Collection 1885, Location no. E97.1 p34, Negative no. 86835, Minnesota Historical Society. http://collections.mnhs.org/cms/display.php?irn=10761959.

"There were quite a number of people living around in your neighborhood at that time who were known to have some white blood, is that true?" Powell charged.

"Yes."

Perfect, thought Powell, now I have him right where I want him. "And when you speak of these people as being of that kind, are you stating that from something you know of their family, or from your general observation of the comparison between them and these others that you know to be mixed-bloods?"

"Well, I should go by my observation and the looks of themselves and their children. You see, at that time there was no such thing—there was no distinction amongst the Indians, full-bloods or mixed-bloods; it is only within the last few years that that has come up," Amik answered.

"They all lived in the same manner?"

"All lived in the same neighborhood; that is, they were all related, you know in groups."

A wide smile came across Powell's lips, he knew this was his chance. "*Many of those*—Isn't this true, that many of those who were known to have white fathers were living as Indians and considered in the tribe as Indians, just as though they had no white father?" he asked accusingly.

"*Yes sir,*" Amik nodded.[8]

"Thank you, Amik; that will be all." Powell was pleased; getting Amik to admit that there were many Anishinaabeg who were biologically mixed-blood was a big step. So many others had been unable to understand what he was trying to ask them. Powell placed a big check mark next to Amik's name and looked for the next witness.

"Will Alice Chi-Makwa please take the stand."

Alice walked forward with confidence. Her hair was pulled back into a tight bun, accentuating the sharpness of her nose. Her young son, Migizi, was sleeping peacefully in a cradleboard on her back.

"Isn't it true that your husband, Gordon Chi-Makwa, was a mixed blood?"

Alice vehemently shook her head. "*He was a full-blood. He made himself a full-blood.*"

Powell raised his eyebrows with suspicion. "*You mean he made himself a full-blood by living like the Indians live?*"

"*Yes, sir, he did not even take a paper to sign as a mixed-blood,*" Alice smiled.[9]

Powell could not believe what he was hearing; what was this woman thinking? Obviously, she had no idea what he was talking about. Her suggestion that her husband could manipulate and control his identity was laughable.

Powell moved on to the next witness, Minogeshig. Minogeshig locked eyes with Powell as he walked toward the front of the room. His dark hair was smoothed back behind his ears, and he wore a black suit.

"Do you know what we mean by a mixed blood Indian?"

"No. No, there was no mixed bloods," Minogeshig answered.

"The question I asked was, do you know what we mean when we say a mixed blood Indian?"

Chippewa woman and baby, White Earth. Inspiration for Alice Chi-Makwa. Photograph collection 1902, Location no. E97.33 r23, Negative no. 31242, Minnesota Historical Society. http://collections.mnhs.org/cms/display.php?irn=10463882.

Minogeshig narrowed his eyes as he responded, "*No; I just stated that I do not know that; I don't understand that word.*"

Powell explained, "*When we say mixed blood Indian we mean that there has been some white blood or other blood mixed with the Chippewa blood?*"

Minogeshig nodded, "*Yes, sir.*"

"*And when we say full blood Chippewa Indian we mean that the Chippewa has not been intermingled with the blood of any other race?*"[10]

"I understand."

"Now, what I want to know is, is Suzette Spruce a mixed-blood?"

Ivy reached out and grasped Suzette's delicate hand at the mention of her name. Suzette was sure she felt her heart skip a beat and held her breath.

"No, she is a full-blood. Her family was part of a group of Ottertail Pillagers that established themselves around the Pine Point area" (Meyer, *White Earth* 49).

Powell was skeptical about Minogeshig's claims and asked a follow-up question to try to get him to admit that Suzette might be a mixed-blood. *"Your statement that she had nothing but Indian blood is based upon the fact that she looked and lived like an Indian, isn't that true?"*

"Yes, sir," Minogeshig admitted. "That is all I know. Suzette's family moved to Pine Point many years ago."

Powell knew he had him. *"If she had a small amount of white blood, coming from (her) grandfather or grandmother, you would not know anything about it, would you, unless it showed in her face?"*

"No, I would not know anything about it."[11]

Powell was pleased with himself. Finally he was getting somewhere with these people! "Thank you for your testimony, Minogeshig. You may step down."

Suzette's mind raced; she didn't know what to do. She knew Minogeshig had done his best, but she worried about what his testimony would mean for her and her family. Would she ever get her allotment back?

"Are you alright?" Ivy whispered.

"I guess so, but I am not going to let this be the end of it. I will testify myself. I'll tell them that I was never paid properly and so I want the land back, mixed-blood or not has nothing to do with it."

"Next, I would like to interview Gekek," Powell announced.

Gekek's presence always commanded attention. He was just over six feet tall, and his face had strong, chiseled features. His good looks made the old ladies shoot sideways smiles and raised eyebrows to each other. His golden brown eyes locked with Powell's as he took his seat.

"Now, I want to ask you some questions about Martin Black. Some people have already testified that he is a mixed-blood. We have already heard accounts that Martin is lighter than the other Indians. Would you agree that Martin is a mixed-blood?" Powell began.

"Let me tell you how I saw him. He used to build a teepee a distance from the other teepees and call other warriors to follow him, and he went forth in the quest of the enemy. Are those the deeds of a mixed blood?"

Powell was annoyed. Why couldn't these Indians just answer a few simple questions with the facts! He tried to redirect the questioning back to the genetic ancestry of Martin. *"He was lighter complected than the other Indians, wasn't he?"*

"I could not say whether he was lighter than the others because it is so long ago. I cannot recollect. I used to see him swallow bones about that long [indicating] in his incantation for eliminating sickness among other fellow men. Is this the practice of a mixed blood?" Gekek was tired of the

stupid questions Powell asked. He knew what Powell was trying to do and he was not going to be a part of it. Gekek refused to give in to Powell's desire for him to say Martin was a mixed-blood.

"You would not call anybody a mixed blood, would you, who wore a breech-cloths, and lived like an Indian and went on the warpath? You wouldn't have thought him a mixed blood unless he wore pants, would you?"

Gekek could see that Powell was upset with his answers, but he made one last effort to get Powell to understand. "*It is no concern to me; I would not have said.*"[12]

Powell decided to change his strategy a bit and ask about Martin's father. If Gekek would not answer questions about Martin, maybe he could get him to say something about Joseph.

"You know Mis-quah-nah-quod, or Joseph Black?"

"Yes, sir, he was here. He lived here."

"Was he a full blood or a mixed blood Indian?" Powell asked.

Gekek smiled. "He was an Indian."

Powell wasn't going to let him get away with evasive answers. "What do you mean by an 'Indian.'—a mixed blood may be an Indian?"

"It must be so."

"You don't know—you don't know whether he was a mixed blood or a full blood?"

Gekek knew what Powell was up to, and he was not going to give him the satisfaction of answering such absurd questions. "*He is dead long ago. I don't know exactly what he was. You can go dig him out of his grave, and then you find out.*"[13]

As Gekek exited, Powell's frustrations reached a breaking point. "Clearly, these Indians don't understand what we are talking about here!" Powell began. "We have explained the definitions of full-blood and mixed-blood time and again, and yet they insist on undermining us by using primitive definitions. Clearly, they do not respect science nor the authority of this investigation! This is not over; I will be contacting the proper authorities," Powell said as he stormed out.

Dibaabiigin: "To Measure Someone (as with Something String Like)"

Powell returned to the reservation a few months later with a new plan to discern which Anishinaabeg were full-bloods and which were not.[14] This time he was accompanied by two anthropologists, Dr. Ales Hrdlicka of the Smithsonian Institution and Dr. Albert E. Jenks of the University of Minnesota.

A cold breeze nearly lifted their hats as they stepped off the train.

"I think you will find the accommodations here to your satisfaction," Powell said. "White Earth has all the modern conveniences."

Powell led Hrdlicka and Jenks down the main street and pointed out the Chippewa State Bank and the post office. Two children sitting on a wooden bench on the platform outside the B. L. Fairbanks Co. Store stared at them as they entered.

The store was large and contained a wide variety of goods. Powell stepped up to the counter and asked for half a pound of peppermints. An elderly Anishinaabe man carefully measured out the red and white candy and collected Powell's dime without comment. The men each popped a piece of candy into their mouths and continued down the street until they entered the fashionable Hiawatha Hotel. Since the government was paying their expenses, they requested the three best rooms.

"We will begin our work first thing in the morning, so get a good night's rest," Powell instructed Jenks and Hrdlicka.

Benjamin L. Fairbanks store, White Earth (village). Photographer: Robert G. Beaulieu. Photograph Collection ca. 1910, Location no. E97.7W r9, Negative no. 6434-A, Minnesota Historical Society. http://collections.mnhs.org/cms/display.php?irn=10813641.

Hiawatha Hotel, White Earth (village). Photographer: Robert G. Beaulieu, Photograph collection 1910, Location no. E97.7W r4, Negative no. 6435-A, Minnesota Historical Society. http://collections.mnhs.org/cms/display.php?irn=10812789.

Powell went to have a word with Simon Michelet, the Indian agent, about the new process that would definitively determine the blood status of the Anishinaabeg before he turned in for the evening.

"So you see, the doctors have created physical tests that can tell—without a doubt—the precise racial ancestry of any individual," Powell explained.

"Fascinating! Science has made such advancements; it is unbelievable to think that a few simple tests can tell us the blood quantum of a person. Now you won't have to bother with any more of those unreliable answers the Anishinaabeg give to your questions and the undeniable facts will be known to all," Michelet responded. "I will get everyone to form a line in front of the examination tent bright and early tomorrow morning. Hmmm . . . I think I will offer an extra ration of salt pork to help motivate them." Michelet smirked as the idea came to his mind.

Ivy was among the crowd that watched the Essens brothers emerge from the tent, and she was curious to know how it turned out. She was skeptical about the work the doctors were doing, but like many of the others needed the extra ration of salt pork so they lined up outside the tent.

"What happened?" she whispered. Everyone craned their necks to hear.

"They are crazy men," the younger brother said.

The two brothers slowly opened their shirts as a small group of Anishinaabeg gathered round. Each brother had a scratch on his chest. Eyes widened in astonishment.

"The doctor man says I am a full-blood and my brother is a mixed blood."

The crowd was silent, stunned. (LaDuke 63–64; emphasis in original)

Just then Ivy was called. She was still reeling from the sight of the Essens brothers' chests. Her mind raced: just who were these so-called doctors? What if they infected those they examined with a disease? Despite her fear, she entered the tent to see for herself just what this examination would be like.
"Please take a seat. I just need to make a few notes and then we can get started," Hrdlicka said. "Don't worry; this won't take long or hurt."
As Ivy's eyes scanned the odd metal instruments laid out on the table, her trepidation increased. Hrdlicka carefully documented her name in his notebook. He then began the task of observing her physical characteristics. He raised her chin to get a better view of her face and began to write down his scientific findings:

Age: 20, estimated
Eyes: Fairly slanted
Hair: Straight, thick, black
Nose: Foot stout, bridge concave, less evolved

She was determined not to show her fear to the doctor, who smiled at her now, apologizing ever so slightly for any discomfort. She tried not to look and closed her eyes when she saw him pick up a set of circular forceps that looked like the jaws of a giant metal bear to her, closing in on her head.

"Do not worry," he explained. "This is nothing but a spreading caliper." He placed the metal tongs on her forehead and she felt the coldness of the steel like a knife blade against her skin. He wrote again in his book, adding lists of numbers, figures, measurements, and observations.

> Cheek bones: Pronounced
> Supraorbital brow ridges: Strong, primatal
> Forehead: Low in appearance, large protrusions
> Occipital bone: Large, protohuman
> Incisors: Shovel-shaped, sharp

He turned to look at her, announcing his prognosis like a benediction: "You will be happy to know that you are of mixed blood descent" (LaDuke 64–65).

Ivy looked him right in the eye, "I am Anishinaabe. I don't care what your nonsense scientific tests say." With that she turned and quickly strode out of the tent. Then suddenly it came to her. Of course, the land sales—these doctors were going to make sure they were all mixed-bloods! Then they would have no way to ever recover their lands. She felt weak, and her stomach seemed hollow as she walked toward the back of the line where the other members of her family awaited their turn. George could see the tears shining in Ivy's eyes as she approached. He knew she was trying to maintain her composure.

"Are you all right?" he asked.

Ivy took a deep breath and closed her eyes. The welled-up tears began to roll down her cheeks. "I know what they are doing but I don't know what we can do about it," Ivy stated.

"What do you mean?"

"The doctor told me that I am a mixed-blood. So now I will never be able to get my land back."

"Well, I will not stand here and let those doctors perform their nonsense tests on me. Let's go home," Ivy's cousin Frances responded.

George disagreed. "You should do what you think is best, Frances, but I am going to stay. Even if they find me to be a mixed-blood, at least my name will appear on the rolls—remember when the St. Clair family didn't collect their treaty annuities a few years ago? Now Michelet refuses them, says they abandoned the tribe; meanwhile, he gets fat from what should go to them. I am going to take my chances with the doctors."

Frances and her husband, children, and father left the line and lost the extra ration of salt pork but thought it their best strategy.

Part 2

Landing Identity

In 1887 the US government passed the Dawes Act, also known as the General Allotment Act.[15] In "The General Allotment Act 'Eligibility' Hoax" John P. LaVelle details the requirements of the act and how it has been misrepresented in scholarship. Contrary to popular belief and previous scholarship, the act did not require an individual to have one-half or more Indian blood. LaVelle asserts: "Indeed, in enacting the 1887 General Allotment Act, Congress imposed no blood quantum-specific 'eligibility' requirement on Indians at all. Instead, Congress made eligibility for allotments under the act depend exclusively on the tribes' own independent membership determinations" (257). Although the act required that those receiving allotments were members of Indian tribes, many tribes did not have official written membership or citizenship policies or complete lists of citizens at this time. Thus, the act signaled the most critical period in the evolution of US involvement in citizenship among tribal nations because this new federal policy required an official census to determine who was a tribal citizen and therefore who would receive an allotment. The resulting "census" effectively became a primary source in determining who was a citizen of a band or nation.[16]

The federal government also wanted to consolidate all the Anishinaabeg in Minnesota onto one or two reservations. As a result, the population at White Earth expanded rapidly during the 1870s.[17] In 1886, Congress appointed a commission to negotiate a formal agreement to move all Anishinaabeg to White Earth. Few Anishinaabeg were willing to agree to this arrangement. In 1889, Congress passed the Nelson Act, which declared that the Anishinaabeg would cede all reservations except for White Earth and Red Lake. Red Lake Anishinaabeg were to take allotments on their own reservation and everyone else would take theirs at White Earth.[18]

White Earth leaders were not impressed with the plan. However, a majority of adult men were finally convinced once they were told that, in direct contradiction with the goal of consolidating all Minnesota Anishinaabeg at White Earth, the act also allowed individuals to take allotments on their home reservations. During the 1890s, about 1,200 of 4,000 individuals whom the Chippewa Commission attempted to relocate to White Earth actually did so. They increased the wide range of diversity already present on the reservation.[19]

Nationally, the Dawes Act resulted in the loss of approximately 90 million acres of land previously held in common by American Indian nations (Peterson 162). The first allotments were made at White Earth in 1901, with 4,372 allotments authorized that year. Eventually, over 12,000 allotments were made.[20]

Legislation in the early 1900s made major changes to the governance of allotments, and White Earth was the center of a national scandal. In her groundbreaking work *The White Earth Tragedy*, historian Melissa Meyer meticulously details the fraud and corruption that occurred at White Earth in the early twentieth century. She delineates dubious legislation that created an avenue for the transfer of legal ownership of thousands of allotments from Anishinaabeg to non-Indian Americans. Meyer examines the complex and dynamic interactions between various political fractions of Anishinaabeg at White Earth near the turn of the twentieth century. She identifies two primary factions during the late nineteenth century as "conservative" and "progressive." She argues that "conservative Anishinaabe bands located at a distance from fur trade outposts maintained a more subsistence-oriented way of life," while progressives "participated more fully in the market economy" (Meyer, *White Earth* 5). Yet she notes, "both groups had adapted to altered conditions from a foundation of continuity with past cultural constructs" (Meyer, *White Earth* 5). The conservative faction were eventually known as "full-bloods" and the progressives as "mixed-bloods," but these labels reflected "culturally determined values," not biological or racial ancestry (Meyer, *White Earth* 118–20, 180–83). My work builds on and expands the various determiners of identity used by the Anishinaabeg that Meyer describes.

In 1906, Congress passed several important pieces of legislation; possibly the most significant for the people of White Earth was the Clapp Rider. It was attached to the Indian Appropriations bill and garnered little attention. The Clapp Rider removed all restrictions to the sale of allotted land in the White Earth Reservation held by adult "mixed-bloods" in addition to those "full-bloods" deemed "competent" by the secretary of the Interior,[21] thus establishing blood quantum as a concept and concurrently correlating it with competency, which continued to be determined on an individual basis.[22] No definitions of "mixed-blood" or "full-blood" were provided in the legislation, which later led to confusion and conflict. Congressman Moses Clapp and his co-collaborator, Halvor Steenerson, claimed to have had the best interests of the Anishinaabeg at heart (Meyer, *White Earth* 142–43, 152–53). This rider opened a watershed, and land offices at White Earth were nearly instantaneously flooded with paperwork for the sale of thousands of acres of land.

There were soon many questions about this problematic and notable legislation. Although the law failed to define who exactly fell into the categories of "mixed-blood" and "full-blood," there was an implicit understanding that these were scientific terms that dealt with literal, biological measures of race. The primary question about the legal definition of "mixed-blood" was: How much European blood did one need to be considered a "mixed-blood"? The US District Court for the District of Minnesota, district 4, sixth division, ruled that an individual must have a minimum of one-eighth "white blood" to be legally defined as a "mixed-blood."[23] The case was appealed, and the US Circuit Court of Appeals overruled the district court finding that a "mixed-blood" was an individual with any amount of "white blood." The US Supreme Court subsequently upheld this "one drop" rule on June 8, 1914 (United States v. First National Bank of Detroit, 234 U.S. 245). Under the law, an individual with any European "blood" was a "mixed-blood," with the exact percentage of "blood" being irrelevant (Meyer, *White Earth* 166–67).

By 1909, a full 80 percent of the White Earth Reservation land had passed into private ownership (Meyer, *White Earth* 159–60). That same year, Warren K. Moorehead, a scholar from Massachusetts and member of the Board of Indian Commissioners, arrived at the White Earth Reservation to investigate the situation. He found confirmation of widespread fraud and began to take affidavits from the individuals who claimed their land had been illegally taken. Moorehead collected a plethora of evidence and delivered it to Commissioner of Indian Affairs R. G. Valentine. Meyer notes: "The results of Moorehead's probing [so] horrified Commissioner of Indian Affairs Valentine that he authorized Moorehead and Edward B. Linnen, a regular experienced Indian Office inspector, to undertake another investigation in July of 1909" (*White Earth* 159–61). Their final report fleshed out Moorehead's original findings. The fraud was so clear and rampant that, as Meyer has observed, "nearly every Indian Office official sent to look into the matter was scandalized by the ways Indians had lost their lands" (*White Earth* 162).

Complaints of disenfranchised Anishinaabeg and the involvement of Indian Office officials soon caused those who had profited from the land sales to realize that their titles could possibly be revoked. With the cooperation of congressmen, including Clapp, these landholders were able to get a provision for establishing a commission to "accurately" determine the blood status of White Earth allottees in the annual Indian Appropriations bill in 1913 that would in turn resolve which land sales were legal in accordance with the Clapp Rider (Meyer, *White Earth* 163). Although a blood classification roll, known as the Hinton Roll, was created in 1910, a new commission was appointed for the same purpose three years later because those who profited from the land deals complained that the roll was seriously flawed.[24] The primary difference between the rolls is that, not surprisingly, many individuals classified as "full-bloods" on the Hinton Roll were reclassified as "mixed-bloods" on the new roll (Peterson 169).

Attorney Ransom Powell was chosen to head the new investigation. He was appointed by the federal government to investigate the genealogy of 200 Anishinaabe families (about 5,000 individual people) and determine which were "mixed-blood," according to the legal definition established in the courts.[25] Interior Secretary Franklin Lane raised some questions about Powell's appointment to this investigation because Powell served as attorney for a host of people and companies at White Earth. Indeed, the investigation of the roll commission expedited cases for which Powell was serving as attorney. Although the conflict of interest was obvious, Powell remained head of the investigation. As Meyer has observed, "Political and economic interests in northwestern Minnesota were obviously on quite cozy terms" (Meyer, *White Earth* 164).[26]

Questionable Identities and Mixed Translations

It is apparent that at best, the conceptions of "mixed-blood" and "full-blood" as biological or racial categories were new to the Anishinaabeg of White Earth in the 1910s. In fact, it was likely that many people rarely (if ever) used these terms or the metaphor of blood as an indication of a biological measure of race as a means to define identity in their own family, community, or nation.

It is not clear when the concepts of full-blood and mixed-blood were introduced among the Anishinaabeg or how these terms might have been initially understood. While blood symbols and rituals are widely distributed throughout cultures, the meanings and metaphors attached to blood are varied and have changed over time.[27] It is not clear what diversity of beliefs Anishinaabeg held about blood in the early twentieth century.[28]

Powell and those who worked under him interviewed numerous Anishinaabeg, asking them a variety of questions to determine who were "mixed-bloods" and who were "full-bloods." The testimonies collected by this investigation provide rare, direct statements by Anishinaabeg of White Earth as to how they understood their identity.[29] However, a number of important factors influenced the interviews. Although the interviews were only recorded in English, language and translation were critical. The English and Anishinaabe language skill level varied greatly at White Earth during this time. Some were fluent in both languages, whereas others had only partial understanding, and others spoke only one language. There is no information about the interviewees' skill levels in English or Anishinaabe; I can only speculate when language and translation became an issue.[30] However, as I will demonstrate, there are cases where translation appears to have influenced the answers of the interviewees.

To establish if an individual in question was a "mixed-blood," an interviewee was often asked if the person had any "white blood." The translation of this term would have been especially difficult even for a skilled translator, because the root of the Anishinaabe word for blood, *miskwi*, is *miskw*. *Miskw* is the color red and probably references the literal color of blood.[31] Consequently, red is inherently tied to the word "blood." Therefore, the term "white blood" was entirely nonsensical for Anishinaabe witnesses who did not understand blood as a metaphor for or literal measure of race or nationality, as used by the investigators. In addition, in the recorded English transcripts the terms "full-blood," "Chippewa Indian," and "Indian" are used interchangeably, which likely caused confusion because of the implication that "mixed-bloods" were not Indian.

Several witnesses were baffled by the investigators' use of the terms "mixed-blood" and "full-blood" because, they claimed, these were not terms and designations with which they were familiar. The simplistic categories based on biology that the investigators insisted on made no sense for many of the Anishinaabe witnesses. The interview excerpt below demonstrates the nature of the exchanges between investigators and Anishinaabe witnesses.

> Q. Do you know whether his father and mother were full blood Chippewa Indians or not?

A. They were Chippewa Indians, I know that.

Q. Do you what we mean by a mixed blood Indian?

A. No. No, there was no mixed bloods.

Q. The question I asked was, do you know what we mean when we say a mixed blood Indian?

A. No; I just stated that I do not know that; I don't understand that word.

Q. When we say mixed blood Indian we mean that there has been some white blood or other blood mixed with the Chippewa blood?

A. Yes, sir.

Q. And when we say full blood Chippewa Indian we mean that the Chippewa has not been intermingled with the blood of any other race?

A. He is a full blood Indian; there is no mixed blood in him at all.[32]

First the witness indicates that the individuals in question are Chippewa Indians. Then he asserts that there are no "mixed-bloods," even though he admittedly doesn't know what the investigators mean by the words "mixed-blood." Translation and lack of an understanding of blood as a metaphor for race and biological ancestry likely played a role in the witness's responses. After being informed about definitions of "full-blood" and "mixed-blood," the witness holds his ground that the individuals in question are not "mixed-bloods." There are several possibilities for the witness's reaction. Maybe he considered the definitions provided by the investigators to be inadequate or inappropriate or might not have understood them at all. Another possibility is that the individuals in question were "full-bloods" as the investigators defined it. The witness's statement could also be a refusal to use the terms and definitions provided by the investigators. He might simply have been persistent in his claim that "there was no mixed-bloods" as a way to deny the terminology and definitions pushed by the investigators.

During the investigation, many Anishinaabeg who were willing to use the terms "mixed-blood" and "full-blood" caused complications for the investigators because their views of these terms were much more nuanced and diverse than a simple calculation of genetic ancestry. For example, during an interview George Morrison (not the famous artist of the same name) argued that there was no designation of who was "full-blood" and who was "mixed-blood" among the Anishinaabeg until the question of land titles became tied to these identities.[33] He asserted that all those who lived with the Anishinaabeg were considered "full-bloods" because of their way of living, not because of their biological ancestry. He stated:

> In old times all who wore the breech cloth and blanket and also affiliated with the Indians, lived in wigwams and didn't live in houses, they were called "Indians"; they were considered the same as the full-bloods on account of their way of living; not on account of their blood, but on account of their—it was their way of living that regulated that.[34]

Morrison clearly argued that lifestyle, not blood, determined who was an Indian. In addition, his use of the term "Indian" in place of "full-blood" furthers his point that racial or biological divisions were not in place "in the old times." We can read Morrison's answer as an act of survivance. He refuses to adhere to the terminal biological definitions provided by the federal investigators and insists that the lifestyle choices made by individuals determined their identity. Anishinaabeg controlled their identity through actions.

Investigators also asked many questions about phenotype, especially skin color, and spent a considerable amount of time attempting to connect skin color with a person's status as either a "full-blood" or a "mixed-blood." Despite their attempts to make skin color a primary factor, Anishinaabe witnesses frequently noted that skin color varied and was not necessarily indicative of an individual's ancestry or their cultural status as a "full-blood" or a "mixed-blood." For example, Bay-bah-daung-ay-yaush did not correlate the darkness of a person's skin with a specific degree of blood. An investigator asked, "Wasn't she light complected?" Bay-bah-daung-ay-yaush replied, "Yes, she was light. Some Indians are light, but she was an Indian."[35] In this case Bay-bah-daung-ay-yaush's use of the term "Indian," not "mixed-blood" or "full-blood," is a subversive way of asserting that the two categories of identity are Indian and non-Indian, thereby undermining and resisting the simplistic biological categories desired by the investigators. When asked a similar question, May-zhue-sah-e-bun-dung refused to correlate skin color with identity by replying, "Yes, he was light, but he was a full-blooded Indian."[36] Like other Anishinaabe witnesses, May-zhue-sah-e-bun-dung may have been applying cultural definitions to the term "full-blood." In these examples, Anishinaabeg rejected the idea that skin color was an important influence on identity.

Resistance to the importance of skin color continued in another form when several people testified that they either could not remember or had never noticed the skin color of certain people. For example, when asked if an individual was "pretty white," Mak-ah-day-wub responded that he had "never taken particular notice."[37] It is possible that witnesses really did not recall the skin color of those they were being questioned about; however, it is more likely that witnesses purposefully refused to recall or describe the skin color of the person in question as a calculated strategy to assert that skin color did not determine an individual's identity.

Measured Identities

The federal government ultimately refused to accept the multiple, fluid understandings of who was Anishinaabe, both "mixed-blood" and "full-blood," and insisted that biological ancestry determined which category a person belonged in. Powell was unable to get the facts he needed from the interviews, so he used a new means to get precise, biological answers regarding the racial ancestry of the people of White Earth. In May 1915, two nationally renowned anthropologists, Albert E. Jenks and Ales Hrdlicka,[38] came to White Earth to administer a series of physical examinations to determine the exact racial makeup of the individuals involved in the land fraud cases and create a blood roll detailing this information.[39] Jenks was confident he could indisputably distinguish "full-bloods" from "mixed-bloods" through various physical examinations (Beaulieu 282, 293–98). The fictional results from the pseudo-scientific tests created fictional results that divided families.

Using the preposterous results from the tests performed by Jenks and Hrdlicka, Powell finally completed his blood roll in 1920. Less than 10 percent of the 5,000 allottees listed on the roll were classified as "full-bloods." The courts approved and accepted the fictional blood roll as final (Peterson 169–70; Meyer, *White Earth* 37). The blood quantum of allottees as listed on Powell's roll became the critical determiner in most of the allotment land fraud cases, and other key evidence was disregarded. Most of the 142,000 acres of land in question were never returned to the original owners or their descendants (Beaulieu 286–96; Soderstrom 71–72; Youngbear-Tibbetts 106–8). White Earth Anishinaabe scholar David Beaulieu has observed: "It is a rare moment in the historiography of the relationship of anthropology and the other social sciences to American Indians to find an example where the colonial nature and political purposes and the uses of academic enterprise seem so obvious and direct" (282). In the land fraud cases, anthropologists' understandings of "full-blood" and "mixed-blood" were considered scientific fact. The diverse, fluid, and nuanced ways the Anishinaabeg classified themselves, on the other hand, were deemed absurd and ultimately irrelevant.[40]

Conclusion

The statements of the Anishinaabeg during this investigation demonstrate that they did not use blood as a metaphor for racial and biological ancestry; to them, this association was illogical and senseless. Those who used the terms "full-blood" and "mixed-blood" insisted that those categories were not bound to biology but were flexible terms generally tied to a variety of lifestyle choices. They insisted that Anishinaabeg controlled their identity through actions; the facts regarding identity could and did change. The designations of "mixed-blood" and "full-blood" in the simplistic and rigid biological understanding pushed by Powell and his investigators were unacceptable and in direct conflict with pliable Anishinaabe understandings of identity. Anishinaabe argued that their identity could not be surveyed and divided the way the reservation had been. There were no clear lines and neat allotments; instead, it was a varied and diverse landscape that changed with the motion of the seasons.

The federal government dismissed Anishinaabe conceptions of identity and insisted on fixed measures of race as the sole determiner of an individual's identity. This focus on race and biology resulted in the legal dispossession of thousands of acres of land. In addition, it legalized the conflation of blood with race and nationality. As the twentieth century progressed, the federal government increasingly relied on "blood" to define the legal status of Anishinaabeg and, more broadly, American Indians. Consequently, the racialization of Anishinaabe identity would have significant and lasting consequences, eventually leading to the fictional erasure of many individuals' legal status as Anishinaabe.

Epilogue: *Wiingashk*

Ivy's granddaughter Anne had gathered the women together in her home to weave sweetgrass baskets.[41] Like their ancestors, the women spun the blades of grass together between their fingers while they spoke of children and politics. A sweet smell filled the room as life was transformed. As the baskets took shape, words stitched the variegated families together. The malleable coils of sweetgrass built on each other like generations, seamlessly connected by skillful women.

Notes

An earlier version of this article was published as "An Anishinaabe Tribalography: Investigating and Interweaving Conceptions of Identity during the 1910s on the White Earth Reservation," *American Indian Quarterly* 33, no. 3 (2009): 295–324.

    1. Anishinaabeg are known by a variety of names, including Ojibwe (also spelled Ojibwa and Ojibway) and Chippewa. I primarily use Anishinaabe(g) in

this essay but will also use Chippewa when using the legal name for government bodies.

2. Gerald Vizenor introduced the term "survivance" in *Manifest Manners*, and although it has a longer history, his uses and definitions have brought it into wide use. Survivance goes beyond mere survival to include resistance to dominance, Native presence, and worldview. Vizenor has written: "Survivance stories are renunciations of dominance, detractions, obtrusions, the unbearable sentiments of tragedy, and the legacy of victimry" (Vizenor, "Aesthetics of Survivance" 1).

3. In the late nineteenth and early twentieth centuries, there were myriad complex systems and social regulations that Anishinaabeg used to determine who were and were not members of their tribe. It would be a mistake to think that these systems functioned without any conflict—undoubtedly, there were disagreements and power struggles. However, Anishinaabeg were in control of these systems, and they worked out conflicts or agreed to disagree, as was their sovereign right; they determined who was and who was not a citizen of the nation.

4. I use "facts" in quotes because there is often an assumption that written documents are "facts," that they hold the truth. In reality, we know that documents can only give part of the story, and there are numerous instances, including the blood rolls that I discuss in this essay, where they have been false.

5. For the title of this section, see "weave" in Nichols and Nyholm 281.

6. Sweetgrass is a sacred plant used in a wide variety of ceremonies. It has a calming smell when dried or burned. It grows in swampy areas and is harvested during the summer. It is often woven into braids and baskets.

7. For the title of this section, see "unravel" in Nichols and Nyholm 277. For Powell, see Ransom Judd Powell Papers, undated, 1843, and 1896–1938, Minnesota Historical Society, St. Paul (hereafter Powell Papers), testimony transcripts from investigation of the blood status of Indian allottees in White Earth regarding the blood status of individual Anishinaabeg, estate claims, and land titles and transfers.

8. Powell Papers, roll 6, 142–43.
9. Powell Papers, roll 5, 422.
10. Powell Papers, roll 4, frame 409, 11.
11. Powell Papers, roll 4, frame 614, 82.
12. Powell Papers, roll 5, 459–60.
13. Powell Papers, roll 5, 69–70.
14. For the title of this section, see "measure" in Nichols and Nyholm 212.
15. This act authorized the president of the United States to allocate reservation land to individual American Indians. The United States would hold the title to the land in trust for twenty-five years as a means of protection for the allotee while he or she learned to use the land to its fullest potential. It was presumed that after twenty-five years the person would have the skills necessary to manage their own affairs and a fee patent, which allowed unrestricted ownership of the

land, would be issued. McDonnell 2. Political rhetoric surrounding the policy was that individual European-style land ownership would teach Indians individualism and selfishness, which were seen as necessary characteristics for the assimilation of Native people into dominant society. O'Brien 78.

16. Individuals who for some reason were left off the list effectively lost their status with their tribe and the federal government. Even though they were recognized as Indian in their communities, officially they were not counted as Indian. Meyer, "American Indian" 232–33.

17. The population increased from about 800 in 1875 to over 1,400 a year later, as the Pembina and Otter Tail Pillager bands joined the Mississippi band already at White Earth.

18. The vague terms used in this legislation caused confusion, and in 1895 the assistant attorney general ruled that for an individual to qualify as "Chippewa Indian" under the Nelson Act, they must have Chippewa Indian blood, have a recognized connection with one of the bands in Minnesota, have been a Minnesota resident when the act was passed, and move to a reservation with the intention of living there permanently. This ruling did not necessarily provide much clarification. In addition, it excluded children of Anishinaabeg women who had married non-Indians but extended qualification to those who had received "half-breed script" under the 1854 and 1855 treaties. Meyer, *White Earth* 59–60.

19. See Meyer, *White Earth* 50–67 for a detailed discussion of the commission and the migration to White Earth. Also see Meyer, *White Earth* 30–34; Graves and Ebbott 45–46.

20. This counts additional allotments that were made after 1904 when the president was authorized to allot pine lands, which had been previously exempted. Peterson 162–65.

21. Of course, "competency" was a term loaded with unspoken implications. Essentially, those Indians who were deemed competent by the federal government had adopted some European and American customs, spoke English, and often had European ancestry.

22. This legislation only applied to the White Earth Reservation. In 1917, Commissioner of Indian Affairs Cato Sells created a policy to unilaterally release all allotted lands held by American Indians of less then one-half Indian blood. While he knew the rationale was not foolproof, he felt "it is almost an axiom that an Indian who has a larger portion of white blood than Indian partakes more of the latter." Only a few years after the implementation of the policy, Sells abandoned it. Sells, quoted in Spruhan 45.

23. "White blood" was the terminology used by the court. It was assumed that "blood" from European countries was "white blood," but the court did not specifically name the countries that were included under this designation.

24. Special Agent John H. Hinton created the Hinton Roll. He attended the September 1910 annuity payment at White Earth and, in consultation with

Anishinaabe leaders, established the blood quantum of each individual to the sixteenth fraction. Meyer, *White Earth* 162.

25. As Meyer observed, "Policy makers interpreted blood status literally at White Earth . . . with absurd consequences" (*White Earth* 172).

26. See index to Powell Papers, undated, 1843, 1896–1938, M455. Powell was well known as an attorney for Minnesota lumber companies and had represented their interests on many occasions. He continued to advise his clients on their cases while he worked on the blood roll. Meyer details the devious and illegal activities Powell engaged in (*White Earth* 163–71).

27. Meyer has observed, "The most widespread metaphorical trope attributes life-giving qualities to blood, both in terms of procreation and agricultural fertility" (*Thicker Than Water* 5).

28. There is a vast literature on the symbolism of blood in a wide variety of cultures. No such study exists for Anishinaabeg, making it unclear what role blood played in society during the nineteenth century. It is possible that the metaphor or belief that blood was directly associated with racial ancestry, as well as physical characteristics and mental abilities, was introduced among the Anishinaabeg during the treaty period.

29. Meyer makes a brief reference to the testimonies collected by this investigation (*White Earth* 169) but focuses her efforts on political factionalisms after the land fraud cases and relies on other sources, including letters, newspaper accounts, and government reports for her analysis.

30. There are occasional instances in which the interpreter interjects to clarify a term and it is recorded in the transcript. For example, a witness was asked, "Did you ever see the trader, George Fairbanks, who used to live here, have a store over here at the old agency, —trading post?" The witness answered, "He was my [*sic*] Frenchman." The interpreter then stated, "That means 'trader.'" Powell Papers, undated, 1843, and 1896–1938, R.4: frame 610, 73.

31. John D. Nichols to Jill Doerfler, personal communication, June 12, 2007. "Blood" and "red" in Nichols and Nyholm 147 and 234.

32. Powell Papers, roll 4, frame 409, 11.

33. This George Morrison was not the famous artist of the same name.

34. Powell Papers, roll 5, 602; roll 6, 51.

35. Powell Papers, roll 6, 50–51.

36. Powell Papers, roll 5, 596.

37. Powell Papers, roll 5, 247.

38. In his dissertation, "Weeds in Linnaeus's Garden: Science and Segregation, Eugenics, and the Rhetoric of Racism at the University of Minnesota and the Big Ten, 1900–45," Mark Soderstrom uses Jenks's life and career to "examine the evolution of anthropology as a discipline within its national context." Due in part to his work at White Earth, Jenks was one of 100 people appointed by the secretary of the Interior to help create Indian policy in 1923 (Soderstrom 49, 70).

Ales Hrdlicka, curator of the Division of Physical Anthropology at the Smithsonian Institution, is the acknowledged "father of American physical anthropology." In addition to his work at the Smithsonian, Hrdlicka was the founder and editor of the *American Journal of Physical Anthropology* and co-founder of the American Association of Physical Anthropologists (Soderstrom 73).

39. For detailed information on the findings of the physical examinations, see Hrdlicka, found at Newberry Library, Chicago.

40. Furthermore, one year after the cases had been decided, Jenks tested the hair of himself and several of his colleagues and found his hair and that of Hrdlicka was of the most typical Negro type. He concluded: "Either the old classification of human races by hair texture is not of scientific value or Dr. Hrdlicka and I are related to the negro" (Beaulieu 305). Numerous investigations have taken up the issue of the legality of the land sales. In her article "Without Due Process: The Alienation of Individual Trust Allotments of the White Earth Anishinaabeg," Holly Youngbear-Tibbetts "focuses on the equity suits filed by the United States on behalf of the Anishinaabeg who had been wrongfully dispossessed" and details the community's response to the White Earth Land Settlement Act of 1987, which might be the last word in the cases" (96–97).

41. For the title of this section, see "sweetgrass" in Nichols and Nyholm 262.

References

Beaulieu, David. "Curly Hair and Big Feet: Physical Anthropology and Implementation of Land Allotment on the White Earth Chippewa Reservation." *American Indian Quarterly* 8, no. 4 (1984): 281–314.

Blaeser, Kimberly. "The New Frontier of Native American Literature: Dis-arming History with Tribal Humor." In *Native American Perspectives on Literature and History*, edited by Alan R. Velie, 38–39. Norman: University of Oklahoma: Norman, 1994.

Graves, Kathy Davis, and Elizabeth Ebbott. *Indians in Minnesota*, 5th ed. Minneapolis: University of Minnesota Press, 2006.

Howe, LeAnne. "The Story of America: A Tribalography." In *Clearing a Path: Theorizing the Past in Native American Studies*, edited by Nancy Shoemaker, 29–50. New York: Psychology Press, 2002.

Hrdlicka, Ales. "Anthropology of the Chippewa." *Holmes Anniversary Volume of Anthropological Essay* (1916).

LaDuke, Winona. *Last Standing Woman*. Stillwater, MN: Voyageur Press, 1997.

LaVelle, John P. "The General Allotment Act 'Eligibility' Hoax: Distortions of Law, Policy, and History in Derogation of Indian Tribes." *Wicazo Sa Review* 14, no. 1 (1999): 251–302.

McDonnell, Janet A. *The Dispossession of the American Indian, 1887–1934*. Bloomington: Indiana University Press, 1991.
Meyer, Melissa L. "American Indian Blood Quantum Requirements: Blood Is Thicker than Family." In *Over the Edge: Remapping the American West*, edited by Valerie J. Matsumoto and Blake Allmendinger, 231–44. Berkeley: University of California Press, 1999.
———. *Thicker Than Water: The Origins of Blood as Symbol and Ritual*. New York: Routledge, 2005.
———. *The White Earth Tragedy: Ethnicity and Dispossession at a Minnesota Anishinaabe Reservation 1889–1920*. Lincoln: University of Nebraska Press, 1994.
Nichols, John D., and Earl Nyholm. *Concise Dictionary of Minnesota Ojibwe*. Minneapolis: University of Minnesota Press, 1995.
O'Brien, Sharon. *American Indian Tribal Governments*. Norman: University of Oklahoma Press, 1989.
Peterson, Edward Michael, Jr. "That So-Called Warranty Deed: Clouded Land Titles on the White Earth Indian Reservation in Minnesota." *North Dakota Law Review* 59, no. 2 (1983): 159–82.
Soderstrom, Mark. *Weeds in Linnaeus's Garden: Science and Segregation, Eugenics, and the Rhetoric of Racism at the University of Minnesota and the Big Ten, 1900–45*. PhD diss., University of Minnesota, 2004.
Spruhan, Paul. "A Legal History of Blood Quantum in Federal Indian Law to 1935." *South Dakota Law Review* 51, no. 1 (2006), available at SSRN, http://ssrn.com/abstract=955032.
Vizenor, Gerald. "Aesthetics of Survivance." In *Survivance: Narratives of Native Presence*, edited by Gerald Vizenor, 1–24. Lincoln: University of Nebraska Press, 2008.
———. *The Everlasting Sky: Voices of the Anishinabe People*. St. Paul: Minnesota Historical Society, 2000.
———. *Manifest Manners: Narratives on Postindian Survivance*. Lincoln: University of Nebraska Press, 1994.
Youngbear-Tibbetts, Holly. "Without Due Process: The Alienation of Individual Trust Allotments of the White Earth Anishinaabeg." *American Indian Culture and Research Journal* 15, no. 2 (1991): 93–138.

Chapter 10

Enduring Critical Poses, Beyond Nation and History

The Legacy and Life of Anishinaabeg Literature and Letters

MARGARET NOODIN

Miikindizi Baapaawinad Jim Northrupibanan
Jim Northrup's Art of Teasing Shakery

Chibenesi dibaajimo, baapaajimo
Great Bird narrates, comediates
ezhi-niimiwaad aandegoog gaashkaading ziigwang
the way crows dance on a crust of snow in spring
ezhi-ikidowinan-nooshkaachinaganiked niibinong
the way he makes baskets for word winnowing in summer
ezhi-mikawaad mekwendaagozijin dagwaaging
the way he finds memory veterans in fall
miidash gikinoo'amawiyangid Anishinaabe-aadizookeyaang biboong.
then teaches us to tell tales the Anishinaabe way in winter.

—Noodin, *What the Chickadee Knows*

In the introduction to *Touchwood*, Gerald Vizenor wrote, "Northrup is an imaginative listener; his direct and humorous stories are inspired by the rich language that people speak on the reservation. The wild and wondrous characters in his stories are survivors in the best trickster humor, no one is a passive victim" (vii). Vizenor knew what the crows know, what the grandchildren know, what stands of rice and sheets of bark know . . . that Jim Northrup's words can make you laugh and cry at the same time, can boil paragraphs down to questions and winnow hulls of meaning away from reality. Northrup's story credentials are extensive. He was a grandpa, a veteran, a longtime journalist, poet, dramatist, and novelist. His stories break the boundaries of the page, disrupt the arc of time, and demonstrate a style of narration that is as interesting across literary traditions as it is rooted in its woodland ways. His tales contain tribal traces that skim like race canoes across lake surfaces, or break down like hearts and engines along the roads of life. He moved on to live beyond this world in 2016, but through his writing, Northrup teaches the elements of Anishinaabe narrative construction and creates his own inimitable way of combining Anishinaabe existentialism, irony, and comedy. *Gii anishaaendamo ohskigagwedwinan, miikindiziyangid miinwaa mazinaigan baapaawinad.* He imagines new questions, teases critical interpretations, and shakes the expectations of his audience.

Aankenootaan: Theory and Translation

Anishinaabe narrative construction is not unlike any other storytelling tradition and in that way, fits into the universe of stories, the storiverse or, *dibaajimo'akii*. Both his American and Anishinaabe identities affected how Northrup wrote, which is why it is important to read him as a world citizen. He could stand beside Vladimir and Estragon asking questions and waiting for Godot. He is also an Anishinaabe author intimately familiar with a specific time, place, and palimpsest of culture.

Many schools of theory offer useful approaches to Northrup's work. A hermeneutic tradition, which includes a close reading of sacred and social perspectives, might be used to show how many of his stories reflect the "big drum" values of the Midewiwin tradition. His work can also be read from a postcolonial stance of deconstructive analysis, not necessarily searching for the same "mastery" Derrida described as beginning "through the power of naming, of imposing and legitimating appellations" (39) but seeking to find connections to the identifying power of language that N. Scott Momaday defines, saying, "our most essential being exists in language" (162). Northrup's writing, and arguably that of other Native authors writing in English, could be seen as an attempt to "master" the language of assimilation while denying the paradigm of the subject and object, the hierarchy of trade economics, possession, and measurement. Northrup's characters are understood through acts of endurance that Vizenor would call survivance. Like Vizenor's infamous postmodern character Griever, Northrup's Luke Warmwater demonstrates how the Anishinaabe have survived colonialism by disassembling and reassembling their culture, and the culture of the traders and missionaries that still surround their ancestral homes. Wry analysis of legal and social histories is often embedded in deceptively simple conversations. Reading Northrup's stories as a form of postcolonial discourse allows his literary contribution to be understood in the context of Native American—specifically Anishinaabe—historical reality. The contemporary emphasis on the revitalization of languages as it relates to indigenous identity offers another possible form of analysis through sociolinguistic and structural interpretation that highlights patterns of meaning and systems of Anishinaabe semiotics found in Anishinaabe and English texts. Northrup builds a story the way a tree measures time, in ever-widening circles that are not mysterious in their make-up and are reflective of highly specific experiences framed by predictable processes. Using multiple modes of theory, readers find that his work connects to the world at large while reflecting the patterns and synapses of Anishinaabe literature.

Literary traditions can be defined by time, location, language, or nation. Indigenous literature often relies on all of these metrics to determine if the author, the intended audience, or the subject and setting are American Indian, Aboriginal, Native American, or more specifically aligned with the epistemology of a single nation. As a linguist and poet, my days are spent explaining patterns of sound and meaning while also celebrating the power of these patterns to reflect a shared sense of wonder cultivated by a group of speakers over many centuries. Over time, they migrated across landscapes, increased collective knowledge, and further defined beliefs, even as they were forced to adopt a second language, sometimes entirely replacing the first. The human capacity to communicate has cognitive elements anchored in the brain, resulting in patterns of sound coming out of mouths. If humans had wings, pollen sacs, or leaves, perhaps the dominant form of encoding communication would be different, but thought to sound distributed from a hole in the front of our head is what we have. Debates have raged over how much of any language is universal and how the patterns of making meaning with sound relates to a society's views of the world. If we follow the logic of most indigenous societies, we are told that distant ancestors of present speakers first described the world, which is the origin of language. Many fascinating hours can be spent unraveling the trails of linguistic genealogy, but the fact remains that every language began with a limited set of sounds and meanings that were used and altered over time by an identifiable set of speakers. In some cases, language blossoms in relative isolation; in other cases, they rise quickly from a deluge of dialogue as cultures collide. Some seek a single point of origin, while others acknowledge multiple sites. Ancient indigenous linguists allude to a time when communication across species and modes of reality was more common. Anishinaabemowin, the language that Northrup considers a heritage language, shares sounds, meaning, and patterns of grammar with languages north of the Equator and west of the longitudinal meridian. It is spoken now primarily in the woodlands and waterways of the Great Lakes and according to legends was originally more focused in a smaller area east of the Great Lakes.

Traces of stories on stone extend back in time. At the site of Mud Portage in the Lake of the Woods area, petroglyphs have been discovered beneath the layers of an Archaic period archeological deposit, which was been dated to 5,000 years ago. Radiocarbon dating at the Nisula site along Lac Cassette, Québec, indicated that the paintings were made about 2,000 years ago (Vastokas). The oldest alphabetic documents mentioning the nations, languages, and stories of the Great Lakes are the diaries of Jesuits who began to visit the area in 1648 and recorded words, phrases, and details about the people in the *Jesuit Relations*. These images and documents are evidence of continued cultural practice, a group of speakers who adapted a shared system of symbol, sound, and meaning to communicate essential information, preserve communal knowledge, and celebrate the sustainability of their culture. Understanding and acknowledging how Anishinaabe language and literature reflect shared experiences is an important part of Anishinaabe narrative analysis, both when Anishinaabemowin was spoken as the dominant language and now as it signifies identity through trace elements in a second language. Especially when the language is semi-dormant and in a state of decline, it is important to uncover and examine the etymological and structural connections original speakers may have taken for granted.

Blending sociolinguistics and literary theory we can read Northrup's work as contributing to other literary traditions from an Anishinaabe perspective. Taking time to interpret structural and cultural elements that are standard in Anishinaabe literature leads to interesting comparative work that allows this literature to be the subject and the critic of other literary perspectives.

Miigwe, Miigwech: Giving Thanks as Story Praxis

A primary element of Anishinaabe narrative is expressed in Anishinaabemowin as *miigwe* (to give) and *miigwech* (to offer thanks for what one has been given). Both echo the discourse marker *mii*, which resists definition but serves to punctuate and accentuate narration. Viewed as various dimensions of a single concept, these units of meaning conform to many complex patterns. Together they represent the Anishinaabe view that stories are part of a highly patterned exchange process that occurs in a specific relationship. Indigenous writing often begins by locating itself in the spiritual, ecological, communal, and familial landscape. Giving thanks, moving narrative along a spectrum of exchange, and framing storytelling as an act of giving are the lessons in Northrup's writing. In all of his books, narrators offer ceremonial thanks to the Creator for life, well-being, and the tangible elements of the Earth that contribute to both. In his early poem "Mahnomin," he includes a "megwetch Munido" [*sic*] for the calm water, the rice, and the cedar (*Walking the Rez Road* 80), and it is one of the few Anishinaabe words used by Luke in the later novel *Dirty Copper* (92). In *Anishinaabe Syndicated* and *Rez Salute*, the notion of "thanks" occurs more than forty times, tracing the concept of gratitude and "thanks" or *miigwech* as a pivot point, an invitation to a narrative conversation that can lead in many directions. He illustrates how the relationship of giving can be complex and filled with many messages. Sometimes "thanks" is a traditional acknowledgment for positive gifts and actions, including thanks given to the Creator for food and a way of life, as when he includes a bilingual passage about maple syrup in *Anishinaabe Syndicated*:

> When we say we are of the earth, it is true. I think there is something in the maple syrup that I need. It makes sense. Countless generations of my ancestors depended on the syrup for food. I will continue to make syrup every spring.
>   Amanj igo apii niinawind ikido niinawind odaadad aki, miish debwe. Niin naanaagadawenim ayi'ii memwech

> megwe-ayi'ii zhiiwaagamizigan manwezi. Mino-inendan, gaawin agim aanikoobijiganag apenimo zhiiwaagamizigan miijiim. Ninwii-zhiiwaagamiziganike akina ziigwan.
>
> We are thankful for the gift of syrup from the Creator.
>
> Niinawind miigwechiwendan debi'zhiiwaagamiziganike onjibaa Gichi-manidoo. (18)

At other times the "thanks" shifts and contains an edge of sarcasm and irony, as in this passage summarizing the "thanks" given at a spear fishing protest:

> FDL spearers would like to thank the Creator for the fish; the game wardens, deputies, and rescue squad for protection; the witnesses for their time and courage; the protesters for their simple-minded opposition; and all Indians who supported the spearers' actions. The spearers would like to especially thank the RBC for their firm "no, yes, no, yes, maybe" decision to allow spearing off the rez. (*Anishinaabe Syndicated* 18)

The verb "to give" can be conjugated to reflect what the speaker is giving or what he or she is given, and meaning can be added to indicate other aspects of the relationship between benefactor and recipient. This manipulation of relationship conceptualization is extraordinarily easy and extremely precise in Anishinaabemowin. By moving along the spectrum of definition with this significant verb, Northrup does in English what is common practice in Anishinaabemowin.

Diba'igan Debwewin: The Truth of Story Time

All stories have time and place, date and setting, days and nights with a background for events. In Anishinaabe stories and the stories of other indigenous traditions, time and place converge to set a stage for action. "In Sawyer, generations of relatives are buried, the air hasn't been breathed by heavy industry, the colors of blue and green rest the eyes and spirits, the quiet makes it easy to hear the spirits and their messages. In Sawyer, the values and traditions of the people are held sacred" (*Walking the Rez Road* 91). The buried past is connected to the active economies of the present. The need to consider multiple temporal layers to fully experience the central present is reflected in the Anishinaabe language and in Northrup's English texts. Northrup's narratives demonstrate how physical location serves as one parallel on which action can be measured. Every story has a setting, and rather than dictating that all Anishinaabe stories must occur on an Anishinaabe reservation, in an urban Anishinaabe neighborhood, or within a certain distance of the Great Lakes, his stories demonstrate there is an Anishinaabe way that time influences the understanding of place that can be used to identify Anishinaabe narratives. "Just doing what grandpa did like his grandpa before him" (*Walking the Rez Road* 78) is a statement that fits within an Anishinaabe worldview in Anishinaabemowin or English. The sense of echoing back in time, which implies that the echo will carry into the future, is a mark of being in an Anishinaabe space.

Time is reflected in two specific and practical ways in Anishinaabe stories: the daily turn of the Earth on its axis and a seasonal journey around the sun. The connection between these concepts is emphasized by numerous etymological connections, the most obvious of which is the term for sun, *giizis* being reflected in the term for day, *giizhigad*. Of further note is that the way to measure time and distance, *diba'iga*, shares sound and meaning with the term for night, *dibikad*. The moon is *dibi-ki-giizis*, literally the night sun, and truth lies in the motion of the Earth, moon, and sun. This does imply a chronology, but it is one that requires acknowledgment of the whole. There is no way to be anchored in this present without full knowledge of the past and future. Northrup's stories demonstrate how Anishinaabe narratives continually move knowingly along both axes. Arguably, this is the case for the stories of most cultures on Earth, but understanding Anishinaabe narrative depends heavily on a need to acknowledge and follow the arc of dawn to dusk while remaining aware of four seasons and four directions. This scientific navigation applied to narrative fixes the Anishinaabe worldview in a matrix of time and provides definition and identity for a community cognizant of the constant motion of space and evolution of the system. The origin of the Anishinaabe intellectual tradition is not recent or in response to a European or classical standard but is a response to the human need to map ideas across generations, for physical, spiritual, and evolutionary reasons.

One of Northrup's recurring characters is named Ben Lookingback. He is a storyteller's storyteller. His name is a reminder that telling a story now, which can be told again in the future, depends on a clear or imagined memory of the past. Anishinaabe stories often begin with the words *mewenzha* or *chizhaazhagwa*, which is much like saying "once upon a time" or "in the big long ago." Whether this preface is offered in Anishinaabemowin or English matters less than the fact that it signifies the beginning and represents only one point on a circumference. Whether the story that follows meets every listener's definition of a "traditional" tale is also sometimes insignificant. What is important is the message that Anishinaabe narrative connects the past to the present. Stories are not simply chronological reports or reactions. Anishinaabe stories combine overt or subtle awareness of the ancient past with living memory as it is being encoded. For example, Northrup models the practice of Anishinaabe narrative construction and transfer when he says, "I can tell you stories about my great-great-great-great-great-grandfather Mikinok who was walking around in 1740—some 30 years before there was a United States. He was living his life with the seasons, probably carrying around a baby in a cradleboard just like this one. And I can tell you stories about each generation since then" (*Rez Road Follie* 233). The long ago is sometimes intentionally elastic and extended. For instance, as he narrates the poem "Tipi Reflections," Jim opens the flap of interpretation, saying, "It could have been yesterday or eons ago" (*Walking the Rez Road* 61). In the novel *Dirty Copper*, Luke says to his Ma, "see you next time" and she replies, "or the time after next," noting that a visit is part of a series across time, not an isolated event (5). Having a voice from the past alive in the present is what assures a voice for the future. This tendency to focus on the present as the center of the past and future is an element of Anishinaabe narrative that can also be related to reflect the concept of *minobimaadiziwin*, living well. In the relation of the words *bimaadiz*, *bimose*, *bimipto*, and *bimode* (to live, to walk, to run, to crawl), there is a sense that living in context is the rasion d'être perhaps stated in Anishinaabemowin as the *waawiyaa ayaayaang*. As Northrup pointed out in his poem aptly titled "End of the Beginning," we need to be cognizant of the cycle of lives, to know our place in time, and to "live each day as if it could be your last" (*Walking the Rez Road* 54).

This concept of living well centered in time is mapped onto location to further define Anishinaabe narrative. For this reason, seasonal markers are essential; they connect what is happening to the cycle of time. Northrup states, "My family and I live our lives with the cycle of the seasons" ("2,000 Seasons" 35). He explains, "Doing what the ancestors have done at the same time of the year just feels right" ("2,000 Seasons" 37). Mapping narratives onto the rhythm of the seasons is akin to using culturally relevant metaphors. Anishinaabe narrative crosses four main seasons, but there is a range, and overlap is encouraged. Understanding a season requires knowing its beginning, middle, and end. Meaning is made by understanding the full circle, not just what is found in the center or at the edges. In the Anishinaabe words for these time periods and in Northrup's English description of actions associated with these times, readers recognize a particular cultural perspective. *Ziigwan*, spring, is when the world melts and water rises. In the spring, Anishinaabe spear fish and boil sap. Northrup shares these traditions not as mystical secrets of the woodland past but as continual proof that generations of relatives are connected by these cycles of harvest. Although his characters may know how things used to be done, they are constantly looking to improve, to find new and creative ways to start a year of growth. "Of course, our culture is ever-changing so in my grandfather's time, they started using number 10 cans to collect the sap. And we're still evolving. We use plastic milk jugs" (*Rez Road Follies* 245). *Niibing*, summer, is a time of full tide, when the *nibii* (the water) is high and there is plenty of work and plenty of sunshine. In Northrup's stories, summer is for basket-making and dancing or visiting at pow-wows. It is the "time to gather bark, another gift from the Creator" (*Walking the Rez Road* 78). *Dagwaagig*, fall, is the balance to spring, a time to hunt and harvest, a time to give and receive at gatherings that mark the shortening of days, lives coming into focus, and the lengthening of stories. In *Walking the Rez Road*, Northrup describes the annual fall harvest time:

> As he drove to the lake, memories of past ricing season came to him. His earliest memories were of playing on the shore while his parents were out ricing. He knew the people enjoyed ricing and there were good feelings all around. Years seemed to melt from people. Grandparents moved about with a light step and without their canes. Laughing and loud talking broke out frequently. (94)

Biboon, winter, is time to tell stories and *booni* (quit) the busy behaviors of other seasons. Because making it through a long winter is an accomplishment, *biboonigizi* is the verb used to indicate age. As Northrup notes, winter is time to rest and "prepare for the next cycle of seasons" ("2,000 Seasons" 38). Occasionally, interseasonal acts connect one time to another and, like a second networked layer, weave a tighter whole between the quadrants. There is always a sense that the cycle of time provides a foundational perspective. In some texts this appears as an overlapping readiness—knockers in spring, regalia in winter, story-making all three seasons to be told in winter. In *Dirty Copper*, Luke's modern existence is measured in hours, days, months, and years, with frequent mentions of time in the astronomical military format. Not once are the seasons mentioned by name, but Luke is Anishinaabe, and seasons are written across the landscape as he mentions maple syrup, cornfields, and wild rice. These variables are the constants, with perhaps the land and water as coefficients, actions serving as signs and the language providing the parameters of Anishinaabe narrative.

Elements of Anishinaabe narrative construction that include viewing the narrative as a complex exchange and locating the story in the multi-layered understanding of Anishinaabe time provide a way to identify and read Anishinaabe text, a way to understand how Anishinaabe literature participates as a citizen of the Anishinaabe textual community, and an Anishinaabe way to read other texts.

Anishaaendamo: Reimagining the Existential

One example of extending the analysis of Northrup's writing to connect with other traditions is to look at how his work suggests a form of Anishinaabe existentialism, irony, and comedy. This can inform how we read the body of Northrup's work with existing theories and terminology and inform how we understand these traditions globally. Northrup's work is often considered unsettling by readers while also being incredibly funny. Ultimately, the pathos he inspires comes from a blend of laughter and shock as he moves from matter-of-fact reporting of terrible events that ignite post-traumatic stress to questions aimed and released so cleanly and swiftly that their sarcasm is only realized after the laughter subsides.

According to literary critic Richard Baker, "It is when humans demand meaning in an unresponsive world that the absurd exists" (2). Reading Northrup's work as part of a world literary tradition of the absurd opens new vistas of exploration, new ways to read the same story, and new ways to think about existentialism, irony, and humor in modern times. Such notable existential texts as *The Trial* and *Metamorphosis* by Franz Kafka connect easily to the surreal experience of an Anishinaabe veteran left wondering how to find honor in serving of the nation that subsumed his culture. In what he says and does not say, an unsettling picture of the settler colonial legacy is outlined. He may be proud to have followed in the footsteps of his relations who became warriors to protect the liberty of their land and community, but he often mentions that death is difficult to justify. In addition, how better to make sense of becoming a stranger in your own land than by adopting a partially existential philosophy and using fiction to understand reality? In *Walking the Rez Road* and *Dirty Copper*, Luke Warmwater relives days in the trenches seeking meaning that is never found. Like Estragon and Vladimir taking off boots and hats again and again while waiting for Godot, the veterans in Jim's novels are unable to step away from the scenes that replay in their minds. Reality becomes unrecognizable, and a lack of stable perception often bleeds from the subconscious to the conscious experience of days and nights. Thinking about the words for thinking, remembering, and philosophizing in Anishinaabemowin, we find that all the words relating to conscious response contain recognizable parts of the verb *inendam*. Sometimes translated as "thought," this root verb takes on many prefixes to become *mikwendan* (remember it), *apiitendam* (to focus thoughts on something), *babaamendam* (to pay attention or worry), *bagosendam* (to hope or wish), *gashkendamo* (to have tangled thoughts or sadness), and *anishaaendamo* (imagination). Of these, *anishaaendamo* is one of the most untranslatable. Related to the phrase *anishaa igo* or *anishaa gonaa*, to be kidding or knowingly presenting an alternate reality, the word implies a gentle nod to that which is not true, or subject to question, without relating to words about truth or knowledge. To think in this way is to explore how far an untruth or teasing tale might go, to question human action and belief systems, to explore existentialism. Although Northrup writes predominantly in English, *anishaaendamo* is visible in his work as his characters transform themselves into something other than soldiers who survive having witnessed, initiated, or longed for death. Writing about the unreality of the war, Northrup recalls,

> Something happened to time. It no longer flowed. Time slowed down and the grunts were no longer aware, but their eyes, ears and minds kept absorbing things as the chopper climbed out of rifle range . . . Luke and the other grunts just stood around outside, trapped inside their minds with the memories of what they saw, heard, and felt. Time returned to normal as the doctor came out and told them the gray marine died on the table. (*Walking the Rez Road* 13)

Northrup describes how rules of time and perception are altered through *anishaaendamo*, or Anishinaabe existentialism. This is more than destabilizing, deconstructive discourse, more than what Royle calls "uncanny politics" (128). Northrup is a dual citizen using language in layered and uncanny ways to dismantle presumed assimilation and reinforce indigenous self-reflection and self-construction. He references and recognizes a state of deconstruction and offers an alter-construction of reality through *anishaaendamo*. He demonstrates how narrative can reflect time out of reality when he allows the story to take control.

> A four year old boy named Joseph and his 42 year old father went for a walk one day. It was a special day. The boy was happy because he had his father's undivided attention. The father was happy because when he was with his son, he could forget past wars, present worries and future problems. Time was put on hold on this bright and sunshiny day as the two began their trip through reality. ("Son and Sunshine" 156)

Northrup's work helps define the structure of Anishinaabe narrative and connects Anishinaabe literature to traditions of time manipulation, allowing the story to move beyond the uncontrollable reality to an existence with the imagination of narration, attempting to see in spaces where sight does not usually exist. As he writes in one story, "Lug stood up to show his sister what it was like standing in the dark. He leaned forward trying to see through the night" (*Walking the Rez Road* 27).

Miikindizi: The Ironic Aim

Equally as interesting and related to *anishaaendamo* is the teasing irony found throughout much of Northrup's work. His invented words, subverted syntax, and rhetorical questions are not what the reader expects. They are the rhetorical evidence of a voice that knows how to unsettle, destabilize, or tease the reader and the English language itself. In Anishinaabemowin, the verb *miikindizi* means to be a tease, a provocateur. In that word, a speaker of Anishinaabemowin will hear the overlay in meaning with the verbs *miikonan* and *miikonaw*, which mean to shoot and hit something or someone. This connection between the two actions is highlighted in Anishinaabemowin narratives and in the English writing of several Anishinaabe authors (Gerald Vizenor, Gordon Henry, Alanis King, and Jim Northrup, among others). The ironic tease is an unexpected confrontation, an aim, taking place at micro- and macro-levels. *Miikindizi*, teasing irony, can untangle and rewrite standard tropes and terminology, disassemble them in whole or part, or create new definitions entirely. As Linda Hutcheon suggests, "irony is the intentional transmission of both information and evaluative attitude other than what is explicitly presented" (11). It has also been described as "language giving the lie to itself yet still relishing its power" (Hartman 146). This use of *miikindizi* as a discursive strategy allows Jim to parody American and tribal social systems, power conflicts, values, and behaviors. "Irony denies us our certainties by unmasking the world as an ambiguity" says Milan Kundera (134). Northrup certainly unmasks many ambiguities and stereotypes about Indians, veterans, Anishinaabeg, and marines, among other categories of confusion. Lori Chamberlain explains, "even while provoking laughter, irony invokes notions of hierarchy and subordination, judgment and perhaps even moral superiority" (98). This politicized, subjective message makes Northrup's work unsettling to readers. However, in the midst of a settler culture, the best storytellers are intentionally unsettling as they reclaim indigenous languages, repurpose the settlers' language, and define their own discursive community.

In Northrup's work, the *miikindizi* takes the form of word play and rhetorical questions. Echoing the multisyllabic, highly flexible qualities of Anishinaabemowin where competing and new definitions for actions and events are celebrated, Northrup crafts phrases with many layers of meaning. In *Anishinaabe Syndicated* he writes, "We have Irish Americans, Mexican Americans, German Americans, Swedish Americans, Japanese Americans, and so on. What does that make us? American Americans?" (12). On the surface, this is about the problem of what to call "Indians." Below the surface it is a comment on ethnic groups in general, the ability to claim heritage after settling in a new nation, and the false implications of "American." Repeated as a suffix, the name sounds especially absurd and calls into question the name of a nation with no current connection to the cartographers who first used the designation in Europe. This subtle focus on names destabilizes the power of naming. Later in the book he focuses more bluntly on the issue, saying, "I am not Indian, I am Anishinaabe. For almost five hundred years my ancestors and I have been called something we're not" (*Anishinaabe Syndicated* 42). By talking about race through irony and teasing, he challenges the reader to question all descriptions related to race. For instance, as he offers a description of Princess Pale Moon, founder of the American Indian Heritage Organization, he says, "she was stylishly dressed in regular white people clothes" (*Anishinaabe Syndicated* 67). Is he teasing Ms. Pale Moon, mocking those who might be impressed by her style, or questioning anyone who thinks they understand what stylish "white people clothes" might be? He likely intends to do all three.

He continues to tease ideas of identities when he asks, "What do you call people who choose to live in the Twin Cities?" His answer, "citidiots," is a tease in the Anishinaabe tradition for sure, creating new words by combining word parts in ways that are both logical and jarring (*Anishinaabe Syndicated* 175). He plays with language and urban identity, redirecting the reservation gaze to the exotic "citidiots" who are defined by their location. Another way he plays with words and identity is to tease two groups at the same time: those who wish to be Anishinaabe and the Anishinaabe who have allowed the language to come apart in strange ways. Asking another question, he writes, "How do you say 'culture vulture' in Ojibberish?" He quickly adds, "Anishaa-wannabee" (*Rez Salute* 31). This is a warning to the culture vultures and speakers of the language. In a single phrase he draws a connection between the vultures who consume what is left for dead and the jibberish that is born of a language surrounded by another culture.

Northrup aims his rhetorical questions at Anishinaabe readers who recognize the embedded assumptions and those unfamiliar with Anishinaabe culture who need their beliefs to be questioned. He explains: "Questions, like families, help make sense of the twists and turns of life. They highlight the humor we're blessed with. They are linguistic tricksters; sometimes the shape of the question shifts before you get the answer, then you see the subject in a new way.... Whenever I think I need to meditate on an answer, I'll ask a question" (*Rez Road Follies* 2). Often, in the tradition of narrative exchange, he throws back questions he has been asked. For example, he was asked, "do you speak your language?" and replied, "yup, yours too" (*Rez Road Follies* 2). When asked if he was "really an Indian," he replied, "no, I'm a spirit, I just look real to you" (*Anishinaabe Syndicated* 4). These didactic questions are aimed at the notion of cultural identity, turning the tables on assimilation and vanishment. Indians may be spirits, but Northrup and other descendants of "Indians" are visible and speak that language of two nations.

Northrup pushed people to confront tribal issues. He questioned historic intentions when he asked, "Why do you call it a 'rez' instead of a 'reservation?'" Listeners probably do not expect the answer, "Because the white man owns most of it" (*Anishinaabe Syndicated* 226). He used these ironic questions to bring the reader's mind to a full stop and reframe the discussion of life as a modern Anishinaabe. One of the real and practical concerns of Anishinaabe today is the question of legal identity, which Northrup examined by telling a story:

> All of this talk about blood quantum reminds me of my only blood quantum story. When I first heard about blood quantum, I was in the first grade at Pipestone, the Federal Boarding school. I was labeled as 15/16ths Minnesota Chippewa Indian. I didn't know which one of my /16ths was something else. Later on when I graduated from Carlton high school in '61, I was checking on scholarships and found that I was 13/16ths Minnesota Chippewa Indian. Hmmmm. . . . The last time I checked, I was 11/16ths. I quit checking because I am losing my blood somewhere. Where did my blood go? Was it those trips to the blood bank? The mosquitoes? I am ever so careful about nosebleeds and shaving. All I know is there is not enough blood for my grandchildren to be enrolled. (*Rez Salute* 23)

Through the public's questions about Native life, he questioned modern political and industrial life. At times he teased the "citidiots" with images of a more peaceful place. When asked, "what do you use for streetlights in Sawyer?," the answer is "the stars, and once in a while, the moon" (*Rez Salute* 18). His answer is not one of hidden traditions but is a reference to the same moon and stars that could be seen by anyone willing to walk outside the city sphere. His writing teases readers and demystifies connections to place by showing that generations or careful stewardship and sustainable living impart simple lessons that are not untranslatable. When asked, "does it hurt the tree when you remove the birch bark?" his answer is, "no, but do you live in a wood house or read a newspaper?" requires that readers see themselves with the Anishinaabe as stewards of the woodland (*Anishinaabe Syndicated* 37). His questions illustrate the disconnect of modernity and serve as a challenge to those willing to understand the answer to "why is some of your syrup dark and some light colored?" has everything to do with local food sourcing, racial color coding, and the syrup itself. His answer, "some of it we boil at night" takes aim at the search for simple solutions and immediate understanding (*Anishinaabe Syndicated* 92).

It is important to find in Northrup's work the reflexive tease as well. He takes aim not only at outsiders but at those lounging across the same living room. One infamous question he asked inspired a negative response from Anishinaabe culture. When he published the question, "Why do Indian men make better lovers?" with the answer, "a lot of them don't have to get up to go to work," he incited the ire of many factions: husbands, wives, politically correct editors etc. (*Anishinaabe Syndicated* 72). The question called attention the economic disparity in America and high unemployment on many reservations, but it was disturbing to many because it dangled on the reader's mind, disconnected from solutions to the problem. Northrup used a combination of existentialism and irony to highlight social and cultural complexity, rattling reality without knowing what the future holds.

Mazinaigan Baapaawinad: Shaking the Page

A third literary tradition to which Northrup contributes is humor. As Vine Deloria Jr. wrote in *Custer Died for Your Sins*, "when a people can laugh at themselves and laugh at others and hold all aspects of life together without letting anybody drive them to extremes, then it seems to me that that people can survive" (167). Like Northrup, Deloria implies a connection between humor and cultural continuity. Northrup's humor could be as subtle as watching a crows in the backyard.

> If we have bread that is starting to turn green, we share it with those guys in the black coats. The crows live in a world where almost everyone else is bigger and is a threat. They first see the food as they are flying by. The crows then land in the pines and just watch the food. Occasionally, they fly to another branch to look at things from another angle. After sitting and looking for a while, they glide down to the food. Their wings flare and they settle gently on the snow. The black feathers on the white snow really stand out, looking like one single word on a page. . . . Sometimes a large crow flies directly at a smaller one, deciding who is top dog in the crow world. One stopped pecking long enough to crow loudly. He sounded like he was happy to be eating. They live in a simple world, fly, eat, sleep, fly, eat, sleep. Maybe a little time out to make some baby crows,

but other than that, fly, eat, sleep. No worries like Bosnia, the Unabomber, and per capita payments. Nothing to worry about but a crow hop. One Sawyer morning I was looking out the window at the crows. I had the powwow tape on loud and I noticed them dancing. Nah, just kidding about the dancing crows. (*Anishinaabe Syndicated* 138)

He is kidding and he is not kidding. The crows teach observers to slow down, be focused, and keep things in perspective. The humor plays with language and the reader's definitions and expectations. It teaches and tests limits, serving as a rhetorical device and a contemporary postcolonial strategy. Describing Northrup's humor in Anishinaabe literary terms requires attention to the fact that *baapi* is to laugh, *baapaagaakwa* is to knock, and *baapagishka* is to shake. Shifting slightly and making a connection to irony, *baapinodaw* is to mock someone. Anishinaabe comedy is something that shakes perceptions, causes dissonance, and tests the limits of teasing.

The *baapaawinad*, the joke, is simple and playful, capitalizing on the two-culture vantage point American Indians often maintain and perhaps others might wish to cultivate. Living in two worlds, having a multifaceted identity provides more options for humor. Sometimes the only word a kid learns in Anishinaabemowin is "no" or "*gaawiin.*" Turning this literally negative reality into a joke, Northrup asked, "How do you say no hotdogs? Answer: Gaawiin-ers" (*Rez Salute* 62). Or he calls someone who plays slot machines "Keno-Sabe" turning the racist Lone Ranger into a casino caricature (*Anishinaabe Syndicated* 172). There is satisfaction for the amateur anthropologist in these jokes because they require knowledge of habits and behaviors not typically in the ethnographic records. For example, the following two questions require a sophisticated but silly level of knowledge about how Anishinaabe people habitually connect with one another.

> Question: What is the past tense of snag? Answer: Snug. (*Anishinaabe Syndicated* 11)

> Question: What do you call a Shinnob with no lips? Answer: Pointless. (*Rez Salute* 125)

Some urban dictionaries offer only one slang term for "snag," "sensitive new age guy" which makes the common pow-wow term "to hook up and find a temporary or long-term mate" even funnier by contrast.

For all the times dances, ceremonies, and traditional gatherings have been documented, it is not easy to find in the archives a description of how to toss your head back just right and send a quick pucker to acknowledge someone in the community. Playing with these words and behaviors solicits a smile and causes readers to remember that people are defined by more than their differences.

In *Humor in Contemporary Native North American Literature: Reimagining Nativeness*, Eva Gruber quotes Wilf Pelletier, who says: "Laughter is a great teacher. You learn from it with your gut more than your head. And what you learn as you are laughing is that nothing should be taken seriously except, perhaps, food and drink. When the Western world learns the art of conquest by laughter, peace will descend upon us and bless us" (4). Gruber further explains, "contemporary Native writers reply on this mediating and didactic capacity of humor, on its transcendence of the purely rational, to renegotiate images of Nativeness that are located in the readers' imaginations" (10). Northrup renegotiates the images of Native Americans and Americans. His work blends TV sit-com tradition with old-time Anishinaabe narrative marketing. His stories offer new views of both the majority and the minority. Writing about TV comedy, Darrell Hamamoto reminds us "the situation comedy as popular art was born amidst labor and capital conflict, interracial hostility, regional and sectional rivalries, and the pressures of Americanization faced by millions of immigrants working in a harsh, competitive environment" (4). Northrup shows how this did not occur in a universe parallel to Native life, but simultaneously as native writers were developing a new narrative tradition. Northrup described his own television tie-in, the play *Rez Jep*, as a portal to new views of native life.

> The play unfolds much like the real game show, with an Anishinaabe twist. The six categories are Ricing, Powwows, Tribal Councils, Higher Education, Casinos & Gambling, and Race Relations. Questions test the contestants' knowledge of life as a Shinnob. After the surprise (don't give it away) ending, the real audience got to ask questions about what they didn't understand. I would estimate 40 percent of what we said went over their heads because they were not familiar with skins and their humor. They might have been looking for legends when we were looking for laughs. For instance, one question

was "When do the dead come to life?" The answer of course is "Just before the election." It is my hope that the ones who didn't understand the play ask the next skin they see about it. Maybe people will understand us better when they see what makes us laugh. (*Anishinaabe Syndicated* 161)

A game show with false advertising, scorekeeping, and stereotypes reteaches tribal political history, redefines Anishinaabe social norms, and makes clear the diversity of the native community. Because so many corrections are juxtaposed with laughter, Northrup was able to knock down previously held assumptions much more efficiently; his *baapaawinad* inserted new views into the conversation more quickly than long debates of definitions. The quick question, "How did Shinnobs survive the Great Depression?" is answered with a wry, "I didn't know it was over," and the story moves on, leaving in that echo of laughter a wonderment about generational trauma, economic inequality, and the highest suicide rate among all American ethnicities (*Anishinaabe Syndicated* 24). Social services and powerful ceremonies may address these problems, but humor is often the release valve, the identifying area, the place where the pain can be poked, prodded, and drained.

A final note about Northrup's comedy fits perfectly with the notion of being physically rattled by humor. Many fluent speakers bemoan the fact that some of the best and bawdiest bits are removed from stories as they translate into English. Of course many twists of meaning are lost in translation, but the romantic notion of the Indian in America has never allowed the direct and dripping passion of the original stories to come through. Northrup works to put a bit of that back into Anishinaabe narrative tradition. While female characters occasionally talk about fending off men, most of his innuendos are in the male voice, or are just plain penis jokes. But what could be funnier than a penis joke? One of the funniest traditional tales is the penis and the moccasin comparing who has a harder life. Thomas Stillday had two versions of this story. In it they are "*maazhendamowaad zaam ogichimaazhidoodaan*," melancholy over their poor treatment, which always inspires a laugh (32). When he poses the question, "What did the Indian say when he saw a white man wading ashore?" you can imagine the snare drum "da dum dum" after the answer, "Is that a treaty in your pocket or are you just glad to see me?" (*Anishinaabe Syndicated* 147). Subtle innuendo about lusting for land and ravaged savages aside, it's hard not to laugh. It's also impossible to resist smiling when he asks, "What is Shinnob Viagra?" and then shares the secret tribal recipe: one part blueberry, one part moose meat, one part wild rice, one part commod pork, one part maple syrup, one part bacon grease, and 94 parts Fix-a-Flat" (*Anishinaabe Syndicated* 225). Again, beneath the *baapaawinad* are allusions to traditional woodland bounty, commodity rations supplied by the government, and good old-fashioned Anishinaabe ingenuity born of solving problems with what is in the garage. Northrup uses *baapaawinad*, Anishinaabe comedy, to blur the lines, test the limits, and deliver hidden lessons efficiently in his texts.

Mii'iw, Miidash: To Be Continued

Question: Why do we still need to ask questions after three hundred years of living together?

Answer: Slow learners. (*Anishinaabe Syndicated* 32)

Northrup's work illustrates elements of Anishinaabe narrative, including ritual exchange and recognition of time as a cycle of past, present, and future tracing the Earth's location and fixing stories in seasons and performance of action. He told stories and asked questions, whether or not the answers were obvious, not matter how fast or slow the learners may be. From existential *anishinaabendamo*, to carefully aimed *miikindizi* irony, to the comedic shake of *baapaawinad*, he wrote as an Anishinaabe contributing to world literature. He gathered important lessons, wrapped them in narrative, layering identity across time. This serious task is tied to the roots of being in and beyond the world. "We teach our children and grandchildren the history and stories of our people" ("2,000 Seasons" 38). Yet these are also the traditions other cultures know, and an Anishinaabe view of these rhetorical stances can inform any literature. In the end, that is the path to evolution, the repetition of invisible threads in a rhythm recognized by storytellers everywhere. We see these stories as clearly Anishinaabe, yet we also see how they fit into world traditions. Like a heart beat or a drum beat, they are the echo of one and many, visible and invisible. Like the image Northrup recalls of his grandpa, "while he was telling the story, he kept time by tapping a drum only he saw. His hand was shaped around an invisible drum stick as he kept time on the arm of his chair" (*Walking the Rez Road* 150). In the story, sight and sound become one and the words make meaning of the invisible.

References

Baker, Richard E. *The Dynamics of the Absurd in the Existentialist Novel*. New York: P. Lang, 1993.

Chamberlain, Lori. "Bombs and Other Exploding Devices, or the Problem of Teaching Irony." In *Reclaiming Pedagogy: The Rhetoric of the Classroom*, edited by P. Donohue and E. Quandahl, 29–40. Carbondale: Southern Illinois University Press, 1989.

Deloria, Vine, Jr. *Custer Died for Your Sins: An Indian Manifesto*. Norman: University of Oklahoma Press, 1969.

Derrida, Jacques. *Monolingualism of the Other: or, The Prosthesis of Origin*, translated by Patrick Mensah. Redwood City, CA: Stanford University Press, 1998.

Gruber, Eva. *Humor in Contemporary Native North American Literature: Reimagining Nativeness*. New York: Camden House, 2008.

Hamamoto, Darrell Y. *Nervous Laughter: Television Situation Comedy and Liberal Democratic Ideology*. New York: Praeger, 1989.

Hartman, Geoffrey H. *Saving the Text: Literature, Derrida, Philosophy*. Baltimore: Johns Hopkins University Press, 1981.

Hutcheon, Linda. *Irony's Edge: The Theory and Politics of Irony*. London: Routledge, 1994.

Kundera, Milan. *The Art of the Novel*, translated by L. Asher. New York: Grove Press, 1986.

Momaday, N. Scott. *The Man Made of Words: Essays, Stories, Passages*. New York: St. Martin's, 1998.

Noodin, Margaret. *What the Chickadee Knows: Poems in Anishinaabemowin and English*. Detroit: Wayne State University Press, 2020.

Northrup, Jim. "2,000 Seasons." In *Do You Know Me Now: An Anthology of Minnesota Multicultural Writing*, edited by Elisabeth Rosenberg, 35–40. Bloomington, MN: Normandale Community College, 1992.

———. *Anishinaabe Syndicated: A View from the Rez*. St. Paul: Minnesota Historical Society Press, 2011.

———. *Dirty Copper*. Golden, CO: Fulcrum, 2014.

———. *The Rez Road Follies*. Stillwater, MN: Voyageur Press, 1997.

———. *Rez Salute: The Real Healer Dealer*. Golden, CO: Fulcrum, 2012.

———. "Son and Sunshine." In *Touchwood*, edited by Gerald Vizenor, 156–58. Minneapolis: New Rivers Press, 1987.

———. *Walking the Rez Road: Twentieth Anniversary Edition*. Golden, CO: Fulcrum, 2013.

Royle, Nicholas. *The Uncanny*. New York: Routledge, 2003.
Stillday, Thomas J. "Bajaaganish Miinawaa Makizinish." *Oshkaabewis Native Journal* 7, no. 1 (2009): 32–39.
Vastokas, Joan. "Pictographs and Petroglyphs." In *The Canadian Encyclopedia* (2012). http://www.thecanadianencyclopedia.com/en/article/pictographs-and-petroglyphs/.

Chapter 11

Enduring Cultural Poses

Memory, Resistance, and Symbolic Sculpture

DAVID STIRRUP

> Why am I wasting my time talking about white men's giant statues? Because they are a form of discrimination.
>
> —John Fire Lame Deer, *Lame Deer, Seeker of Visions*

> A monument is a deposit of the historical possession of power.
>
> —Ruth B. Phillips, "Settler Monuments, Indigenous Memory"

If the title of this book carries a double connotation, so does the title of this chapter. The inference of the word "enduring," which can indicate stamina, longevity, persistence, but also a sense of the long suffering, is that the "poses" we encounter here, whether critical or cultural, are simultaneously strong and pervasive and potentially damaging, limiting, and imposed. I stress the latter, and the poses I address are literal: the frozen poses of victimry established in the form of colonial memorial statuary and in the broader vernacular of memorialization and commemoration. While my ostensible focus is on two plays written and first performed in the 1990s—Gerald Vizenor's *Ishi and the Wood Ducks* and E. Donald Two-Rivers's *Chili Corn*—I begin with a more general discussion of monuments and memorials to establish precisely what is at stake in both Native and non-Native representation of Indigenous peoples and spaces.[1]

To say that public art has a social function is of course to utter a truism, but the very nature of that social function is multifaceted—it produces meaning differently for different audiences. In many cases, those meanings can have negative, even damaging consequences. For the two Anishinaabe authors in this conversation, the social production of meaning in particular spaces is paramount for the ways that static monuments to the past can render that past invisible, or alternately reiterate hegemonic mythologizing, which inevitably obscures the realities of the present. The paradox that memorialization tends to prescribe forgetting underscores the particular interactions the writers under scrutiny have with statuary and memorialization, and with the notion of public sculpture that demeans, undermines, delimits, or refuses Native agency and sovereignty. Ultimately, I argue that these interactions effect decolonizing gestures enact what Dean Rader calls "engaged resistance" to the assumptions of colonial historiography and call attention to the histories and realities said statuary obscures.

Historic Monuments and the Power of Scale

To be clear, it is far from my intention to deride all public art and memorial employing Native images, forms, and names as dishonorable or misguided. There are many cases of well-intentioned memorials and an increasing number of powerful pieces of Native public art. Some of these seek simply to re-place indigenous-inspired forms and motifs in specific landscapes; others are more interventionist, seeking to resist stereotype and reclaim primacy of representation.[2] Dean Rader discusses the "public statues and sculptures of Native Americans in Santa Fe" which "now carry a meaning beyond themselves" (184). He notes their commercial, touristic potential, of course, asking, "are these sculptures an homage to the Indians who once occupied the areas around Santa Fe, or are they part of the municipal semiotics that bring tourists and their credit cards to the plaza?" (184). Their specific iconography—not least their bare-chested and befeathered forms, both sexualized and mythicized—is key to a vernacular of the noble savage. More recent than the Santa Fe statues, a forty-foot-tall statue of Kluscap towering over the Glooscap Heritage Centre and Mi'kmaq Museum (and Highway 102, for that matter) in Millbrook, Novia Scotia, is an excellent example of both participating in and challenging that problematic vernacular. The statue affirms for many the importance of cultural revival—symbolic of the Mi'kmaq broadly, its depiction of the mythical Kluscap significantly avoids the standard reification of individuals or memorialization of events common to the monumental tradition.

Although the Klusap figure replicates the classic bare-chested and feathered warrior, context and location—as well as the detailed information boards that accompany the statue—help prevent its subsumption into colonial (and colonizing) representation. Not inconsequentially, the Kluscap statue also puts the Glooscap Heritage Centre on the map of giant roadside statue in Canada's Atlantic province, invoking the tourist dollar adjacent to a historical-educational endeavor rather than a purely commercial one. The first answer to Rader's question in Santa Fe, then, is probably "both." Yet in the sense that memorials are designed as much to give permission to forget as to remember, as many have argued, that "homage," a memorial function, ironically writes Native peoples out of the landscape—generating myth rather than, as with Kluscap, drawing *from* myth. More to the point, the logical corollary to Rader's description that the Santa Fe memorials "are woven into the tapestry of the town's landscape; they are part and parcel of the argument Santa Fe makes about itself" is precisely that they render the Native absent while indigenizing the town's self-narrative. As he writes, "Indianness has come to be inexorably linked with Santa Fe's identity" (190). In other words, they represent not simply the Indianness of Santa Fe but the very Santa Fe–ness of Santa Fe, semiotically encoded as indigenous (or, in Rader's words, fiercely marketed as "one of America's most indigenously embodied municipalities"; 190).

In other words, space—the space of the monument, public or private—is every bit as significant as intent in generating affect and effects. Intent, of course, is not necessarily always readable, but there is clearly a line between cultural self-representation and the implicit effects of monuments and memorials that, as has been written recently in relation to Holocaust memorials in Germany, constitute "the not so subtle attempt at *Entsorgunug*, the public disposal of radiating historical waste" (Huyssen 32). Where colonial monuments tend to commemorate individual accomplishments on one hand and mark historical traumatic events or significant victories on the other, much monumental sculpture made by Native artists and on behalf of Native communities veer toward generalized representation and even abstraction. Whereas the former obscure and absorb Native sovereignties into colonial narratives, the latter point to

Indigenous presence and the Indigenous present, eschewing closure—one objective of memorial—and enacting resistance by articulating (aesthetic) sovereignty and survivance.

The particular problematics of this issue are perhaps best briefly exemplified with an infamous response to the most monumental and iconic of memorials—the Crazy Horse Memorial at Thunder Mountain in the Black Hills (Páha Sapá) of South Dakota. Writing in 1972, following a protest against Korczak Ziolkowski's work on the memorial, John Fire Lame Deer said:

> This genius [Ziolkowski], I am told, makes more than 100,000 green frog skins a year tax-free from tourist admissions and by selling plaster models of his statue from three dollars up—tax-free, because he is doing all this for us poor Indians. Somewhere in, or under, that statue is supposed to be a fifty-million dollar university for Indians, maybe in the big toe or hoof, I'm not quite sure where, but I'm fairly sure that we Indians never got any money out of this. (94)

Referring to the balance between commercial advantage and motivation, Lame Deer makes two particularly salient points. On one hand, he addresses the condescending paternalism behind the "plight" narrative that, quite literally, justified such work in the 1940s when it began. On the other, he points out the irony of "poor" Indians—the community at Pine Ridge Reservation in South Dakota numbering among the most disadvantaged groups in the United States—receiving an expensive sculpture rather than the money it generates.

Lame Deer reveals some of the best intent behind the memorial, alluding to its beginning in a request from Henry Standing Bear on behalf of Lakota leaders unhappy with the desecration of Mount Rushmore and seeking a gesture of acknowledgment of the "true history" of Western settlement. Despite the deaths of Ziolkowski in 1982 and his wife, Ruth, in 2014, work continues, and the planned university has been launched as a collaboration between the Memorial Trust and the University of South Dakota. Good intentions, though, are a limited currency for Lame Deer:

> The time has passed when a white man could simply decide for us to build a monument on our behalf according to what

he had in mind, in our sacred hills, without asking us. When he started it all over thirty years ago, he could still find Indians who were flattered that a white sculptor-genius wanted to do a statue of an Indian chief. But these days are over. (94–95)

In even blunter terms, he continues, "He might have good intentions, but he doesn't see that all that gigantic carving up of our sacred mountains is just another form of racism" (95).

The fundamental prejudice implicit in the assumptions and presumptions behind such projects are perhaps clearest in the words of Gutzon Borglum, Ziolkowski's one-time boss and creator of the Mount Rushmore monument. Like Ziolkowski, Borglum "had a dream, 'dear to his heart' . . . to create an enormous memorial to the Sioux Indians in the Pine Ridge foothills near Chadron, Neb." (Wagner). Borglum had played with Indians as a boy, Wagner reports: he was "'brought up on the tales of those old chiefs,'" and believed that "the Lakota were a people of great 'integrity,'" unlike those who oppressed them. In an Associated Press story from 1938, Borglum described the crimes perpetrated against the Lakota by their mendacious, rapacious colonizers, hoping that one day a memorial such as he envisaged would "serve as a vehicle for righting some of [those] wrongs" (Wagner). Again, in a speech in 1940 at the foot of Mount Rushmore, he declared

> We are standing on territory once belonging to the Sioux Indians—that great warlike race, like the Romans, who ruled everything from Wyoming to Chicago. I wish we had treated them better, in a more noble manner. We are standing on their very land, for which we never paid a cent—just stole it from them and lied about it. Well, these are the things we probably will do something about some day. (Wagner)

If Lame Deer articulates a sense of cynical exploitation and paternalism in response to the Crazy Horse memorial and by extension Borglum's earlier plans, Borglum's descriptions of treaty-breaking and his general sense that the Native communities of North America had been monumentally wronged are sentiments that are largely irrefutable.[3] As hard as it is to escape the deep irony of committing millions of dollars to sculptural projects designed to "right the wrongs" of acts perpetrated on the lands of one of the most disadvantaged tribal nations in the United States, the desire to ensure or restore a historical balance is surely positive. The fact that it is being constructed, just like Mount Rushmore, on those same sacred lands taken from and still under dispute with the Lakota remains an ambivalent spoke in the wheel of philanthropy.

On many levels, such memorials are simply further colonial impositions on Indigenous peoples and environments. Shaped by the forces—and prejudices—of their times, some clear markers of complicity in the forces of violence that Borglum (for instance) berates are explicit in his language. His use of past tense along with his implicit mythologizing of the Lakota participate in a rhetoric of vanishing that sees Native Americans only in terms of the past and as variously doomed or conquerors/colonizers/immigrants themselves, as if this somehow explains or justifies European colonization of the Americas. This latter is intricately imbricated with a self-justificatory narrative of Manifest Destiny on one hand and cultural assumption of Native absence or invisibility on the other. The present-day Lakota, on whose treaty-promised land Borglum stood, become entirely obscured in the process.

In "Identity and Exchange," Hartwig Isernhagen footnotes another of Borglum's pronouncements on the issue of memorialization, this time from the "Sioux Memorial" special issue of *Nebraska History*. Isernhagen quotes Borglum's rather pompous pronouncement that "it is a particularly gracious act for us, as the victorious nation, to put up a memorial to those who preceded us here—not merely as a historical record, but to honour them as a brave and valiant race" (194 n.32). As Isernhagen points out, Borglum's acknowledgment of the Lakota is always already past tense. It prompts the question, as does the Crazy Horse Memorial, about the conditions of life—the circumstances of survivance—of the present-day Lakota in the vast edifice's shadow.

Two things are at stake here. On one hand, the weighty baggage of notionally paying "honor" to Native Americans inevitably evinces a devastatingly misleading sense of their pastness. Again, the iconography described by Rader is abundantly clear in the Crazy Horse memorial, celebrating Native survival via a static rendition of a nineteenth-century bare-chested Indian—albeit a Native "hero." As loudly as it proclaims nobility, it does so using the grammar of noble savagery and inevitable demise. On the other hand, the space in which the memorial is constructed engenders a profoundly paradoxical scenario in which colonial imposition is at once erased and repeated, asking who, ultimately, the memorial is for. Does it honor the brave, or does it assuage a guilt?

The Plays

The two plays I discuss reflect on earlier times—the 1910s of Ishi's residence at the University of California, Berkeley's Museum of Anthropology, and the 1970s of direct political action—but carry that spirit of renewed engagement and resistance to historical and invented representations of Native peoples. I do not rehearse their respective plots in great detail here, but a quick sketch may be useful. Two-Rivers's two-act play *Chili Corn* is set in an apartment in Chicago, where Benny Red-Beaver, a Canadian-born Ojibwa and director of the Chicago chapter of the American Indian Movement (AIM), flirts with a woman, Vanessa (Chili) Corn.[4] An "urban Chippewa" from northern Minnesota,[5] Benny has brought Chili to his apartment as part of an urban protection scheme for vulnerable women. While she is there, Benny takes phone calls and then a visit from Gabriel Peoples, a Menominee and AIM street coordinator. It becomes clear that they are planning a demonstration—which Gabriel intends to escalate—against a statue outside the Chicago Historical Society of an "Indian" scalping a white woman. Gabriel brings in Rosario, just arrived from Mexico, because he believes she can provide explosives. Like Chili, she is on the run, an exiled member of late 1960s dissent in Chiapas. Gabriel believes she is a bomb-maker, contributing to the play's dramatic irony as the audience sees early on that he has his wires crossed. Toward the end of act 1, Chili's abusive boyfriend, Waabooz, appears—in shadows, as a voice on the answer machine, and as a disembodied voice outside the apartment.

Waabooz (rabbit), often associated with the Ojibwe trickster Nanabozho, closes out scene 2; Rosario is convinced she has killed him by randomly shooting, as police sirens roll up in the street. Act 2 reveals a number of surprises. Rosario, it turns out, is not Gabriel's official Mexican contact, who was shot dead crossing the border. Gabriel determines to leave for the History Society with what he believes is a bomb in spite of the apparent stakeout. Tensions mount between the four, and Gabriel starts threatening to shoot Benny. A phone call informs them that it is too late, the statue has already been moved. Preparing for a showdown with the police, the developing relationship between Rosario and Gabriel is accelerated before the comic deflation of a phone call that reveals Waabooz was not killed but has been arrested and that the stakeout was related to a raid on a dopehouse in the same building. The bomb, it turns out, is a bottle of mezcal, which loosens Benny's tongue into telling of how his girlfriend, Donna, who has phoned periodically throughout the play, likes him to dress up as a brave and perform aggressive sex with her. As the cast disperses, Benny prepares to visit Donna again.

Ishi and the Wood Ducks is a very different prospect. Driven by humor and equally focused on the legacy of colonial damage, it takes a more cerebral, less physical approach to its subject matter. Subtitled *Postindian Trickster Comedies*, trickster plays a slightly different role here—a more explicitly comedic role—where in *Chili Corn* Waabooz's role is disruptive and sinister, but ultimately he brings about catharsis of sorts. The prologue is set outside a federal courtroom, where Ishi—the so-called last of the Yahi, who lived his final years at the University of California's Museum of Anthropology under the auspices of Professor Alfred Kroeber—sits talking to an elderly woman, Boots Story. The four acts then take place, in turn, in the Museum (during Ishi's lifetime); at the Mount Olivet Cemetery Columbarium (present moment); at Kroeber Hall, University of California (present); and finally inside the federal courtroom (indeterminate). Although each act putatively takes place in a particular moment in time, the indicators of time are rendered deliberately ambiguous, not least through the presence of the characters of Alfred Kroeber and Ishi himself, long after their deaths.

Ishi takes in many of the issues already touched on here, not least in act 3, where a panel discusses the possibility of renaming the fictitious Kroeber Hall "Ishi Hall" in his memory (and a direct, deliberate inversion on Vizenor's part of how achievements are memorialized—"Ishi made my name . . ." ["Ishi" 321] says Kroeber, the proposer). In act 4, Ishi tries—and fails—to prove his credentials as an artist according to the remit of the Indian Arts and Crafts Act (1990), passed at the very beginning of the decade in which Vizenor's play was written, which also saw the passage of the Native American Graves and Repatriation Act (NAGPRA 1992). Act 2, meanwhile, follows the artist Zero Larkin into Mount Olivet Cemetery's Columbarium, where, accompanied by a reporter and photographer, he seeks inspiration from Ishi's burial urn for his own sculpture. All of this follows from act 1, which takes place in and around Ishi's *wickiup* in the Museum of Anthropology, during which Vizenor stresses Ishi's role as ironic tease and subverter of common assumptions.

Literary Activism, Agents of Change

The statue around which the plot of *Chili Corn* fails to unfold is very real. Resituated in the foyer of the Chicago Historical Society from Fort Dearborn in 1931, it depicts the rescue by Potawatomi Chief Black Partridge of Margaret Helm, who struggles in the grip of a young warrior with tomahawk raised to strike. The events it portrays took place during the Battle of Fort Dearborn in the War of 1812, and the message it infers is intriguing. On one hand, the bare-chested warrior, brutal enough to kill a defenseless woman, imparts a clear message of savagery that can be readily internalized by individuals and the wider community. As Daniel Heath Justice says in interview with Sam McKegney, "the male body is seen as capable of and a source only of violence and harm. When that's the only model you have, what a desolation, right?" (McKegney 144). This in turn fuels the internal justifications underpinning Manifest Destiny, perpetuating stereotypes that Gerald Taiaiake Alfred identifies as "instrumental to someone else's agenda . . . it's meant to be killed, every single time" (quoted in McKegney 79). The statue was protested in Chicago in the 1970s by Native American groups (including Two-Rivers), after which it was removed. Reinstalled once more in the 1990s at 18th Street and Prairie Avenue—a catalyst for Two-Rivers's play—it was later removed for conservation and remains in storage, the hidden subject of resistance by Chicago's American Indian Center. On the other hand, the depiction of Black Partridge, bare-chested but nobly raising his hand against the warrior's strike, imparts another message. This time, bedecked in leggings (the warrior wears only a breech-cloth) and carrying what looks like a flintlock rifle in contrast to the warrior's knife and hatchet, he tells a story of emerging civilization, the redemptive potential of alliance. He even stands over what appears to be a cherub, cementing his association with heroic (civilized) iconography. In the context of the War of 1812, when the American nation further reinforced its credentials in opposition to the British, this apparent interpolation of the Native into a narrative of America's resistance to savage aggression is significant. Like the statue in the play, its association with the particular institutional space of the historical society communicates a deeper truth to the depiction.

Of course, devoting too much attention to the statue partly misses the point. There is no doubting its damaging aspect, a fact addressed directly when Benny describes to Chili the nature of the protest for which he and Gabriel are preparing. Having told Chili what the statue portrayed ("this big-assed statue of a white woman getting scalped by an Indian," Two-Rivers 105), he explains his reasons for organizing a demonstration:

> BENNY: A busload of kids was running about . . . When they see us standing there they looked really scared and went way around us. At first I was wondering to myself, what's wrong with these little guys? Then I spotted the statue and this cabinlike thing . . .
> There was this sign that said, "American Indians—Friend or Foe?" then they showed a few farming implements and a whole wall full of weapons. (Two-Rivers 106)

Two-Rivers is explicit about the specific damage such representations can cause:

> BENNY: . . . Now, you ask yourself what would that make a little kid think?
>
> CHILI: Man, you talk about your racist statements!
>
> BENNY: No jokin', Sherlock. Some hippie came up with the idea that it's actually against the Illinois constitution to have a statue like that because it incites hate against Indians. (Two-Rivers 106)

As flippant as Benny's comment is, it is incontestable that such representations fuel negative stereotypes, which may generate or reinforce prejudice. Indeed, the Illinois constitution, redrafted in 1970 and adopted in 1971, does address rights pertaining to race and ethnicity. Section 20 of Article I, the Bill of Rights, which refers to individual dignity, states that "communications that portray criminality, depravity or lack of virtue in, or that incite violence, hatred, abuse or hostility toward, a person or group of persons by reason of or by reference to religious, racial, ethnic, national or regional affiliation are condemned."[6] Although tribes cannot sue for civil rights violations, as a 2003 Supreme Court Decision confirmed (*Inyo County v. Paiute-Shoshone Indians* [No. 02-281], 538 U.S. 701 [2003]), Native Americans are covered by state constitutions as individuals in the same way that other citizens are.[7] Section 20 was intended to cover insulting statements; by 2001, only one recorded case had offered interpretation of Section 20, and that involved a discriminatory note written by a shopkeeper (Kopecky and Harris 48). Nevertheless, in the context of Two-Rivers's purposes here, the statue as text encodes "depravity" in a way that may be read as incitement to prejudice. Stretched as that possibility is (I certainly wouldn't like to present the case in court), it imparts a clear understanding of the relationship between hegemonic representations of past events and generalized understandings of present-day Native peoples.

The statue casts a secondary shadow of male–female violence on the other central subject of the play's plot, which revolves around two women fleeing different forms of persecution, including serious domestic abuse. Chili initially describes her abuse at Waabooz's hands in simple terms: "Asshole wants to kill me. You know what I mean?" (Two-Rivers 111). There is the faintest of echoes of the statue here—a vulnerable woman pursued by an aggressive man. To go beyond the description of the statue in the play to the actual monument, she is "saved" by a politically committed intercessionary, Benny. The related politics (Black Partridge was a mediator, whereas AIM's image in the mid-1970s was anything but one of mediation or moderation) may well resist any closer reading of statue and plot, of course, but the truly chilling moment comes later, just before the play's denouement, when Chili is trying to figure out her future:

> CHILI: And he treated me real bad . . .
> I ended up with such low self-esteem. I didn't feel very pretty . . . or desirable. (*Pause.*) You understand? (*Pause.*) Sometimes I even felt like I deserved it when he's beat me up. (*Pause.*) Then one time he stuck his gun in my mouth. He had removed the bullets, but I didn't know that. He pulled the trigger, and I fainted. When I regained consciousness, he was raping me. (Two-Rivers 133)

The stark brutality of this moment seemingly throws the statue into relief. The two situations—protesting a negative representation and violent physical abuse against women—appear momentarily, preposterously dichotomized. Yet herein lies the subtle cleverness of the play.

That these two things are both aspects of the contemporary lived experience of Native communities is confirmed by Two-Rivers in his preface to *Briefcase Warriors*. Describing the need for Native playwrights to start writing real Indian characters for the theater—another aspect of the stereotype-debunking remit of much of his work—he recounts a conversation with his long-term partner, Beverly Moeser, in 1994 in which AIM activist turned actor Russell Means comes up: "You know I'm an old AIM man myself. Hell, woman—I led a demonstration right over there across the street. At the Hysterical [*sic*] Society. What do you think?" (vii). Confirming this as inspiration for Benny's demonstration in the play, he notes, "As I wrote the play, a young woman in my life was actually undergoing the same sort of mistreatment from her boyfriend that my character Chili was" (viii–ix).

At first glance, we might be tempted to read the play as insisting the later event of abuse renders the earlier demonstration trivial; that so-called Native warriors like Gabriel attend to the insignificant at the expense of serious, pressing issues. What does a marble statue in a stuffy institution matter when vulnerable people are abused and damaged? This, however, is where the statue itself participates in the spirit of engaged resistance, Rader's "controlling metaphor," for a "fundamentally indigenous form of aesthetic discourse that engages both Native and American cultural contexts as a mode of resistance against the ubiquitous colonial tendencies of assimilation and erasure" (1). It is significant that although sometimes ridiculous, Benny and Gabriel are not explicitly ridiculed by Two-Rivers, an AIM man himself. Of course, it is significant that they are rendered "real." There are three clear ways this rendition of engaged resistance manifests. Despite never actually seeing the statue, since it is removed before Benny and Gabriel even leave the apartment, many of the issues associated with the type of representation it stands for and the ideological function such representations serve are laid bare, producing a narrative of resistance to the type of erasure such statuary effects. That is the first, most obvious level. Second, one of those stories of erasure—the failure to acknowledge and adequately deal with the disproportionate levels of violence against Native American and First Nations women—is brought to the surface precisely through the ironic absence of the monument. Third, the story and all its elements are packaged in a way that does service to Native-centered discourse, which absorbs the colonial imposition into its essential comedy and renders a tale of Native communities articulating and negotiating their own challenges. Through the honest illumination of domestic abuse, through the day-to-day intimacy, humor, and love that develop in its midst, to the deliberate invocation of Waabooz, rabbit, trickster, of an Anishinaabe signifier for making sense of and working through the obstacles the play erects, the depiction of male violence against women is literally laid at the feet of such representations as the statue depicts, but resisted and reworked as a story of survivance not victimry.

The question of memorialization is rendered quite differently in *Ishi and the Wood Ducks*, where, among other plot points, Vizenor effectively opposes the renaming of Kroeber Hall with Zero Larkin's desire to absorb the artistic spirit of Ishi by taking a rubbing of the name on Ishi's funerary urn for use in his memorial sculpture. In turn, he opposes Zero, "native sculptor with a vision," seeker of mystical connection, with Ishi the artist, who cannot "prove" his authenticity because the Yahi are not a recognized tribe under the auspices of the Indian Arts and Crafts Act (IACA). The absurdity of the latter scenario is of course in ironic tension with how Ishi satiates a need for Indigenous presence for other characters, such as Kroeber and Zero. Vizenor serves this irony up, as ever, linguistically. In act 4, where the Kroeber character is transformed into a tribal judge, he asks: "Mister Ishi, are you represented by counsel to answer these charges, that you are not an established tribal character?" ("Ishi" 327). Use of the word "character" triples in this short exchange, appearing to refer at first to his moral character—under scrutiny because other artists have complained that he is "not a real Indian," in other words, that he is committing ethnic fraud—then to a generalized tokenism as Kroeber makes reference to the fictitious but perfectly titled "Minority Character and Judicial Reform Act." The deliberate ambiguity of the first phrase is choice. It could refer to a perceived (stereotyped) moral character in a person of ethnic minority, the implications of which then infer the potential for racial profiling and institutional racism through legislature such as the Indian Arts and Crafts Act. On the other hand, it also renders Ishi a cartoon-like caricature, a token *indian* to accompany other minority clichés invented by the majority culture. This ultimately renders him, in the third instance already quoted above, a tribal character, not a man of character.

The exchange continues:

KROEBER: What tribal character does he intend to claim?

POPE: Yahi, of the Yana.

ASHE: The Yahi, your honor, is not a federally recognized tribe. ("Ishi" 327)

The nuances of the word implicitly render the people and groups it is associated with here—Ishi, the tribal—as ambiguous constructions. The tribal character he may or may not claim becomes simultaneously a moral quality, an essence or distinctive aspect, a reputation, an invention, even a symbol. Blurring possibilities speaks to the ways such figures, such "tribal characters," serve the needs of the hegemonic culture to stand in for particular qualities or synecdochically take on the guilt/bravery/fate/endurance/anger/promise or other emotive or emotional baggage of particular episodes of US history. The so-called Last of the Yahi becomes, in other words, a monument. The paradox such monumentalization presents is neatly demonstrated by Vizenor in this scene, showing that the "remains of the stone age," as Kroeber calls Ishi's heritage—remains, incidentally, that highly ironically the "Counsel . . . agreed not to romance"—while serving the anthropological narrative of indigeneity also simultaneously fall foul of the mechanism by which indigeneity becomes regulated in the modern world. The ultimate irony: the IACA, and tribal enrollment more generally, depends a lot on instruments like blood quantum, another anthropological invention.

If controlling and policing Indigenous bodies is one goal of legislation, then, consuming Indigenous cultures is variously shown to be a facet of the institutional scenarios Vizenor depicts here. Anishinaabe artist Andrea Carlson pursues a similar line of intervention in paintings like "Cannibal Ferox" and "Soldier Blue" from her 2008 *VORE* series. Dealing with cultural consumption more broadly, both literally and as metaphor for exploration and assimilation, and the consumption—both ideological and cultural—of Indigenous peoples in the service of popular culture and popular cultural mythology in the United States, Carlson produces representations of classical statuary literally cannibalizing body parts. "Cannibal Ferox" references the Italian exploitation film by the same name written and directed by Umberto Lenzi (1981). A follow-up to Ruggero Deodato's *Cannibal Holocaust* (1980), which is also referenced in another of Carlson's paintings, *Cannibal Ferox* claimed to be the most violent film ever made. Facing Carlson's painting, one is confronted by her signature abstract landscape background, which references Anishinaabe designs and timescapes, with two large circles reminiscent of the eyes of skulls, before which float two classical marble statues chewing on human limbs. Across the bottom of the painting but written backward (in its mirror image) are the words "CANNIBAL FEROX." While the exploitation films, revolving around the discovery, provocation, and mutual slaughter of Indigenous South American communities by white Euro-Americans, purport to reflect the hypocrisy and moral depravation of modern "civilized" society back to itself, Carlson resists merely presenting the mirror image. Instead, onlookers stand in an ambiguous space, potentially facing or standing behind the mirror, in turn questioning their own culpability as voyeurs in the film's moral ambiguity and as consumers (cannibals?) themselves. The "satisfying" subject position that such self-reflection as the films permits is thus further unsettled.

In using the statuary, Carlson reinforces the examination consistent across her oeuvre of how culture is (and cultures are) consumed and cannibalized in the name of Western entertainment and edification. Museums, as in other paintings like "Vaster Empire," are the ostensible object of critique here, for their participation in the consumption and assimilation of other cultures and peoples. The paintings seem to suggest a museumification of culture, in which the self-reflexive becomes another means of mythologizing the spectacle or permitting its consumption in the name of justice. Such representations recall the critique of the museum's consumption of culture, and reproduction of mythic cultural products, in Vizenor's work. Susan Bernardin notes that "Rather than embodying a static past tense that one finds in pronouncements of a stone age Ishi, stones are living texts" in Anishinaabe culture. Thus, Carlson's paintings and Vizenor's play subtly juxtapose the living text against "a different story of stone, stone taken to build monuments to manifest memory, to keep 'bound' within its walls the wealth of other cultures" (Bernardin 76).

In *Ishi and the Wood Ducks*, although there are no monuments or statues per se, there are two forms of memorialization: the first, the renaming of Kroeber Hall (an analogue for Dwinelle Hall) Ishi Hall; the second, Zero's planned sculpture, which begins with rubbing the name engraved on Ishi's funerary urn. Both involve Ishi's name, which is significant, and it allows for a visceral juxtaposition of the linguistic trace of Ishi's presence in the naming of the hall and the ossified tracing of his name for Zero's sculpture. Simultaneously, the two represent resistance to and direct representation of the "romance of the stone age" the real Ishi came to symbolize and that Vizenor refuses as he "writes a literature of restoration that recasts Ishi as a Native storier of presence" (Bernardin 67).

In act 3 of *Ishi*, then, as in Vizenor's campaign to have Ishi recognized in the nomenclature of the University of California, emphasis is laid on the renaming of Kroeber (Dwinelle) Hall as a means of recognizing the residence of the man called Ishi without ultimately burdening his memory with the tomblike stasis of monumentalization. Vizenor inserts several notes of subversion, chief among them the decision to have Kroeber insist on Ishi replacing his name, even suggesting that his doctorate ought to have been transferred to Ishi. The true act of engaged resistance in this moment, though, has to do with his emphasis on story as an open form, in opposition to the terminal creeds of taxonomic labeling. Discussing an earlier proposal to rename Kroeber Hall "Big Chiep Hall" after Ishi's name for the professor, Kroeber explains: "Ishi honored me with a nickname, in the same sense that we gave him his name (*Pause*), the contradiction, of course, is that our name for him is romantic, while his name for me is a story" ("Ishi" 322). Quoting Vizenor, Bernardin relates:

> "Ishi was not his native name; he was rescued by cultural anthropologists and named by chance, not by vision" . . . Every time Vizenor writes Ishi's name, it is with the full sense of both the silences Ishi deliberately maintained, and the absences he was meant to embody: those of indigenous peoples in California in the early twentieth century. Accordingly, Vizenor's writings sustain the contradictions comprising Ishi in the official record and Ishi *as* storier: "ishi is the subject, the object, the absence, the presence, and the main characters in his stories." (67)

Naming Ishi Hall (or, in reality, Ishi Court) therefore puts a moniker to a colonial site that is in fact a non-name, that signifies an imposition, a misnomer, and an invention that is itself, through Ishi's own character (as opposed to Ishi the character) a site of engaged resistance.

Using Ishi's name for the hall/court renders the whole of the university building a memorial—again, Bernardin notes, "In his tragic-comic account, Vizenor remaps the University of California, Berkeley, as a state monument, which for Ruth B. Phillips, signifies 'a deposit of the historical possession of power'" (69). Ishi's trace in memory unsettles that deposit, a constant reminder of how that power was achieved in relation to Indigenous Americans, and a re-presenting of Indigenous agency. Drawing on Freud, Michael Levine notes that "Through the memorial, trauma is edified to limit the damage. One remembers in order to forget" (124). Memorializing through name—particularly through the fluidity of Ishi's name in Vizenor's hands—resists the edification of trauma or loss, replacing it with an image of survivance. Where Andreas Huyssen notes, "Recalling Robert Musil's observation that there is nothing as invisible as a monument . . . The more monuments there are, the more the past becomes invisible" (32), Vizenor's naming, in contrast to Zero's planned sculpture, precisely invokes an active trace that is intrinsically uncontainable: "The trace in nature is an event in language," Vizenor insists, "as *bimikawaan*, a track, or footprint, is a presence of an absence in nature and narratives. The trace is natural reason, a native presence" (*Fugitive Poses* 26). As Justice Gary Strankman noted at the time, "'to call this place Ishi's court does not give it his name . . . Ishi was not his name. You have bestowed on this bit of earth an alias, not a name—aka wild Indian, aka Ishi, aka man. He, in his existential dignity; he in his brown presence; he is beyond your power to name'" (quoted in Bernardin 71). As such, the naming of Ishi's court evokes the trace of presence and counters "the culture of the *indian* [as] a simulation" that resides in the historical document (Vizenor, *Fugitive Poses* 26). In this regard, the double connotation of "Ishi Court," the final memorial, is deliciously ironic, particularly in light of his "authenticity trial" in act 4. Deliberately invoking both the presence and the absence of the real, the naming puts on trial the processes and mechanisms of colonial erasure, in which the university itself, and the museum specifically, are complicit.

Ruth Phillips reminds us that monuments, whatever their intent, are subject to processes of "destruction, erosion, and accretion" (281). Through Vizenor's renaming, the University of California as monument begins to take on significance as a site that connotes and resists naming and containing Indigenous bodies. Its absorption into a dramatic narrative further enhances its textuality—or the possibility inherent in its textuality. As Phillips attests, "the cultural construction of a painting or other object *as* monument is altered by evolving narratives of history and art history" (281). Bernardin reminds us that "Berkeley's founding role as a state institution cannot be separated from its founding role in the development of American anthropology, which was largely built on the study of California Indians, including, most notably, Ishi?" (68). To bring Ishi's name officially into the cartography of the University of California at Berkeley campus, indeed, to associate it with and even implicitly overwrite the names of Kroeber in the play and Dwinelle in reality,[8] not only puts Ishi at the heart of its (and California state's) origin story but reinforces that Indigenous presence as, by turns, self-naming and ironically constructed, the "actuation," in the play "of [his wood duck] stories, the commune of survivance and sovereignty" (Vizenor, *Fugitive Poses* 37).

The absence of irony, on the other hand, characterizes Zero's antics as sculptor, evoking a particular kind of new age mysticism in relation to Ishi's name that also evokes an attitude of indigenization implicit in settler-colonial consumption of indigenous cultures. Despite the fact that

Zero is Native, he seeks to authenticate his Nativeness by association with the romance of Ishi, a critique of the *penenative*, "the *autoposer*, the autobiographical poseur, or the almost native by associations and institutive connections" (Vizenor, *Fugitive Poses* 15). Where for Vizenor, Ishi's name generates an associative matrix of ideas and stories, for Zero it represents a static identifier into which he can tap. Introducing himself as "Zero Larkin, native sculptor with a vision" ("Ishi" 316), Zero attempts to channel Ishi the artist-shaman, the first denied Ishi by definition, the second imposed on him by romantic tradition.

While Angel Day (manager of the cemetery association) answers the questions of Ashe Miller (reporter) about Ishi's black funerary urn, Ishi and Boots Story sit in the shadows and observe. Boots comments on the claims that constitute the romance:

> BOOTS: Angel said you made that black pot and then you wrote your name on it before you died, is that true?
>
> ISHI: My family never made pottery, we made baskets. . . .
>
> BOOTS: But she said you wrote your own name.
>
> ISHI: My signature, but if you look closely you can see that the letters on the black pot are printed . . . ("Ishi" 318)

This commentary enables a simple satire on the autoposeur, in this case the artist who would seek to enhance or otherwise affirm his Nativeness through mystical attachment, no better (or worse) than the white wannabe shaman. Indeed, Zero's pronouncements are clear: "Ishi is a name with sacred power . . . Ishi gives me my power as an artist . . . Ishi is with me, our spirit is one in his sacred name . . . I'm going to blast his sacred signature, right from this rubbing, at the bottom of my stone sculpture, my tribute to his power as an Indian" ("Ishi" 319). Here is where Ishi's earlier comment on the name on the urn—"the letters on the black pot are printed (*Pause*), very modern" ("Ishi" 318) take on their force, and not because a genuine signature would not be modern. Vizenor is steadfast in his objection to the removal of Indigenous peoples and cultures from the categories of the modern. A modern printed name, though, is inauthentic to the romance, to the simulation of stone-age stasis that the "Indian" Ishi and his sacred power represent to Zero and others. That power is visceral: "I can feel his spirit," Zero declares; "Ishi is with me, his spirit is coming through my fingers . . . The greatest power of my life, the spirit of my people" ("Ishi" 320). "Northern California?" asks Ashe, an incredulous and ironic tease, to which Angel provides the key: "He means a universal tribal spirit" ("Ishi" 320). The continued simulation, the penenative contemplation, in other words, requires only the desire and not the material artifact for its power.

Zero's own name, of course, feeds this trope. "Zero is the same cipher either way," says Ishi, to which Boots replies, "Zero, Zero, and the cemetery liars" ("Ishi" 319). In keeping with Vizenor's psycholanalytic dissections of the motivations of the poseur, Levine notes that "In Lacanian terms, memorials can be theorised as expressing our desire to be the Other; our desire to be heroes for instance because we know that we are not" (124). Under Ashe's scrutiny, Zero reveals that his sculpture is to be placed in the Kroeber Hall where, despite Ishi's lack of children, it will be surrounded by children to secure the next generation. The satirical point is subtle but clear: generations of Native children have had their identities, their cultural understanding, and even their senses of self limited under the pernicious influence of clichés and stereotypes, received through popular cultural misperceptions, bad history, academic misdirection, and so on. Statuary, both of the colonial, triumphalist kind and of the misguided romantic kind such as Zero fashions, is a definite contributor to that generalized understanding: to that absence of the Native in the presence of the *indian*. There is arguably little to distinguish Zero's consumption of Ishi and broader ideas of Native culture, from that of the museums of Carlson's art, or from the indigenizing institutions of settler-colonial society more generally.

Conclusion

The plays discussed herein, both set in the 1990s, invoke and attempt to move beyond the static signifiers of the *indian*, noting the urgency of twentieth-century life and survivance over and above preoccupation with the monuments and memorials of the past. For Two-Rivers, the statue becomes almost a distraction from the immediate problems of his urban Native community. Although a legitimate site of protest, his play seems to ask whether the priorities of the 1990s need to be realigned, ensuring the safety and protection of women like Chili Corn as arguably the ultimate goal of that will to challenge misrepresentation. His male characters are drawn in by their female companions, both distracted from the warrior performance demanded of them as AIM activists. There is a light mocking but no real derision here—more a gentle nudge away from the spectacle toward the substantive need. At the same time, the sculpture, in its monumental visibility, renders invisible those issues he raises. The predicaments of Rosario and Chili, and the implicit racism of the statue along with the prejudice it generates, become masked by the romanticism of the Chicago Historical Society statue. In challenging its significance and its effects, Two-Rivers renders a variety of lived experience visible and effectively reclaims access to public space—a public space made inaccessible to Native Chicagoans through the political, colonial, topography of the space of the monument.

For Vizenor, the dual discourse of memorialization—in the name (excuse the pun) of tricksterish deferral on one hand and a mix of romanticism and artistic self-aggrandizement on the other—speaks directly to indigenous–settler relations. Settler colonial forms of commemoration have had the effect of erasing and silencing North America's first peoples, but forms of memorial that seek to address those silences run equivalent risks of merely re-presenting the *indian* in the absence of the real. Both plays, then, engage the memorial sculpture, albeit in different ways, as sites of engaged resistance to discursive imposition. For Two-Rivers, the resistance is principally performative; for Vizenor, it is primarily linguistic. That the issues they both raise are still pertinent is revealed in Carlson's subject matter and echoed in the work of many other artists, writers, and activists.

Among them, I want to close with brief consideration of the work of two artists who engage the same monumental space. Although not Anishinaabe artists, Jeff Thomas (Iroquois/Onondaga) and Greg Hill (Kanien'kehá:ka; Audain curator of Indigenous Art at the National Gallery of Canada) have worked on projects around the so-called Anishinaabe Scout figure that once knelt at the front of the Samuel de Champlain monument at Nepean Point in Ottawa. The now official name of the figure ties him—and the artists (albeit tongue in cheek) to the Anishinaabe focus of this chapter, although it is used to refer to Quebec founder Champlain's alliances with Algonquian peoples and therefore more generally than it is otherwise used here. Champlain's alliances with Algonquian peoples, to further underscore the irony, were forged at least partly in collective opposition to Haudenosuanee peoples, who were more hostile to his trade settlements in the Great Lakes region.

The Anishinaabe Scout, variously referred to as the Indian Scout or the Kneeling Indian Tracker and renamed in 2013 Kitchi Zibi Omàmìwininì, is a life-size bronze, sculpted and cast by Hamilton McCarthy, who also designed the Champlain statue. Added to the earlier (1915) monument in 1924, the Scout, attired only in a breech-cloth, a feather in his hair, and a quiver of arrows, was intended to "mark the participation of 'loyal' Indian tribes in Champlain's explorations" (Lauzon 82). In the original composition, Champlain literally towers above the Scout, who, slightly twisted as if looking up to him, kneels before him as both advance guard and (metaphorically at least) supplicant. Thomas and Hill have responded in photograph, performance, and film to the statue, since a campaign for its removal was launched in 1996 by then national chief of the Assembly of First Nations, Ovide Mercredi (Cree).

The ideological undertow of a monument such as this is considerable, not least because a plaque declares Champlain as the "First Great Canadian," immediately interpolating those who identify with the white Frenchman into a narrative of European settlement, which forms the originary discourse of the nation. Representative of what goes (kneels) before, the Scout becomes viscerally symbolic of that range of tropes, from vanishing Indian to "primitive" inferior, invoked partly in justification of settlement and the varied violence it produces. The insinuated narrative—confirmed by commentators such as the sculptor's great-great-granddaughter, Charlene MacCarthy—is one of friendship, collaboration (Aubry), but as Lauzon elucidates,

> the presence of the scout would seem to erase the history of exploitation, forced relocation, and attempted eradication that characterized European–Aboriginal relations well into the twentieth century—a history subsumed by the narrative of partnership and cooperation between Champlain and the Anishinabek and Wendat Nations he encountered. But the cooperation invoked by the monument is by no means imagined as a partnership between equals. Indeed, the visual contrasts in the juxtaposition of Champlain and the scout are significant, and advance the narrative of colonial surety. (82–83)

Both Thomas and Hill, then, engage the statue as a site of erasure or collective amnesia and thus as an explicit opportunity to unsettle colonial narratives, unpack and re-present the clichés and realities of contemporary (and especially urban) Native people, and recenter Indigenous presence in the capital city (and thus in the nation) through artistic activism.

Beginning in the mid-1990s, when controversy over the Scout was becoming particularly heated, Thomas began a series of photographs titled "Scouting for Indians," taking in a range of images of "Indians" in Ottawa. This led him to further work juxtaposing Native subjects such as his son with the statue ("F.B.I." 1998) to interrogate "the limited and limiting nature of mainstream representations and understandings of Aboriginal authenticity" (Lauzon 84).[9] Echoing some of the romance interrogated through Vizenor's representation of Zero, Thomas uses the statue not to invoke his subject's authenticity, as Zero Larkin does, but to challenge hegemonic representations that fossilize the *indian* as a typologically static, antimodern primitif.

Following the Scout's removal and relocation in 1999 to Major's Hill Park, where he kneels in front of Parliament and looks back toward Champlain—a more unintentionally ironic process and outcome is scarcely imaginable—Thomas and Hill have embarked on projects that address the Scout and the empty plinth beneath Champlain. Hill's performance pieces "Joe Searches for Cigar-Store Lasagna" (2001) and "Real Live Bronze Indian" make use of the plinth and the pose of the Scout, referencing the Oka confrontation of 1990 through camouflaged clothing and undermining stereotype—as he did with an earlier replica canoe—by wearing a cereal-box headdress. Directly evoking that narrative of relocation and removal, subtly indicting the asymmetries of power masked by the myth of equality and collaboration, these pieces actively revisit the moving of the statue to Major's Hill Park. Thomas also imagined the statue on the move in *Scouting for Indians* (1992–2007) and, more recently, has worked with a number of sitters, including Hill in his cereal-box canoe, to reimagine and revivify the empty plinth through portrait photography (*Seize the Space*; since 2000, with particular emphasis on the 400-year anniversary of Champlain's arrival in the Ottawa area in 2013).

These interventions into the codified narratives that monumental sculpture represent are clearly significant and bear relation to the literary interventions into memorial of both Vizenor and Two-Rivers. For Thomas in particular, the removal of the statue—a victory for the black-and-white rationalizations of protest against the imagery it conveyed—is historically, culturally, and artistically as problematic as its continued presence. This is partly because of the double erasure its removal enacts: if the monument flattens out the violence and coercion of the past, the empty plinth removes even the compromised Indigenous presence from Champlain's story *and* erases that original erasure. "While acknowledging the AFN's concerns regarding the scout's subservient position and demeaning attire," Lauzon reports, "Thomas maintained that the continued presence of the scout would offer 'an example of how Canadian history has diminished the role of Aboriginal peoples today'" (85–86). His intervention becomes a "tactical interruption of normative discourse in the very sites of its enunciation" (Lauzon 80), which, I suggest, expresses something about the interventions of all of the artists and writers I have addressed here. In all of these instances, memorial and monument and the artistic engagement with sites of memory destabilize the ideological and political functions of nation-state discourse manifest in monumental form; simultaneously, though, they ask questions of the ongoing implications of revision as a strategy of correcting historical wrongs and re-envisioning contemporary identities. Removal and renaming newly complicate the particular relations of power and histories of alienation, suppression, and tension that characterize much of the history of settler–Indigenous relations and of course present opportunities to examine and indeed rupture those same histories precisely in the commemorative spaces that participate in their construction and lend them their discursive authority, opening up, in Thomas's words, a space for dialogue.

Notes

1. The Black Lives Matter protests in summer 2020, which focused much attention on the presence and impacts of statues of European explorers, frontier settlers, and memorial "Indians," occurred too close to the proof stage of this book to integrate meaningfully in this chapter. The objects of analysis here, however, demonstrate the long history of that struggle over the maintenance and dismantling of racialized and settler hierarchies through the built environment, embodied in the construction of and opposition to certain kinds of memorial.

2. For an excellent if inevitably too brief discussion of contemporary public art by Native practitioners in comparison to conventional "Native" public art, see Rader's chapter "Roofs, Roads, and Rotundas: American Indian Public Art" in *Engaged Resistance* (183–205).

3. I say "largely" in acknowledgment of the fact that such sweeping generalizations are rarely helpful.

4. This play was first performed in 1997 at the Great Lakes Naval Station in Waukegan, Illinois.

5. Chippewa is the common legal-political term for the Ojibwe (Anishinaabe) in the United States. Two-Rivers spells Ojibwe "Ojibwa" here (Ojibway and other variations are also common). It is becoming more common for Ojibwe peoples in the United States and Canada to refer to themselves simply as Anishinaabe. Chippewa, though still in use, is increasingly viewed as a government term and has no origin in any of the Anishinaabe autonyms.

6. See Constitution of the State of Illinois, http://www.ilga.gov/commission/lrb/conent.htm (accessed December 4, 2014).

7. Sincere thanks to David Carlson and Matthew L. Fletcher for confirmation of this distinction.

8. Dwinelle was an assemblyman and author of the Organic Act through which the university was founded in 1868.

9. For images of Thomas's work, see his website, http://jeff-thomas.ca.

References

Aubry, Jack. "Sculptor's Family Vows to Fight NCC." *Ottawa Citizen*, October 7, 1996.

Bernardin, Susan. "Almost California: Returning to Elemental Vizenor." In *The Poetry and Poetics of Gerald Vizenor*, edited by Deborah L. Madsen, 63–79. Albuquerque: University of New Mexico Press, 2012.

Huyssen, Andreas. *Present Pasts: Urban Palimpsests and the Politics of Memory*. Stanford, CA: Stanford University Press, 2003.

Isernhagen, Hartwig. "Identity and Exchange: The Representation of 'The Indian' in the Federal Writers Project and in Native American Literature." In *Native American Representations: First Encounters, Distorted Images, and Literary Appropriations*, edited by Gretchen M. Bataille, 168–94. Lincoln: University of Nebraska Press, 2001.

Kopecky, Frank, and Mary Sherman Harris. *Understanding the Illinois Constitution*. Springfield: Illinois Bar Association, 2001.

Lame Deer, John Fire, with Richard Erdoes. *Lame Deer, Seeker of Visions*. 1972; New York: Simon & Schuster, 1993.

Lauzon, Claudette. "Monumental Interventions: Jeff Thomas Seizes Commemorative Space." In *Imagining Resistance: Visual Culture and Activism in Canada*, edited by Kirsty Robertson and Keri Cronin, 79–93. Waterloo, ON: Wilfrid Laurier University Press, 2011.

Levine, Michael P. "Mediated Memories: The Politics of the Past." *Angelaki: Journal of the Theoretical Humanities* 11, no. 2 (2006): 117–36.

McKegney, Sam. *Masculindians: Conversations about Indigenous Manhood*. East Lansing: Michigan State University Press, 2014.

Phillips, Ruth B. "Settler Monuments, Indigenous Memory: Dis-membering and Re-membering Canadian Art History." In *Monuments and Memory, Made and Unmade*, edited by Robert S. Nelson and Margaret Olin, 281–304. Chicago: University of Chicago Press, 2003.

Rader, Dean. *Engaged Resistance: American Indian Art, Literature, and Film from Alcatraz to the NMAI*. Austin: University of Texas Press, 2011.

Two-Rivers, E. Donald. *Briefcase Warriors: Stories for the Stage*. Norman: University of Oklahoma Press, 2001.

Vizenor, Gerald. *Fugitive Poses: Native American Indian Scenes of Absence and Presence*. 1998; Lincoln, NE: Bison Books, 2000.

———. "Ishi and the Wood Ducks: Postindian Trickster Comedies." In *Native American Literature: A Brief Introduction and Anthology*, edited by Gerald Vizenor, 299–336. New York: Longman, 1995.

Wagner, Sally Roesch. "Borglum's Vision." *Rapid City Journal*, August 10, 1991. http://www.dickshovel.com/BorgVision.html.

Afterword

The Songs We Are Given

GORDON HENRY JR. AND MARGARET NOODIN

Some years ago, an old man arose among us at a Thirsty Dance ceremony. The old man told all of us he wanted to give us a song. He wanted to give a song because he felt we were doing something good and right in continuing the ceremony. "I am going to sing this song," he said. "Remember it and you can take it with you. Sing it to your children when they are sick. Sing it when someone needs healing."

The man sang the song four times through. He sang in Anishinaabemowin, and not all of us caught the song, or remembered it immediately, but some of the people who were there remembered, and they continue to sing the song and we continue the ceremony. The song tells us:

Gichi-manidoo ningii-miinigoonaan gaagige-minawaanigoziwang.
The Great Spirit gave us a path/way to everlasting life.

Each year more people are able to sing the song in Anishinaabemowin, and we have come to understand the song as a healing song. It continues to heal by confirming ongoing relationships and confirming the enduring Anishinaabe spirit.

While the views expressed by the song or the use of the song as a coda to this discussion of Anishinaabe letters may seem essentialist or reflective of some general metaphysical leanings, the song speaks directly to the profound underlying qualitative cultural capacities carried by tribal traditions. It also speaks directly to an acknowledgment of an enduring continuum of life.

This volume, with its emphasis on connections made through personal experience, also expresses an affiliative, attunement, to Anishinaabe scholar, Lawrence Gross's views, in his article, "The Comic Vision of Anishinaabe Culture and Religion." Gross offers this opening note to his work:

> One of the challenges I have faced as an academic is the manner in which I should discuss my own people, the Anishinaabe. The fact of the matter is, I am an Anishinaabe academic, no matter how much the term sounds like an oxymoron. I feel I can no longer use the third person in discussing my people. The experience of the Anishinaabe is my experience, and there is no way I can imply the Anishinaabe are the "Other." As such, I have made a conscious decision to use the first person in my academic writing on the Anishinaabe. In one respect, I am surrendering the scholarly goal of supposed objectivity for a larger goal—academic precision. To the degree my comments approach the latter aim, my writing will serve the interests of both the Anishinaabe and academic communities, thus encouraging dialogue between the two. In the final analysis, if we are to move beyond treating people as the other, just such a dialogue is necessary. (2002, 436)

Gross points to a lasting tension in the work of Native academics, whether Anishinaabe or from different tribes. The academic, critical perspectives signing the fields of literary, cultural studies, and American Indian literature often seem far removed from the cultural continuum, associated with the healing song quoted above. The academic world and the world of letters often strike poses and hack reposes in a system of virtual production, where trends and conventions of theory and sign and professional appointments reinforce market communities and powers of production that seem based on how one displays valued positions in research and letters to maintain a position in institutions and scholarly communities of affiliation. For those of us who are scholars or writers and Natives, researching and writing from the remote vistas of the academy, Edward Said's words from *The World, the Text, and the Critic* still resonate:

the contemporary critical consciousness stands between the
temptations represented by two formidable and related powers
engaging critical attention. One is the culture to which critics
are bound filiatively (by birth, nationality . . . ; the other is the
method or system acquired affiliatively (by social and political
conviction, economic and historical circumstances, voluntary
effort and willed deliberation). (1983, 25)

In some respects, the powers of filiation and affiliation, with the potential to inform our critical attention, might be the driving forces in how scholars in American Indian studies develop the conviction of critical positions, as we sign our names and create academic texts, reflecting such positions, as we affiliate with organizations, attend conferences in our disciplines and fields relative to our "convictions" and "willed deliberations." Moustafa Bayoumi explains that authority "depends on this consolidation," of filiation and affiliation (2004, 59). Bayoumi also claims that an examination of such consolidation "at any time, in any system . . . can "reveal cultural logics at discrete moments" (2004, 59).

At this moment, the filiative roots that bind us have given way to the more powerful demands of affiliation. If we develop critical positions for ourselves and create strong enough, widely valued critical, political, institutionally affiliated positions, our affiliations will extend further and our work, our production, and our effort will produce greater recognition and even more powerful possibilities for affiliation. For most scholars in American Indian studies, engaging the powers Said associates with filiation remains less promising for developing a valued critical position than giving oneself over to the powers of affiliation. Under the current structural conditions in the academy, how we position our work socially and politically will provide greater institutional and professional, economic, and historical reward and recognition than will filiative community work driven by voluntary effort and willed deliberation. But the latter, the community, the relatives at home, the grandparents, mothers, fathers, aunts, uncles, cousins, the love they impart, the storied lives they have shared remain at the heart of our continuance. At this moment, under current economic and historical circumstances, although consolidation of the forces of filiation and affiliation may be necessary, the need to marshal the influences of filiation seems to be diminishing. Academic affiliation seems more potent, a seemingly better lightning rod for popularity, notoriety, and reputation. This is important, as Bayoumi reminds us in his review of Said's work: "Affiliation is, in other words, the manner in which cultural authority is built, and unmasking its connections and networks is the first step toward inaugurating political change" (2004, 57).

To put it another way, the "powers" of filiation and (perhaps more so) affiliation, legitimate individual and institutional social, professional, and cultural identity, activity, and work, giving authenticity to individuals, based on authority derived from filiation and affiliation. It follows that cultural authority, in fields such as American Indian studies, remains vested in the generative power of authenticity, associated with Native filiation, ascribed most directly through family and tribal community ties; on the other hand, cultural authority stands in relationship to the illusive power of influence required to legitimate authority in the academy as garnered through the power and influences of affiliation. Of course, no modern or postmodern, contemporary, conceptual dynamic, constructed between poles such as filiation and affiliation, should ever be simplified into discrete either/or propositions. Said's message is clear in that regard; cultural authority involves a consolidation of the power of filiation and affiliation. In American Indian studies, this seems to be as true as it could be in any other range of academic disciplines connected by such a vast and diverse array of cultural people and possibilities, although the clout of having influential affiliations seems to hold more authoritative power for American Indian studies scholars and organizations. Moreover, cultural authority is often contingent on context. An individual Native scholar may have legitimate cultural authority in a classroom or while delivering a presentation at a conferences of affiliated peers, but that same person might have little or no authority in a different setting—at a community feast or at a tribal funeral, a family gathering, in tribal governance, or in decision making involving tribal communities, for example. Affiliations powered by work and associations in the academic world may hold little sway in contexts where we must return to our filiative roots and community-based affiliations.

Let us all willingly attend to, contend with, and engage with the ways filiative and affiliative poses bring us back to the terms and conditions, the construction, distribution, and reception of our academic and creative work as representations in this context of our marked, lettered poses and further consider how those critical poses might support greater cultural continuance with an enduring sense of ethical engagement and care for the people and communities we work in and live through. As we profess to understand one another and the world, we are part of an enduring Anishinaabe continuum. Let us all remember the songs that heal us and bind us to one another, the songs of strong women who are daughters of the sky, the songs of old men who lead Thirsty Dance ceremonies, the songs of children not yet sung into the world.

> *Gimiigwechiwigo Gichi-manidoo gaa-miizhiyaang o'o gaagige-bimaadiziwin.*
> We thank you Great Spirit for giving us this path/way to everlasting life.

References

Bayoumi, Moustafa. "Our Philological Home Is the Earth." *Arab Studies Quarterly* 26, no. 4 (2004): 53–66.

Gross, Lawrence W. "The Comic Vision of Anishinaabe Culture and Religion." *American Indian Quarterly*, 26, no. 3 (2002): 436–59.

Said, Edward W. *The World, the Text, and the Critic*. Cambridge, Mass.: Harvard University Press, 1983.

Contributors

Nichole Biber is a Waganakising Odawa Anishinaabekwe and jingle dress dancer who lives with her family in East Lansing, Michigan. Organic gardening and walks in urban patches of woods and wildlife motivate her political activism on local and national levels. Nichole graduated from Michigan State University, earning a PhD in English. She is known as Dr. B by the K–5 elementary school children for whom she works in a local public school library. She writes an occasional blog at https://insightoutfit.wordpress.com/.

Susan Berry Brill de Ramírez was the Caterpillar Professor of English at Bradley University in Peoria, Illinois, where she taught and lived for over twenty years. During this period, she authored several books, including *Wittgenstein and Critical Theory* (1995), *Contemporary American Indian Literatures and the Oral Tradition* (1999), *Native American Life-History Narratives* (2007), and *Women Ethnographers and Native Women Storytellers* (2014). With Evelina Zuni Lucero, she also coedited *Simon J. Ortiz: A Poetic Legacy of Indigenous Continuance* (2009). Brill de Ramírez guest-edited a special edition of *Studies in American Indian Literature*, and she served on the editorial board for *PMLA*. In addition to her body of scholarship, Brill de Ramírez was an active contributor to the Bahai communities around the world and the writer of two trade books on academic success geared toward first-generation college students. At the time of her passing in October 2018, she was directing the graduate program at Bradley, teaching literature courses, and hard at work on study of place in contemporary Native American literature.

Jill Doerfler is Professor and Department Head of American Indian Studies at the University of Minnesota, Duluth. Her primary area of scholarly interest is American Indian (specifically Anishinaabe) identity with a political focus on citizenship. She has taken a community-engaged approach to research, working closely with the White Earth Nation on constitutional reform efforts from 2007 to 2015 and in 2016 coestablishing a grassroots community group, Zaagibagaang, which is focused on governance and nation building. Her most recent book, *Those Who Belong: Identity, Family, Blood, and Citizenship Among the White Earth Anishinaabeg* (2015), examines staunch Anishinaabe resistance to racialization and the complex issues surrounding tribal citizenship and identity. She coauthored *The White Earth Nation: Ratification of a Native Democratic Constitution* (2012) with world-renowned Anishinaabe scholar Gerald Vizenor and coedited *Centering Anishinaabeg Studies: Understanding the World Through Stories* (2013) with Niigaanwewidam James Sinclair and Heidi Kiiwetinepinesiik Stark.

Gordon Henry Jr. is an enrolled citizen of the White Earth Anishinaabe Nation in Minnesota. He is Professor in the English Department at Michigan State University and a Gordon Russell Visiting Professor at Dartmouth College. He serves as senior editor of the American Indian Studies Series and the subimprints Mukwa Enewed and Sovereign Traces at Michigan State University Press. He has received an American Book Award for his novel *The Light People* and his poetry, fiction, and essays have been published extensively in the United States and Europe. He is author of a mixed-genre collection, *The Failure of Certain Charms*, and his writing has appeared in journals and anthologies and in translation in Spain, Greece, Hungary, Italy, the United Kingdom, and Germany. Henry has served as an Anishinaabe Oshkawbaywis for a variety of ceremonies, as passed on to him by the late Turtle Mountain elder and spiritual leader Francis Cree and his brother, Louis Cree. Henry has been participating in and helping conduct ceremonies for over thirty-five years.

Sharon Holm earned her PhD in Native American Literature from Birkbeck, University of London, and works with Native, First Nations, Inuit, and indigenous literatures focusing on indigenous law, sovereignty, and environment. Her current project involves the intersection of Native American poetry with concepts of the Anthropocene, the environmental humanities, and issues of climate change. She has taught Native American, indigenous, and African American literatures at various UK universities and presently is an associate lecturer at the Centre for Lifelong Learning at the University of York. Forthcoming publications include an article on the work of two Inupiaq poets, dg nanouk okpik and Joan Naviyuk Kane, in *The Art of Resistance and Resurgence* (vol. 2, edited by Padraig Kirwan and David Stirrup, 2020) and an essay, "Indigenous (Other-) Worldings, Indigenous Ecopoiesis: 'World Literature' and a New Onto-Epistemological Politics."

Padraig Kirwan is Senior Lecturer in the Literature of the Americas at Goldsmiths, University of London. He specializes in contemporary Native American literature, and his book *Sovereign Stories: Aesthetics, Autonomy and Contemporary Native American Writing* appeared in 2013. Padraig is currently coediting and contributing to two forthcoming essay collections: *Famine Pots: Choctaw and Irish Exchanges 1848-Present* (with LeAnne Howe) and *The Art of Resistance and Resurgence* (two volumes, with David Stirrup). Kirwan has published essays in *NOVEL: A Forum on Fiction*, *Comparative Literature*, and the *Journal of American Studies*. He has also written articles for the *Times Higher Education* magazine and *The Conversation*. Kirwan is the *Literary Encyclopaedia*'s area editor for Native American Literature and Culture. In 2015 he was awarded a Public Engagement Award by Goldsmiths for his work on the relationship between the Choctaw Nation and the people of Ireland.

Chris LaLonde is Professor of English at SUNY Oswego, where he also directs general education and serves as interim associate director of the Honors Program. His publications include books on the early fiction of William Faulkner and on the novels of mixed-blood Choctaw-Cherokee-Irish writer and scholar Louis Owens and essays on Native American literatures, hip-hop, and film, with particular attention to the works of White Earth Anishinaabe writers Gerald Vizenor and Kimberly Blaeser. His most recent publications include essays on Owens and California (2019), on the documentary film *This May Be the Last Time* by Seminole-Creek filmmaker Sterlin Harjo (2018), on novels by Karen Tei Yamashita (2018), and on Vizenor and ghosts (2107).

Deborah L. Madsen is Professor of American Literature and Culture at the University of Geneva, Switzerland. She has published widely in the field of indigenous North American literatures, focusing in particular on the work of Gerald Vizenor and Louise Erdrich. Her recent work engages with indigenous digital media; part of this project is the essay "Indigenizing the Internet" (in *The Cambridge History of Native American Literature*, ed. Melanie Benson Taylor), which analyzes Heid Erdrich's video poems ("poemeos") and video games designed by Elizabeth LaPensée.

Carter Meland is a tall, left-handed man of White Earth Anishinaabe heritage. He takes writing seriously but does so with good humor. His novel *Stories for a Lost Child* invokes the waters of Lake Superior and the Mississippi River and the deep woods voice of Misaabe (Bigfoot) to help his characters make sense of the problems in their lives. His creative and critical work has appeared in journals like *Studies in American Indian Literature, Yellow Medicine Review*, and *Lake*. By day he teaches students in American Indian studies at the University of Minnesota Duluth about the wicked smart, moving, and profound things that Native writers have to say about the world; by night he tries to rise to the standards they set. *Stories for a Lost Child* was a finalist for the 2018 Minnesota Book Award.

Margaret Noodin earned an MFA in creative writing and a PhD in linguistics from the University of Minnesota. She is currently Professor at the University of Wisconsin-Milwaukee where she also serves as Director of the Electa Quinney Institute for American Indian Education. She is the author of *Bawaajimo: A Dialect of Dreams in Anishinaabe Language and Literature* and *Weweni*, a collection of bilingual poems in Ojibwe and English. Her poems are anthologized in *New Poets of Native Nations, Sing: Poetry from the Indigenous Americas, Poetry*, the *Michigan Quarterly Review, Water Stone Review*, and *Yellow Medicine Review*. With her daughters, Shannon and Fionna, she is a member of Miskwaasining Nagamojig (the Swamp Singers) a women's hand drum group. To see and hear current projects visit http://www.ojibwe.net where she and other students and speakers of Ojibwe have created a space for language to be shared by academics and the native community.

Stuart Rieke is an English, humanities, and guitar instructor at the Turtle Mountain Community College in Belcourt, North Dakota, on the Turtle Mountain Reservation. He has presented twice at the Native American Literature Symposium, in 2010 on James Welch's novel *Fools Crow* and most recently with his wife, Monique Vondall-Rieke, on how the art and symbolism of George Morrison relates to Indian law. He co-presented with Monique at the Michigan State University Law and Literature Conference in 2007 where he spoke about natural law from a tribal perspective. He earned a master's degree in English from the University of North Dakota in 2008 after completing his thesis on the work of Gordon Henry Jr., discussing Henry's novel *The Light People* and poetry book *The Failure of Certain Charms*. He co-produced a rock album from Ben Balivet called *Twenty Thousand Daydreams under the Sea* (2019).

David Stirrup is Professor of American literature and indigenous studies at the University of Kent, in the United Kingdom. He is author of *Louise Erdrich* and *Picturing Worlds: Visuality and Visual Sovereignty in Contemporary Anishinaabe Writing* and a number of articles and book chapters on indigenous literatures and visual arts. Always keen on collaboration, Stirrup has also coedited *Tribal Fantasies: Native Americans in the European Imaginary* with James Mackay; *Parallel Encounters: Culture and the Canada-US Border* with Gillian Roberts; *Theorising the Canada-US Border* with Jeffrey Orr, and is currently editing two volumes under the title *The Art of Resistance and Resurgence* with Padraig Kirwan. Stirrup is a founding coeditor of the online, open-access journal *Transmotion* and has coedited special issues of *Wasafiri*, the *European Journal of American Culture*, the *American Review of Canadian Studies*, and *Comparative American Studies*.

Index

aabaabiigin (unwind), 200
aadizooke (tell a teaching story), 2; *aadizookeyaang* (we are telling a teaching story), 227
abandon, 21, 121, 211, 222
abduct, 178, 187
abuse, against children, 127, 141; against women, 70, 259; domestic 258–60
acknowledge violence, 260
adapt, 2, 3, 10, 26, 34, 38, 59, 212, 230
Alexie, Sherman, 51, 56, 70–71
American Indian Movement (AIM), 67, 255, 259–60, 268
andopawatchigan (seek your dream), 26
anishaa (be kidding), 237; *anishaaendamo* (imagination), 228, 236–38; Anishaa-wannabee, 240
apiitendam (focus thoughts on something), 237
appropriate, 23, 128, 150–52, 162–63, 166, 168–71
arrest, 256
ascribe, 39, 42, 278
assign, 41, 45, 111, 184
assimilate, 10, 34, 36, 131, 151, 188–89, 222, 229, 238, 240, 260, 262–63

Asutru Folk Assembly, 168
attack, physical, 120; tribal rights 63, 88
Aubid, Charles, 133–34
ayaa (be something), 234

baapaagaakwa (knock) 243; *baapaaseog* (woodpeckers), 87
baapagishka (shake) 243
baapaajimo (comediate), 227; *baapaawinad* (a joke), 227–28, 242–46; *baapi* (laugh), 243; *baapinodaw* (mock someone), 243
baatayiinadoon (be many of something), 2–3
babaamendam (pay attention or worry), 237
bagosendam (hope or wish), 237
Bakaawiz (brother of Nanabozho), 1, 10
basket-making, 235
Battle of Fort Dearborn, 257
Benjamin L. Fairbanks store, 207
Biber, Nichole, 10
biboon (winter season), 227, 235; *biboonigizi* (verb to indicate age), 235
biidaabin (dawn), 25
Bimaadiz (person), 60, 62; *bimaadizi* (to live), 60, 234; *bimaadiziwin*

Bimaadiz (person) *(continued)*
  (to live a good life) 138, 142, 153, 159–60, 162, 164, 170–72, 234, 279
bimipto (to run), 234
bimode (to crawl), 234
bimose (to walk), 234
Black Partridge, 257, 259
Blaeser, Kimberly, 3, 5, 8, 10, 79–80, 89–104, 123, 178, 196
blood; classification roll, 208, 214, 218; full, 200–204, 206, 209, 213–19; mixed, 90, 120, 203, 206, 213
boil sap, 235, 241
Borrows, John, 124
brainwash, 21
Brave Heart, Maria Yellow Horse, 173
Brill de Ramirez, Susan Berry, ix, 10, 13
Brinton, Daniel, 11, 178, 182
Broker, Ignatia, 8, 149
bury people, 64, 232; bury religion, 182
Butler, Judith, 123

Cannibal Ferox, 262
Carlson, Andrea, 149, 262
Champlain statue, 269
Chatters, James, 166–69
Chicago Historical Society, 255, 257, 268
Chili Corn, 12, 249, 255–57, 267
colonize, 49, 151; colonizer, 253–54
commemorate, 251
conventional translation equivalents (CTEs), 46–48
conjugate, 232
Coyote, 179, 190–91
Crawford, Suzanne, 150–51, 168–71
Crazy Horse Memorial, 252–54
critical poses, 1, 12
cultural poses, 12, 249
cultural revival, 251
cut, body parts, 120; trees, 41

dagwaagin (fall season), 227, 235
dance, general, 12, 87, 116, 227, 235, 243; fancy-dancing, 51–52, little war, 40, 42
Dawes Act, 211–12
debwe (true, correct), 232; *debwewin* (truth), 232
decolonize, 66, 250
derealized others, 123
Derrida, Jacques, 155
devalue, 124
diba (measurement), *dibaabiigin* (measure someone), 206
dibaajimo (narrate), 86, 227; *dibaajimo'akii* (storiverse), 12, 228; *dibaajimomin* (storytelling), 12; *dibaajimowin* (story), 3; *diba'iga* (story time), 232
Diné, 157
Dirty Copper, 231, 234, 236–37
discrimination, 249, 258
disrespect, 44, 184
displace, 60
Doerfler, Jill, 5, 11, 64–66, 69, 125, 138, 223
dream song, Anishinaabe, 167, 172
drive vehicle 26, 89–92, 101
drum, 12, 28, 85, 98, 228, 245–46, 284; drumbeat, 97
dry, 92
Duran, Bonnie, 173
Duran, Eduardo, 173
Dwinelle Hall, 263

edawayiing (come from both sides), 48
E. Donald Two-Rivers, 8, 12, 249, 255, 257–60, 267–68, 270, 272
endanakii (homeland), 82–83, 85–86, 95, 103

endure, 2, 6, 10, 11, 81, 100, 150
engaged resistance, 250, 260, 264, 268
epistemology, 153, 156, 159, 161, 163, 229
eradicate, 128, 169
Erdrich, Heid E., 103, 149–72
Erdrich, Louise, 5, 8–11, 19–30
escape, thoughts, 42; Eurocentrism, 117
exceptionalism, American, 11, 128, 150–51, 153–54
execute, 121

fall, down, 40, 107, 112–13, 161; off, 20; of solarism, 191; season, 55, 200, 227, 235
Fine-Dare, Kathleen, 151–52, 163
fishing, rights, 63, 132; spear, 232, 235
Frost, Robert, 153–59, 172–74
Fuss, Diana, 170–71

gaagige (everlasting), *aadizooke* (place of infinetly renewed stories), 2; *bimaadiziwin* (life), 279; *minawaanigoziwang* (happy life), 275
gashkendamo (to have tangled thoughts or sadness), 237
gather, supply, 41, 235; together, 40–41, 183, 197, 201, 209, 220, 235, 244, 278
genocide, 120, 124–28, 134, 137–40
Genocide Tribunals, 11, 119, 124–25, 127, 133–41
giggle, 51
giiwe (goes home), 83, 86
gikinoo'amaw (to teach), 227
Goeman, Mishuana, 172
going, along, 111, 179; home, 83, 86, 92; to a pow-wow, 90–91, 94–95
Gray, Jeffrey, 172
Great Lakes, 1, 4, 230, 233, 268

Gross, Lawrence, 159, 276
grow, beards, 47; population, 63, 152; sweetgrass, 221; tired, 46; to a shape, 48

haiku, 167, 172
hang (suicide), 120, 123
Haraway, Donna, 171
harvest, 41, 221, 134–35, 235
hate against, 258
head home, 90–94
heal, 24–25, 27, 89, 96, 98–101, 108, 134, 137, 139–40, 275–76, 279
hear, Coyote, 179; instances, 120, 206; laugh, 90, 93; Ojibwe, 66, 238; spirits, 232; stories, 28, 60, 167; testimony, 135
Henry Jr., Gordon, 8, 10–11, 71, 79–81, 84, 89, 95–103, 108–16, 196, 239
Hiawatha Hotel, 207–208
Hill, Greg, 268–70
Hinsley, Curtis M., 152, 162
Holm, Sharon, 11
honor, 29, 66, 86, 88, 141, 236, 254–55, 264
Howe, LeAnne, 12, 64–68, 71–72, 196
hunting, animals 40, 42, 60, 121, 235; rights, 132
Hutcheon, Linda, 239

ikido (speak), 232; *ikidowinan* (words), 227
imaginative stories, 126, 135
in absentia, 11, 119, 125–26
Indian wars, 130, 141, 150
indigenize, 97, 251, 265, 267
inendam (think a certain way), 237; *inendan* (think of it a certain way), 232
inscribe, death, 22; landscape, 161; monuments, 164; narrative, 169

intermingle blood of different races, 204, 216
International Criminal Court (ICC), 125–28, 134, 141
interrogate, 20, 270
invasion, 126
Ishi, 12, 249, 256, 261–67
Ishi and the Wood Ducks, 249, 256, 261, 263
izha (it is near), 83, 86

Jesuit Relations, 230
Jiibayaaboozo (brother of Nanabozho), 1–2, 11
Johnston, Basil, 1–2, 7, 25, 36, 44
Jones, William, 44
Jung, Carl, 11, 178, 189–90
Jural "third space," 139
Jurisgenesis, 136

Kafka, Franz, 8, 236
Kennewick Man, 153, 166–71
kill, 13, 40, 44, 129–30, 179, 255–57, 259
King, Alanis, 239
Kirwan, Padraig, 10, 55–56, 67, 70, 72–73
knock, 87, 243
Kroeber, Alfred, 256, 261–67
Krupat, Arnold, 13, 52

LaDuke, Winona, 8, 24–26, 29, 41, 209–10
LaLonde, Chris, 9–10
Lame Deer, John Fire, 249, 252–53
laugh, 44, 90, 92–93, 228, 235–36 239, 242–46
learn, 3, 28–29, 36, 58–59, 166, 282; Anishinaabemowin, 25, 243–44; from nature, 44; in school, 116; survival, 91; to read, 113; use land, 221

Leaving Smoke's, 107–16
Lurie, Jon, 51

maajaa (leave), 86–88, 91
Madsen, Deborah, 5, 11–12, 172
Majikawiz (brother of Nanabozho), 1, 9
Manibozho, 178–80, 183–91
Manifest Destiny, 128, 150–54, 157, 254, 257
Marshall Trilogy, 129, 131
Maungwudaus, 8, 10, 33–49
Mbembe, Achille, 173
McGuire, Randall, 168
McNally, Michael, 159
McNickle, D'Arcy, 34–36, 190
mekawiyaanin, (be reminded), 82, 85; *mekwendaagozijin* (memory), 227
Meland, Carter, 11, 72
memorializing, 12, 150, 256, 264
Metacomet ("King Philip"), 150
Michabo, 178–79, 182–91
Michelet, Simon, 199–200, 208, 210
midewiwin (Anishinaabe medicine society), 28, 98, 184–85, 228
migrate, 167, 188, 229
miigwe (to give), 231
miigwech (offer thanks), ix, 191, 231, 279; *miigwechiwendan* (be thankful), 232
miikindizi (to be a tease), 227–28, 238–39, 246
miikonan (shoot and hit something), 238
miikonaw (shoot and hit someone), 238
mikaw (find someone), 227
mikwendan (remember it), 237
mock, 240, 243, 268
Momaday, Scott, 190, 228
Morrison, George, 217, 223
Mount Rushmore, 252–54

Müller, Max, 180–86, 191–92
murder, mass, 125, 128; of Sand Creek, 120–21, 124
murmuring petitions, 41
museum, 150–52, 168–69, 172, 250, 255–56, 263, 265, 267

naagadawendam (think about it), 1; *naagadawenim* (think about someone), 9, 231
Naanabozho, 11, 177–78, 186, 188–90
Native American Fiction, 52–57, 60–61, 66–68, 70–73
Native American Graves and Repatriation Act (NAGPRA), 151, 168, 256
niibidoon (weave something), 197
niibin (summer season), 227, 235
niimi (dance), 87, 227
Noodin, Margaret, 5, 8, 10, 12, 71–72, 79–97, 100–104, 135, 227
Northrup, Jim, 8, 12, 72, 227–46

O'Connell, Sarah, 51, 66
ontology, 123, 153, 156, 159, 162, 170
oshkidibikad (dusk), 25

paradigm of "indianness," 68, 121, 129, 133, 138, 251
Parker, Robert Dale, 91, 156
Parkhill, Thomas, 151
pictograph, 28–29, 161, 184
Pine Ridge Reservation, 252
Powell, Ransom, 200–208, 214–15, 218–19, 221–23
prejudice, 117, 124, 128, 133–34, 253–54, 258–59, 268
preserve, 1, 63, 141, 161, 185, 230
protest, 12, 232, 252, 257, 259, 267, 270, 271
purchase, 199

racial profiling, 261
racism, 63, 89, 93, 120, 131, 140, 196, 253, 261, 268, 271
Rader, Dean, 71, 99, 153, 159, 250
Radin, Paul, 11, 178, 189
Randall, William Lowell, 59
rebellion, 24
receive something, 197, 199, 222, 68
recover, 19, 89, 124, 160, 210
reinforce, 238, 258, 265, 276
rename, 24, 256, 261, 263–65, 269, 271
repatriation, 132, 151, 256
respect, 27, 43, 153, 160, 163–65, 171, 206
restore, 96, 100–101, 154–55, 168, 172, 186, 254, 263
revitalize, 2, 186, 229
Rez Life, 10, 55, 58–59, 62–70, 72
ricing, 235, 244
Rieke, Stuart, 10–11
Riel, Louis, 24
rights, 63, 126–29, 131–36, 138–39, 141–42, 258

sacrifice, 13, 129, 164
salute, 43
Santa Fe, 250–51
Sarris, Greg, 151
scalp, 120–21, 255, 258
scatter, 107, 112
Schoolcraft, Henry Rowe, 162
Schoolcraft, Jane Johnston, 7, 10, 79–103
Schweninger, Lee, 151
Sebald, W. G., 20
separation, mother's, 83; political, 66; threat of, 21–22
settler-state, 11, 122, 128–30, 134, 138–39, 141–42, 162
shake, 243, 246
Shakespeare, William, 81, 165, 166

shiver, 107, 112
shoot, 40, 190, 205, 238, 255
sit, 20, 66, 90, 92, 99, 201, 207, 242, 266
skin, 179
solarism, 180–82, 189, 191
South African Truth and Reconciliation Committee (T.R.C.), 127
sovereignty, 9, 36, 58, 69, 80, 88, 100, 122, 124, 126, 128–30, 133–36, 138–42, 153, 156, 159, 171–72, 188, 250, 252, 265, 282
spring season, 227, 231, 235–36
stakeout, 255–56
state of exception, 130
St. Columba Episcopal Church, 198
stereotype, 40, 42, 55, 70, 129, 169, 196, 239, 245, 250, 257–59, 261, 267, 270
steal, 151, 159, 170, 253
Stillday, Thomas, 245
struggle, 27, 49, 80, 103, 119, 123, 156, 159, 221, 257, 271
Stirrup, David, 5, 12, 149
suicide, 11, 63, 71, 119–21, 245
summer season, 47, 179, 221, 227, 235, 271
surrender, 154
survive, 21, 35, 40, 49, 89, 91, 101, 116, 122–26, 133–40, 159, 196, 221, 229, 237, 242, 245, 254

Taylor, Christopher, 52, 57, 72
terminal creeds, 122, 128, 131, 264
textual tease, 12, 136, 228, 237–43, 256, 267
The Hiawatha, 53, 55–56, 72
the Indian, 35, 45, 61, 121, 128–29, 150, 170, 183, 190, 199, 203, 208, 212, 217, 245, 250–51, 256, 265, 267–70

The Tempest, 81, 165
Thirsty Dance ceremony, 13, 275, 279
Thomas, Dylan, 166
Thomas, Jeff, 268–72
threat, 21, 242, 255
translate, 44, 56, 60–61, 129, 159, 184, 191, 237, 245
trap, 121, 237
treaty, 130, 135, 201, 210, 223, 245, 253–54
tremble, 1, 107
Treuer, David, 8, 10, 51–73
tribalography, 11–12, 64–65, 72, 195–97, 220
tribunals, 125–28, 132, 134–41
trickster, 1, 11, 122, 140, 177–79, 185–89, 192, 228, 240, 255–56, 260
Tuan, Yi-Fu, 151
twirl, 195

Ulin, David, 60, 62, 68–69
University of California, Berkeley, 169, 255, 264–65

Vaster Empire, 149, 263
Verdery, Katherine, 122–23, 140, 171, 221, 249, 260
victimry, 196
visit, people, 234–35, 255–56; places, 29, 43–45, 48, 113, 230
Vizenor, Gerald, 1, 5, 7, 9, 11–13, 26, 37–38, 52, 65, 67, 71–72, 80, 87–88, 98–102, 111, 113–14, 119–28, 132–41, 150, 177–78, 187–90, 196, 221, 227–29, 139, 249, 256, 261–70

walk, 46, 87, 203, 210, 234, 238, 241
Walking the Rez Road, 231–38, 247
Warmwater, Luke, 229, 237
weave, something, 172, 197, 220; textual, 153, 189, 195–97, 235; motion, 89, 92, 101

White, Dane Michael, 11, 119–24
White Earth Reservation, 12, 92, 120, 198, 212–13, 220, 222
winter season, 27, 181, 183, 227, 235–36
Wolfe, Patrick, 172
write, 28

Yellow Horse-Davis, Susan, 173

zhiibendam (endure, strength of mind), 2–3
zhinaagwazi (look like someone), 48, 87
ziigwan (spring season), 227, 232, 235

www.ingramcontent.com/pod-product-compliance
Lightning Source LLC
Chambersburg PA
CBHW021214240426
43672CB00026B/85